The Traveler's Guide to the Information Highway

The Traveler's Guide to the Information Highway

Dylan Tweney

Illustrated by
Gary Suen

ZIFF DAVIS PRESS
EMERYVILLE, CALIFORNIA

Development Editor	Valerie Haynes Perry
Copy Editor	Carol Henry
Technical Reviewer	Bob Flanders
Project Coordinator	Ami Knox
Proofreaders	Carol Burbo and Ami Knox
Cover Illustration	Gary Suen
Cover Design	Carrie English and Kenneth Roberts
Book Design	Dennis Gallagher/Visual Strategies, San Francisco
Screen Graphics Editor	Dan Brodnitz
Technical Illustration	Gary Suen
Word Processing	Howard Blechman
Page Layout	M.D. Barrera
Indexer	Carol Burbo

Ziff-Davis Press books are produced on a Macintosh computer system with the following applications: FrameMaker®, Microsoft® Word, QuarkXPress®, Adobe Illustrator®, Adobe Photoshop®, Adobe Streamline™, MacLink® *Plus*, Aldus® FreeHand™, Collage Plus™.

If you have comments or questions or would like to receive a free catalog, call or write:

Ziff-Davis Press
5903 Christie Avenue
Emeryville, CA 94608
1-800-688-0448

ISBN 1-56276-206-0

Manufactured in the United States of America
10 9 8 7 6 5 4 3 2

Table of Contents

Acknowledgments

I am grateful to the many people whose help, ideas, and hard work have contributed to this book.

Above all, I thank Karen Jensen, without whom I never could have begun. She has my gratitude first for encouraging me to write the book, and then for putting up with me while I was writing it. But her ideas, suggestions, and lucid criticisms have also shaped the book from its beginnings, to say nothing of the research assistance she provided. I truly couldn't have done it without her.

I thank Matthew Lake and Ron White, whose advice, example, and good words got me started. It was Matthew whose editorial finesse and technical wizardry helped me to learn something of the twin crafts of writing and wasting time with computers. Ron convinced me that I could write a book and helped me get this project off the ground. He truly is a role model for me. I am grateful to both Matthew and Ron for their help.

Valerie Haynes Perry helped refine my writing and clarify my ideas immeasurably. Thanks to her sure editorial sense, this book is both more interesting and more useful than it would have been otherwise. It was a pleasure working with her.

Carol Henry's acute eye and tireless pencil discovered and corrected more infelicities in my writing than I thought possible. Without Carol, the following pages would be much less readable. I'm grateful for her patience and her deftness in improving my words.

Dennis Gallagher and Gary Suen are responsible for taking my naive sketches and turning them into sophisticated, clear, and exciting illustrations. I thank them both for creating what are surely the heart of this book: the maps.

For advice on the Internet and on UNIX, I'm indebted to my brother, Christopher Tweney. He knows more about computers than I ever will, and somehow he even manages to make using UNIX seem like fun. A tip of the hat to Ed Krol as well, whose book, *The Whole Internet User's Guide and Catalog*, proved to be a valuable resource.

Finally, I am grateful to the many people in the on-line industry who provided assistance and information while I was researching this book: Amy Arnold and Margaret Ryan of America Online, Janet Bowers of CompuServe, Barbara Byro of GEnie, Gwenn Gauthier of Schwartz Communications, Mark Lavi and Nancy Morrisroe of Delphi, Mary McElhiney of ZiffNet, Caroline Wallace of Prodigy, and Gail Williams of The WELL. Thanks, everyone!

Introduction

The on-line universe is expanding rapidly. Millions of people now use on-line services to telecommute, find information, shop, and communicate. There are more commercial on-line services to choose from than ever before, and each of them offers a greater variety of resources. But finding your way around these services isn't always easy, and on-line travelers find themselves on the electronic equivalent of dirt roads more often than on interstates.

That's where *The Traveler's Guide to the Information Highway* comes in—it will help you navigate the complicated highways, side roads, and alleys of the on-line universe. This book is a travel guide for all the major commercial on-line services, plus the Internet. It gives you everything you need to know in order to become a savvy on-line traveler. Its maps will help you get your bearings instantly, no matter where you choose to go. And they will point the way to some of the most interesting, useful, and valuable resources to be found on each of these on-line services.

Who This Book Is For

Whether you're a novice modem user or a seasoned on-line traveler, this book has something for you. It's designed to be a useful roadmap and handbook for *anyone* who is interested in commercial on-line services or the Internet.

If you're currently trying to decide which on-line service will best meet your needs, you'll find a wealth of information here to help with your decision. This book covers every major commercial on-line service, plus the Internet. There are details about each on-line service's strengths and weaknesses, pricing, "look and feel," and more. The maps give you an overview of what's on each on-line service, and you can browse the service resource descriptions to learn about the highlights of each one.

Once you subscribe to an on-line service—or if you're already a member of one—*The Traveler's Guide to the Information Highway* will help you get the most out of that service. Each chapter includes a detailed description of how to get around, including summaries of the most useful commands. The resource descriptions will point you to some of the best features found on each service. The maps will help you find what you're looking for quickly and easily. Or, if you're just browsing, use the maps to get acquainted at a glance with what's available on the various menus.

If you're already a sophisticated on-line traveler, you'll find that the maps

provide a convenient way to locate resources you're interested in as quickly as possible. The maps also give you the big picture and may suggest possibilities you hadn't considered, or didn't know about. (Most on-line services are huge, and it's almost impossible to be aware of all the resources available.)

A Short Tour of the Chapters

Chapter 1 covers the basics of getting on line. If you've never used a modem—even if you have no idea what *on line* means—read this chapter for a quick but thorough introduction to on-line travel. You'll find everything you need to know to get started. And on-line travelers at all levels of experience will find the e-mail guide at the end of this chapter useful: It shows you exactly how to send e-mail between the major on-line e-mail systems.

Chapter 2 is a collection of useful Travel Tips that tell you more about on-line customs, about where to get help when you need it, how to keep costs down, and more. If you want to make the most of your on-line experiences, don't miss the tips in this chapter.

Chapters 3 through 9 are the heart of the book. Chapters 3 through 8 cover the largest and most important on-line services in the U.S. today: CompuServe, ZiffNet, Prodigy, America Online, Delphi, and GEnie. Each of these chapters gives a basic introduction to the service or network covered, tells you how much it costs and how to sign up, and provides instructions for getting around. The maps give you a bird's-eye view of each service, and

the resource descriptions following each map describe and evaluate that service's highlights. Chapter 9 covers the Internet, which is not a commercial service, but rather a public data network spanning the entire globe. *Note:* You'll find three-page foldout maps of CompuServe and the Internet at the back of this book.

If you're looking for on-line resources on a particular topic, be sure to check out the Index at the back of the book. It's the quickest way to scan all the on-line services for a topic you're interested in. You'll also find the On-line Traveler's Dictionary, a glossary of on-line terminology, at the back of the book.

How to Use the Travel Guide

If you know how to use a map, you know how to use *The Traveler's Guide to the Information Highway* to find the information you need, fast. Each chapter covers one major information service and includes a roadmap of that service. The maps show you, in a visual way, the major areas into which the service is divided and how they're connected. When you're browsing a new network, use its map to help you find your way.

The central hub of each map represents the on-line service's main menu. The spokes radiating from this central hub are choices on that main menu, and they lead to menus for each of the service's main subject areas. Branching submenus and sub-submenus on the map correspond to menus you'll find within the on-line service. Turn the page to see a sample map.

How to Read the Travel Guides

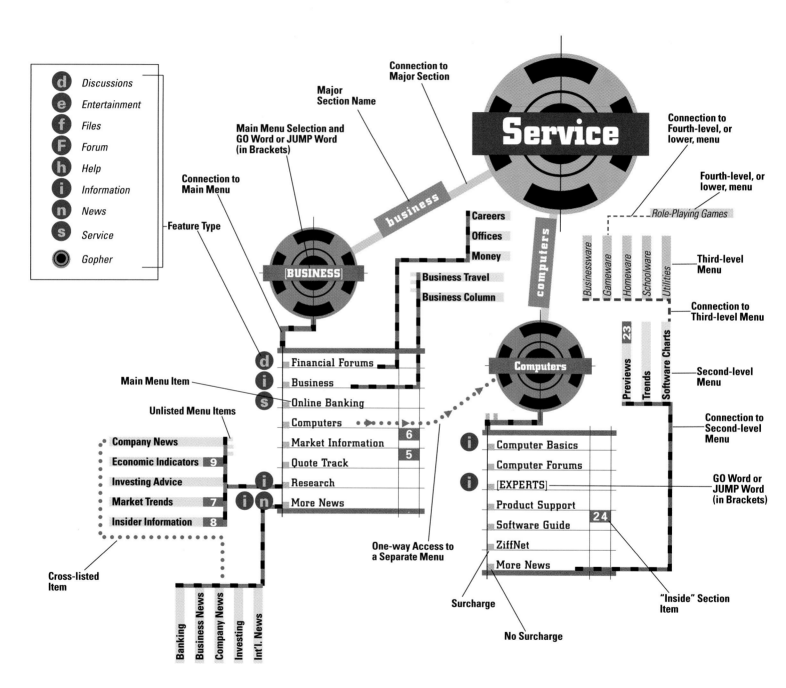

Legend:

- **d** Discussions
- **e** Entertainment
- **f** Files
- **F** Forum
- **h** Help
- **i** Information
- **n** News
- **s** Service
- **◉** Gopher

Service

Connection to Major Section

Major Section Name

Connection to Fourth-level, or lower, menu

Main Menu Selection and GO Word or JUMP Word (in Brackets)

Fourth-level, or lower, menu

Role-Playing Games

Connection to Main Menu

business

Feature Type

[BUSINESS]

Careers
Offices
Money
Business Travel
Business Column

computers

Businessware
Gameware
Homeware
Schoolware
Utilities

Third-level Menu

Connection to Third-level Menu

Computers

Previews 23
Trends
Software Charts

Second-level Menu

Connection to Second-level Menu

- **d** Financial Forums
- **i** Business

Main Menu Item

- **s** Online Banking

Unlisted Menu Items

- Computers ····▶····▶ 6
- Market Information 5
- Quote Track
- **i** Research
- **i n** More News

- Company News
- Economic Indicators 9
- Investing Advice
- Market Trends 7
- Insider Information 8

i Computer Basics
i Computer Forums
[EXPERTS]
Product Support 24
Software Guide
ZiffNet
More News

GO Word or JUMP Word (in Brackets)

Cross-listed Item

One-way Access to a Separate Menu

Banking
Business News
Company News
Investing
Int'l. News

Surcharge

No Surcharge

"Inside" Section Item

Following each map are pages describing and evaluating the best and most popular resources on that on-line service. Each description is preceded by a number that refers to a location on the map, so you can use the map to find any resource you've just read about. Or, when you see a number on the map, turn to the corresponding number in the listing to read more about the resource in that place.

Each resource description includes two visual keys to help you evaluate the item at a glance. The quality of each resource is indicated by the number of triangles pointing up (or a triangle pointing down). The cost of the item (amount of surcharges, relative to other resources on the same on-line service) is shown by the number of dollar signs.

With the maps and resource descriptions in hand, you'll find it's easy to locate just the resources you need.

A Note to Readers

The on-line world is a large and rapidly changing place. Although I checked the accuracy of each map carefully, on-line services frequently change and rearrange their menus. As a result, some resources may have moved from their position on the map. If you don't find a resource where it is shown, chances are it will probably be on a nearby menu—or the service may have discontinued it. If in doubt, visit the on-line service's index of resources and search there for the missing item, or check with their on-line customer support or member assistance area.

Also, because of the immense size of many of these on-line services, it was impossible to include every item on the menus. To save space and to make the maps more readable, I left many redundant or cross-listed resources unlabeled, so sometimes a map shows only a representative selection of the items on a menu. However, the maps clearly indicate incomplete menus.

Of course, the resource descriptions only cover a fraction of the resources in each on-line service. I've listed what I think are the best and most popular resources, concentrating on those of interest to the largest number of people. I focused on resources that are especially clever, useful, exciting, or just plain cool; and these naturally fared better in my evaluations than resources that are ordinary, dull, difficult to use, or aimed at a small audience of users.

Of course, my evaluations and decisions about what to include are subjective. If you know of an outstanding resource that I overlooked, or if you want to comment on my evaluations, please let me know. Send me a letter or an e-mail message telling me what on-line service carries the resource, exactly where it can be found, and why you think the world ought to know about it. Write to

Dylan Tweney
c/o Ziff Davis Press
5903 Christie Avenue
Emeryville, CA 94608

Or send e-mail to my CompuServe address, 72241,443 (Internet address 72241.443@compuserve.com). I'd love to hear your suggestions!

Going On Line

CHAPTER 1

What's on line? Everything!

Going "on line" is a simple matter of using a modem to connect your computer to another computer via ordinary telephone lines that transmit data between the two. The possibilities that open up to you by going on line are immense because you can tap into pipelines of data so expansive they've been termed, quite appropriately, "the data highway."

Right now there is no one single "data superhighway" connecting everybody. Instead, we have many large but mostly separate data highways, each one a major conduit of information and resources. All of the on-line services covered in this book are, in this sense, data highways of various sizes. At some points these highways connect to each other (often by means of the largest of data highways, the Internet), but for the most part they run through different parts of the on-line universe, rarely intersecting with each other.

Once you get on line, you'll have access to information you can't get in any book. You'll be able to talk to people you might never be able to meet otherwise. You can get news, weather, sports, games, graphics, and great advice on any subject—it's all available on line.

Think of going on line as upgrading your desktop PC to a NASA-class supercomputer. Think of it as plugging into a worldwide web of electronic intelligence. Think of it as putting a graphical interface on your telephone that lets you chat with people in Taiwan, in Iowa, and in Germany—all at the same time, and for the price of a local call.

There's a wealth of information waiting for you on line, and all you need to know is how to find it. The Internet, CompuServe, Prodigy…these are just a few of the massive information services you can tap into with a modem, right from your desk. When you do, you'll be transforming your personal computer from a mere word- and number-cruncher into a sophisticated communicator. Anywhere data can flow, you can go, once you're on line.

And the benefits of getting onto these networks are substantial, whether you need demographic data to help you hone your company's marketing efforts, or you want to share your thoughts with people halfway around the world.

Going on line brings the world of information to your desktop computer

But when you want to go on line, you're going to need some orientation to keep from getting lost. The on-line universe is big, and it's hard to find what you need unless you have directions. That's where this travel guide comes in.

We've mapped all the major on-line services, so you can find your way around them quickly and easily. And just like a traveler's guide to a city or country, this travel guide gives you advice about the best places to visit, how to get around, and what to watch out for. Even if you're just browsing, this guide will help you make the most of your on-line time. And when you want to find something *fast*, the index will help you zero in on the right source, so you can get what you need as quickly as possible.

Going on line is like going to a foreign country. You will be dealing with unfamiliar customs, using new modes of transportation, and passing through territory you've never seen before. The Netiquette Travel Tip in Chapter 2 will help familiarize you with the customs, and the "Getting Around" sections of each chapter will make it easier for you to transport yourself from one place to another. As you explore the on-line universe, this book will help you become a savvy traveler.

On-line Basics

If you're already an experienced electronic traveler, you can skip this section. But if you're new to the world of on-line information, read on to learn the basics of going on line.

In order to get into the on-line universe, you'll need a few tools. For starters, of course, you must have a computer, a modem, and software to control the modem. And there are a few additional tools you'll find essential.

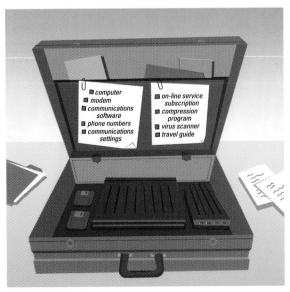

Packing list for the Data Highway traveler

The Computer

The computer can be anything from the humblest Apple II to the fastest, newest Pentium-based machine. You name it: Macs, IBM-compatibles, Amigas—it doesn't matter. You can get on line with all of them.

Of course, the type of computer you use is going to determine what kind of modem and modem software you'll need. But modems and a variety of communications software programs are available for just about every personal computer ever made. If you're in doubt as to what will work with your computer, check with your dealer.

The Modem

The second required component is a modem. A modem is the hardware that makes the connection between your computer and the outside world, using your telephone line to transmit data to and from other computers. It does this by converting digital information from your computer into sounds that can be transmitted over the phone line. On the other end of the line, another modem "listens" to these sounds and converts them back into electronic data, passing the data on to the receiving modem's own connected computer. This process works the same way in reverse, so that a remote computer can send data to your computer; your modem "listens" to this data and passes it on to your computer. In the language of electronics, converting digital signals into sounds and back into digital signals again is called *modulation* and *demodulation*—and that's where your modem gets its name; it's a "MOdulator-DEModulator."

Modems can be internal or external. An internal modem is a card you plug into an expansion slot inside your computer. The internal modem doesn't take up space on your desk, and it draws its power from your computer's power supply. Once you've installed an internal modem, all you need to do is plug it into the phone jack in the wall. In contrast, an external modem is a box that

sits on your desk and is connected via a cable to your computer. An external modem has lights on it that flash as the modem communicates, so you get some additional information about your connection; for instance, you can see if the connection has been broken. On the other hand, an external modem takes up space. And instead of one wire, you have to worry about three: the serial cable that connects the modem to your computer, the modem's power cord, and the line going to the phone jack.

Both types of modems sport an additional phone jack, into which you can plug your telephone, so that it will continue to operate normally whenever you're not using your modem. If you don't have the luxury of having a separate phone line just for your modem, this extra jack is indispensable.

Most modems also have speakers, so you can hear what happens during connections. When you're making a connection, the first thing you'll hear (assuming the modem speaker is turned on) is the modem dialing the number you've requested. When the receiving, or *remote modem*, picks up, it sends out a "hailing tone" that identifies it as a modem (as opposed to a human being who's just picked up the phone). Your modem sends a higher-pitched tone in return. Then you'll hear a hissing noise, which is called the *handshake*—the two modems are exchanging information about how they can communicate, and resolving how they will do it. Once this handshake is complete, the modem turns its speaker off, and you're on line, ready to send data to or receive data from the remote modem. If the modem speaker were to remain on during your communications session, you'd be able to overhear this exchange of data; it sounds much like the hissing of the modems' handshake. Since this hiss is pretty much unintelligible (not to mention annoying) to human ears, the modem turns the speaker off.

The Modem's Face Lights

The modem's face lights

An external modem has lights on its face that give you valuable information about what's going on during a communications session. These lights are especially useful in diagnosing problems if your terminal screen freezes up, if you have trouble connecting, or if something else goes wrong. Here's what the labels on each light stand for, and what they mean when lit:

HS (High Speed) The modem is set to its highest transmission speed.

AA (Auto Answer) The modem is set to answer incoming calls automatically.

CD (Carrier Detect) The modem is connected to a remote modem.

OH (Off Hook) The modem has picked up the line (taken the phone off the hook).

RD (Receive Data) This light flashes as the modem receives data over the phone line.

SD (Send Data) This light flashes as the modem sends data over the phone line.

TR (Terminal Ready) The modem is receiving a ready signal from the comm software running on your computer.

MR (Modem Ready) The modem is turned on.

The Software

Once you've got a modem connected to your computer, you'll need a communications program to handle the data going back and forth. This program takes data sent by the remote computer and displays it as text on screen (or saves it as a file on your disk, if you so choose); it also takes your own keystrokes and commands and sends them as data to the remote computer. In this way, communications software (*comm* software for short) coordinates your modem, your computer, and you. The comm software also engages the proper protocol to transfer data to your computer when you request a file from an information service.

A general-purpose comm program will give you everything you need to connect to most of the information services described in this book. Most general-purpose comm software has many options for customizing the way you communicate. The software may contain phone lists of frequently dialed information services and bulletin boards; modem settings required for connecting to those numbers; information about the type of emulations and protocols used by the services; and so forth. Many comm programs also include the ability to record and replay *scripts*, which automate tedious or repetitive processes such as logging on or downloading files. The most elementary scripts are simply macros that "type" characters for you; the most complicated scripts are full-blown programs in their own right. The kinds of scripts you can create and replay will depend on the software you choose. General-purpose comm programs tend to accommodate the most sophisticated script capabilities.

A wide variety of general-purpose communications programs are available for just about any computer platform. If you're using a DOS-based PC, Procomm Plus and Crosstalk are two of the most popular full-featured communications packages, featuring many emulations and download protocols, powerful scripting capabilities, and easy-to-use interfaces. You won't go far wrong with either of these programs, and Windows versions of both are available. On the Mac side of the world, MicroPhone II is probably the most typical full-featured communications program.

Some services, such as Prodigy and America Online, require their own specialized comm programs, or "front-ends." These programs provide a graphical interface to the information service for which they're made, and without the program, you won't be able to connect to the service. (Likewise, you can't use the front-end program to connect to any other information service.) When you sign up for an information service that requires a special interface program, this software is usually included with the sign-up fee.

A third kind of comm software is the optional front-end. Some information services have awkward command structures, are difficult to use, or are not very visually intuitive. Many programs have appeared on the communications scene to make connecting to these services easier and more efficient. For example, CompuServe has its own optional front-end, the CompuServe Information Manager (CIM), which puts a friendlier, more graphical face on the CompuServe service. Programs like these are designed for a specific service and won't work with any other—but they're not absolutely required to connect to the service.

The Phone Numbers and Communications Settings

Now you're almost ready to go on line. All you need to get connected are the phone numbers of some information services and bulletin boards, and the *communications settings* required to connect to them.

The communications settings determine the way your modem exchanges data with another

modem, and these settings are what the two modems are discussing during their handshake. If you don't specify the correct settings before you connect to a service, you'll probably see a lot of "garbage characters" appear on your screen. If that happens, just give your comm software the command to hang up the line, and double-check your communications settings.

The three most important settings for a communications session are the number of data bits, the parity used, and the number of stop bits. Don't worry about the technical side of these arcane terms! All you need to know is that the most common setup is 8 data bits, no parity, and 1 stop bit—frequently abbreviated "8N1." If your comm software is set to 8N1, you'll have no problems connecting most of the time. The second most common setup is 7 data bits, even parity, and 1 stop bit, abbreviated "7E1." Using either 8N1 or 7E1, you'll be able to connect to just about every information service there is.

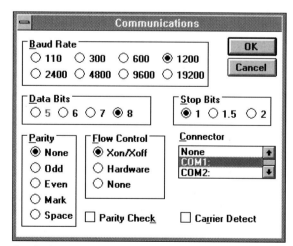

A typical comm program's settings dialog, currently set for 8 data bits, no parity, and 1 stop bit

The On-line Service Subscription

The process of going on line can be as simple as setting up your comm software to dial up your local bulletin board and log on. In the case of most major information services described in this book, however, it's a little more complicated: You need to have an account or a subscription before you can connect. Many commercial information services let you dial up their main access number with your modem in order to sign up for the service; others require that you actually make a telephone call (yes, with your voice) or purchase a membership kit in a store. When you sign up, the information service gives you instructions about how to connect to it, what numbers and communications settings to use, and what commands to use once you're connected. That's all you need to get started!

Most on-line services impose some combination of a monthly membership fee plus hourly connect-time charges. The pricing gets somewhat complicated with some services, so it's a good idea to pay close attention to what's included in your basic fees and what's considered a surcharge. Spend a few too many long, carefree evenings on line, and at the end of the month you'll get a vivid illustration of the principle that "information is not free."

The Compression Program

When you start browsing the on-line world, collecting files and programs, you'll run into *compressed* or *archived* data files. These files aren't readable, viewable, or executable—they've been compressed so that they're smaller and don't take as much time to download. A compressed file can contain one or many files. Before you can do anything with them, you'll either need to extract (expand) them using the same compression program that was used to compress them, or use a counterpart decompression program.

The standard compression/decompression programs for PC files are PKZIP and PKUNZIP. Files compressed with PKZIP are identified by their .ZIP file name extensions. Both of these programs are available on most bulletin boards. They're shareware, and it costs only $49 to register the pair.

For Mac files, the standard compression program is StuffIt!, and in order to decompress StuffIt!-compressed files, you'll need to get a program called UnStuffIt!. You can download UnStuffIt!, which is freeware, from any bulletin board or information service that uses this compression program.

Some archived files are *self-extracting archives*, which means the archive file has been converted to an executable program. When you run this program, it "pulls out of itself" all the files that were archived in it—which you can then use.

The Virus Scanner

Whenever you download software from a bulletin board or an information service, you don't need to be *paranoid* about viruses, but you should be *cautious*. Most *sysops* (system operators) are responsible individuals who scan every file they get, and only put virus-free files on line. Still, some viruses will escape detection, and not every sysop will check every file. For that reason, a good virus-scanning program is indispensable. Get one and use it: Scan *every* program you download *before* running it. Run periodic scans on your hard disk and floppy disks, too. And exercise common sense: A file you download over the Internet or from a neighborhood BBS run by young hackers is probably more likely to have a virus than a file downloaded from a major commercial information service, for the simple reason that the commercial information service has a stake in providing clean files only; they'd go out of business if their files were overrun by viruses.

Note that viruses can only infect your system through executable (program) files. Data files (text files, word-processed documents, and graphics images) can't contain viruses. If you don't know whether a file is executable or not, scan it. Also, always scan compressed files *after* decompressing them—unless they're in a self-extracting archive, in which case you should scan them *before and after* extracting them.

The Travel Guide

You wouldn't go on a vacation to Rio or London without a travel guide, now, would you? When you go on line, you'll want to be sure that you keep *The Traveler's Guide to the Information Highway* with you so you don't get lost. It'll show you the commands you need to negotiate each information service, point out the highlights, and let you know what dangers to watch out for. So plug in that modem, pilgrim, and get on line!

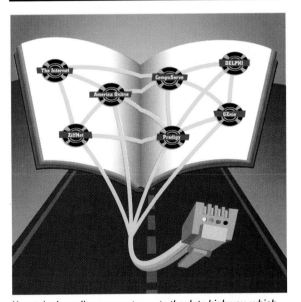

Your telephone line connects you to the data highway, which you can take to any of the information sources in this book.

How to Send E-Mail Anywhere

Most information services include some sort of electronic mail, or *e-mail*, facility. E-mail allows you to send electronic messages to other members of the service no matter where they are. But what do you do if you want to send e-mail to your next-door neighbor, who's got an e-mail address on a *different* information service?

It's simple. Most information services provide e-mail *gateways* to other mail networks. A gateway simply takes messages from one network and hands them off to another network for delivery. To use a gateway, you usually just need to format your message's address correctly, and off it goes. In some cases you need to take additional steps, but it's usually not very hard once you know the basic approach.

Most major e-mail services, such as CompuServe, have an Internet gateway. If this is true of your e-mail service, you can use the Internet to send messages to people on any other service that also has an Internet gateway. Your service doesn't need a direct connection with the other service to use this gateway. The Internet serves as a middleman. You send a properly addressed message to the Internet, and the Internet passes it on to the proper e-mail system for delivery to the recipient. Many of the examples below show you how to send e-mail from one service to another.

The drawback to using e-mail gateways is that you need to know your recipient's exact e-mail address ahead of time. Usually there's just no way for you to look up someone's address when they subscribe to another e-mail system. In addition, some of your e-mail options may be limited, as well. For example, many gateways don't support return receipts or attached files.

To simplify sending mail through gateways, the next sections provide e-mail formatting instructions for sending mail between the various information services. Just replace the sample address with your recipient's actual e-mail address, and format the TO: line of your message exactly as shown. In some cases you'll notice a few additional steps that are required.

Caution Most e-mail addresses must be formatted exactly as shown in these examples, without extra spaces or punctuation other than that shown. In some cases, capitalization is also important.

Sending Mail from America Online

Here's how you send e-mail from America Online to each of the following on-line services.

To CompuServe: To send e-mail to the CompuServe address **71234,56**, address your message to **71234.56@cis**.

To Delphi: To send e-mail to the Delphi user **JAMESJOYCE**, address your message to **jamesjoyce@delphi.com**.

To GEnie: To send e-mail to GEnie user **joyce**, address your message to **joyce@genie**.

To the Internet: To send e-mail to an Internet address, you don't need to use any special codes. Just address it to the Internet address—for example, **joyce@ulysses.edu**.

To MCI: To send a message to James Joyce, whose MCI address is **123-4567**, address your message to **1234567@mcimail.com** (be sure to remove the hyphen). You can also use your recipient's MCI user name. For the user name **JJoyce**, for instance, address the message to **jjoyce@mcimail.com**. If more than one MCI subscriber has that user name, however, your message won't be delivered. It's better to use the mailbox number if you know it, because the number is guaranteed to be unique.

To Prodigy: To send a message to the Prodigy account **abcd12e**, use the address **abcd12e@prodigy.com**.

Sending Mail from CompuServe

Here's how you send e-mail from CompuServe to each of the following on-line services.

To America Online: To send a message to the America Online user **J Joyce**, address your message to **INTERNET:jjoyce@aol.com**. Be sure to remove all spaces from the America Online address, and use only lowercase letters after the colon. Also, messages must be no longer than 8K and will arrive with all nonprinting ASCII characters converted to spaces.

To Delphi: To send e-mail to the Delphi user **JAMESJOYCE**, address your message to **INTERNET:jamesjoyce@delphi.com**.

To GEnie: To send a message to the GEnie user **joyce**, send your message to **INTERNET:joyce@genie.geis.com**.

To the Internet: To send a message to the Internet address **joyce@ulysses.edu**, address your message to **INTERNET:joyce@ulysses.edu**.

To MCI: To send a message to the MCI address **123-4567**, send your message to **MCIMAIL:123-4567**.

To Prodigy: To send a message to the Prodigy account **abcd12e**, address it to **INTERNET:abcd12e@prodigy.com**.

Sending Mail from Delphi

Here's how you send e-mail from Delphi to each of the following on-line services.

To America Online: To send e-mail to the America Online user **J Joyce**, address your message to **internet"jjoyce@aol.com"**. Be sure to remove all spaces from the America Online address, and use only lowercase letters. Also, messages must be no longer than 8K and will arrive with all nonprinting ASCII characters converted to spaces.

To CompuServe: To send a message to the CompuServe address **71234,56**, send your message to **internet"71234.56@compuserve.com"**. Be sure to use a period in place of the comma in the CompuServe address.

To GEnie: To send a message to GEnie user **joyce**, use **internet"joyce@genie.geis.com"**.

To the Internet: To send e-mail to an Internet address, you don't need to use any special codes. Just address it to the Internet address—for example, **internet"joyce@ulysses.edu"**.

To MCI: To send a message to James Joyce, whose MCI address is **123-4567**, address your message to **internet"1234567@mcimail.com"** (be sure to remove the hyphen). You can also use your recipient's MCI user name. For the user name **JJoyce**, for instance, address the message to **internet"jjoyce@mcimail.com"**. If more than one MCI subscriber has that user name, however, your message won't be delivered. It's better to use the mailbox number if you know it, because the number is guaranteed to be unique.

To Prodigy: To send e-mail to the Prodigy account **abcd12e**, address your message to **internet"abcd12e@prodigy.com"**.

Sending Mail from GEnie

Here's how you send e-mail from GEnie to each of the following on-line services.

To America Online: To send a message to the America Online user **J Joyce**, address your message to **jjoyce@aol.com@INET#**. Be sure to remove all spaces from the America Online address, and use only lowercase letters except for the final **INET#**. Also, messages must be no longer than 8K and will arrive with all nonprinting ASCII characters converted to spaces.

To CompuServe: To send a message to the CompuServe address **71234,56**, address your

message to **71234.56@compuserve.com@INET#**. You must use a period in place of the comma.

To Delphi: To send e-mail to the Delphi user **JAMESJOYCE**, address your message to **jamesjoyce@delphi.com@INET#**.

To the Internet: To send a message to the Internet address **joyce@ulysses.edu**, send it to **joyce@ulysses.edu@INET#**.

To MCI: To send a message to James Joyce, whose MCI address is **123-4567**, address your message to **1234567@mcimail.com@INET#**. You can also use your recipient's MCI user name. For the user name **JJoyce**, for instance, address the message to **jjoyce@mcimail.com@INET#**. If more than one MCI subscriber has that user name, however, your message won't be delivered. It's better to use the mailbox number if you know it, because the number is guaranteed to be unique.

To Prodigy: To send a message to the Prodigy account **abcd12e**, address it to **abcd12e@prodigy.com@INET#**.

Sending Mail from the Internet

Here's how you send e-mail from the Internet to each of the following on-line services.

To America Online: To send e-mail to the America Online user **J Joyce**, address your message to **jjoyce@aol.com**. Be sure to remove all spaces from the America Online address, and use only lowercase letters. Also, messages must be no longer than 8K and will arrive with all nonprinting ASCII characters converted to spaces.

To CompuServe: To send e-mail to the CompuServe address **71234,56**, address your message to **71234.56@compuserve.com**. You must use a period in place of the comma in the CompuServe address.

To Delphi: To send e-mail to the Delphi user **JAMESJOYCE**, address your message to **jamesjoyce@delphi.com**.

To GEnie: To send a message to GEnie user **joyce**, use the address **joyce@genie.geis.com**.

To MCI: To send a message to **James Joyce**, whose MCI address is **123-4567**, address your message to **1234567@mcimail.com** (be sure to remove the hyphen). You can also use your recipient's MCI user name. For the user name **JJoyce**, for instance, address the message to **jjoyce@mcimail.com**. If more than one MCI subscriber has that user name, however, your message won't be delivered. It's better to use the mailbox number if you know it, because the number is guaranteed to be unique.

To Prodigy: To send e-mail to the Prodigy account **abcd12e**, address your message to **abcd12e@prodigy.com**.

Sending Mail from MCI

Here's how you send e-mail from MCI to each of the following on-line services.

To America Online: To send a message to James Joyce, whose America Online user name is **J Joyce**, type **James Joyce (EMS)** at the TO: prompt. Enter **INTERNET** at the EMS: prompt that appears next. Then enter **jjoyce@aol.com** at the MBX: prompt (remove all spaces from the user name and use only lowercase letters). Messages must be no longer than 8K and will arrive with all nonprinting ASCII characters converted to spaces.

To CompuServe: To send a message to James Joyce, whose CompuServe address is **71234,56**, type **James Joyce (EMS)** at the TO: prompt. Then enter **compuserve** when the EMS: prompt appears. When the first MBX: prompt appears, enter **P=CSMail**. At the second MBX: prompt, type **DDA=ID=71234,56** to complete the address.

To Delphi: To send a message to James Joyce, whose Delphi member name is **JAMESJOYCE**, type **James Joyce (EMS)** at the TO: prompt. Enter **INTERNET** when the EMS: prompt appears. Then enter **jamesjoyce@delphi.com** when the MBX: prompt appears.

To GEnie: To send a message to James Joyce, whose GEnie user name is **joyce**, type **James Joyce (EMS)** at the TO: prompt. Enter **INTERNET** at the EMS: prompt that appears next. Then enter **joyce@genie.geis.com** at the MBX: prompt to complete the address.

To the Internet: To send a message to James Joyce, whose address on the Internet is **joyce@ulysses.com**, type **James Joyce (EMS)** at the TO: prompt. Enter **INTERNET** when the EMS: prompt appears. Then enter **joyce@ulysses.com** when the MBX: prompt appears.

To Prodigy: To send a message to James Joyce, whose Prodigy address is **abcd12e**, type **James Joyce (EMS)** at the TO: prompt. Enter **INTERNET** when the EMS: prompt appears. Then enter **abcd12e@prodigy.com** when the MBX: prompt appears.

Sending Mail from Prodigy

Here's how you send e-mail from Prodigy to each of the following on-line services. (Note that you *must* use the Prodigy Mail Manager in each case.)

To America Online: To send e-mail to the America Online user **J Joyce**, start a new message in the Prodigy Mail manager and select **Internet E-Mail** in the Delivery Method dialog box. Enter **jjoyce@aol.com** on the TO: line and continue writing your message. Be sure to remove all spaces from the America Online address, and use only lowercase letters. Also, messages must be no longer than 8K and will arrive with all nonprinting ASCII characters converted to spaces.

To CompuServe: To send e-mail to the CompuServe address **71234,56**, start a new message in the Prodigy Mail Manager and select **Internet E-Mail** in the Delivery Method dialog box. Enter **71234.56@compuserve.com** on the TO: line and continue writing your message. You must use a period in place of a comma in the CompuServe address.

To Delphi: To send a message to the Delphi user **JAMESJOYCE**, start a new message in the Prodigy Mail Manager and select **Internet E-Mail** in the Delivery Method dialog box. Enter **jamesjoyce@delphi.com** on the TO: line and complete your message.

To GEnie: To send a message to GEnie user **Joyce**, start a new message in the Prodigy Mail Manager and select **Internet E-Mail** in the Delivery Method dialog box. Then enter **joyce@genie.geis.com** on the TO: line to address your message.

To the Internet: To send a message to James Joyce, whose address on the Internet is **joyce@ulysses.com**, start a new message in the Prodigy Mail Manager and select **Internet E-Mail** in the Delivery Method dialog box. Enter **joyce@ulysses.com** on the TO: line and continue writing your message.

To MCI: To send a message to **James Joyce**, whose MCI address is **123-4567**, start a new message in the Prodigy Mail Manager and select **Internet E-Mail** in the Delivery Method dialog box. Enter **1234567@mcimail.com** on the TO: line of your message (be sure to remove the hyphen from the MCI address). You can also use your recipient's MCI user name. For the user name **JJoyce**, for instance, enter **jjoyce@mcimail.com** on the TO: line. If more than one MCI subscriber has that user name, however, your message won't be delivered. It's better to use the mailbox number if you know it, because the number is guaranteed to be unique.

Now that you know the basics of going on line and how to send e-mail all over the world, there's only one thing left to do: Get on line! Use the following chapters to decide which on-line service or services you want to subscribe to. Then, once you've got your subscription (or if you have one already), use the maps in this travel guide to help you find your way around. You'll discover that the on-line universe is a fascinating, rapidly changing place, with every bit as much variety and excitement as the real world. Have fun exploring the new electronic frontier. *Bon voyage!*

CHAPTER 2

Travel Tips

When you're roaming around the on-line world, you should know a thing or two about the customs, habits, and dangers of your virtual surroundings. Here are some tips to help you become a savvy on-line traveler, whether you're exploring the wilds of the Internet or strolling the more cultured avenues of a commercial information service. From net etiquette (*netiquette*), to shareware, to keeping costs down, the following tips give you important information to make your on-line travel pleasant and productive.

Minding Your Manners with Netiquette

As in any other community, the electronic community has its do's and don'ts. It's all too easy to unintentionally annoy your fellow denizens of virtual space, especially when you're new to the medium. Keep the following guidelines in mind when you're on line, and you'll avoid much needless conflict.

▶ ***Think before you type.*** *Remember that when you're on line, your words are all anyone ever sees of you. It's difficult to convey subtle shades of meaning in plain, unadorned text, so choose your words carefully. If someone has sent you a message or posted a public message that makes you angry, don't instantly fire off a reply. Wait a while, write a response off line, and look at it again in a couple of hours. Once you send the message, you can't take it back, so make sure it says exactly what you want it to.*

▶ ***Don't publicly quote private messages.*** *If someone sends you a private e-mail message, it's bad form to quote that message in a public forum without the sender's permission. The sender probably would have posted the message publicly if it were OK for everyone to read it.*

▶ ***Use emoticons with humorous or ironic statements.*** *Irony is one of the most difficult tones to convey on line. If the recipient of your message misses your ironic intention, your message may cause anger, mislead, or portray a mistaken impression about you. It's a good idea to include an emoticon (see the next travel tip) signifying irony or humor after any such statement, just to make sure the reader "gets it." If you don't like the little smiley ASCII faces, at least use <g> to show that you're grinning or <s> to show that you're wearing a smile.*

▶ ***DON'T SHOUT!*** *If you post your messages in all capitals, it looks to readers like you're shouting. Use standard capitalization, except when you really do want extra emphasis for a few words or a phrase.*

▶ ***Don't use italic, <u>underlining</u>, or other special characters.*** *E-mail systems vary widely as to the characters that they're capable of transmitting and displaying, and so do the computers that people use to get their e-mail. Limit yourself to ordinary letters and punctuation that are common to all systems. When you do need to indicate an underlined word (in a book title, for instance), put it between two _underline marks_ or surround it with *asterisks* to set it off.*

▶ *Check your spelling. As mentioned above, all anyone can see of you on line is your words. Poor spelling reflects badly on you. If you can't spell well yourself, use a spelling checker—they're widely available and are included with most of today's word processing software.*

▶ *Use specific, detailed subject lines. Whether you're posting a message in a public discussion area or sending a private letter to a single person, your message is more likely to get read if its subject line says exactly what the message is about. For example, "Need help" is a much less effective subject line than "Can't get Word-Immaculate to print." For the best results, be precise and concise.*

▶ *Use quotations sparingly in replies. Many mail and public message systems let you quote part or all of a message when replying to it. This is useful for reminding readers exactly what you're responding to, but don't overdo it. One or two lines is usually enough; having to read more than that is not only annoying but a waste of readers' time. And if they're paying connect-time charges, it's a waste of their money, too.*

▶ *Treat others with respect. Just as in the real world, people want to be treated with respect when they're on line. Most "flame wars" (on-line arguments that have turned nasty, also known simply as flames) start because disagreements turn personal, and respect breaks down. Avoid personal attacks, don't insult people, and don't let yourself get drawn into personal arguments.*

Expressing Yourself with Emoticons

Do you know what :-) means? If someone tells you that they are ROF,L, does that mean they're into massage? Should you be upset if someone tells you to RTFM? If you don't know the answers to these questions, you need a quick lesson in *emoticons*, the emotion icons used in the on-line world to convey shades of meaning or feeling that can be difficult to get across on an unforgiving computer screen.

When posting messages to a bulletin board or via e-mail, your range of expression is severely limited. All you've got to work with are the 26 letters (upper- and lowercase) plus a handful of punctuation marks. There's no easy way to include in a computer message the gestures, expressions, and body language that enrich face-to-face communication. Emotions and inflections are very hard to communicate on line.

To work around this difficulty, many people employ emoticons: typographical symbols that indicate subtle shades of meaning. Some of these emoticons are sideways pictures—that is, turn your head to the left and you'll see the "faces" that illustrate the emotional messages. Other emoticons are simply abbreviations for frequently used phrases.

Here are some of the most common emoticons and their meanings:

:)   Smiling face; I'm happy

:-)   Variation on smiling face

;)   Winking and smiling; I'm joking; indicates irony

;-)   Variation on winking and smiling face

:(	Frowning face; I'm unhappy
:-(	Variation on frowning face
:-/	Wry face; indicates ambivalence
:->	Evil grin; smirk
<S>	Smile; I'm smiling or I'm happy; I mean well, so don't be offended
<G>	Grin; I'm grinning; don't take what I just said too seriously; I'm kidding
<BG>	Big grin; that was a joke; I'm kidding
BRB	Be right back
BTW	By the way
FWIW	For what it's worth
G,D&R	Grinning, ducking, and running; follows a comment spoken in jest that you expect to provoke a strong reaction
IMHO	In my humble opinion
LOL	Laughing out loud; what you wrote was funny
PITA	Pain in the (expletive deleted)
PMFJI	Pardon me for jumping in
OTOH	On the other hand
ROF,L	Rolling on floor, laughing; what you wrote was hilarious
RTFM	Read the (expletive deleted) manual
TIA	Thanks in advance
TTFN	Ta-ta for now
>	Punctuation used at the beginning of each line in a quotation (instead of quotation marks), especially when quoting parts of a message to which one is replying

Use emoticons sparingly—overdo it and you risk coming across affected or too clever. But do use them; a well-placed <G> can avert a possibly disastrous misunderstanding, and save you hours of agonizing apologies and explanations.

Cutting Costs

If you spend much time exploring the on-line universe, be prepared for some rather steep costs. Commercial on-line services all have their monthly fees. In addition, most charge an hourly rate for the time you're connected to them (called *connect-time charges*), and often there are additional surcharges for using certain features. Plus, if you need to make long-distance calls to access the service, you'll have phone bills to consider, too.

The first step in keeping your on-line costs down is figuring out your primary use for on-line services. Will you use it mostly for e-mail? Getting news and weather reports? Or will you use on-line databases to do product and market research? Pinpointing what you use, and how often, will enable you to determine what combination of on-line services is best for you.

Most commercial on-line services offer several pricing plans, each one aimed at a particular type of user. If you use the service rarely, a plan with a low monthly fee and high hourly costs is probably the best for you. If you spend more than a few hours per month on line, however, you're probably going to save money with a plan that offers the lowest hourly cost. Usually this type of plan is the most economical for users who spend more than five or ten hours per month on line.

If the features you're most interested in are standard news and information features, look for an on-line service that offers these features for a flat rate. You don't want to worry about hourly fees while you're reading the headlines, after all.

On the other hand, if you're most interested in research databases such as Dialog or IQuest, you may just have to bite the bullet and pay their steep hourly rates. In that case, it's a good idea to plan your searches carefully, *before* you sign on, so that you can minimize the time you spend connected to the surcharged service. Take the time to read any available manuals. If you will be using Dialog, try to attend one of the training seminars offered around the country, and learn the most efficient way to use this very complicated system. See the sidebar, "Dialog: The Mother of All Databases" in Chapter 7, for more information on Dialog.

When you make long-distance calls to access your favorite information service or bulletin board, wait until late at night or on the weekend, when the phone company's rates go down. Also, connect at the highest speed possible. Many commercial services now offer 9600 baud access, and some offer 14,400 baud access. If you're downloading large files over a long-distance telephone connection, you'll save a lot in long-distance charges by connecting at the highest baud rate supported by the information service.

Finally, if you're interested in the Internet, be sure to shop around. Commercial providers of Internet access have varying rates, and it makes sense to go with the cheapest one—assuming your long-distance charges to access the service won't outweigh the savings. You may even be able to get Internet access for free. If you're a student, staff member, or teacher at an educational institution or university that has Internet access, then you may qualify for a dial-up Internet account there. Be sure to ask about this before you shell out any money for a commercial provider!

Asking For Help

Sooner or later, you'll inevitably run into some problems on line that you don't know how to solve. Maybe you can't figure out how to use a certain database, or you don't know how to download a file you want. So where do you turn for help?

On the commercial information services, help is never far away. There's always an easy-to-access customer service area, where you can read answers to common questions, get advice, or request help from a customer service representative. Often, responses will be e-mailed to you within a day or so; sometimes you can even get help on the spot. Usually the help you'll get is limited to basic information about using the service and getting around in it; more detailed information about specific features may not be available. Still, on-line customer service is the first place to look if you need help.

Some features within an on-line service may have their own help resources. Certain commercial databases (for example, IQuest) have a live customer-service option, so you can get help while you're using the database. Discussion areas on many services are monitored by sysops, who are also usually a good source of information. Remember that sysops are usually overworked and underpaid (if they're paid at all), so be nice to them and don't give them a hard time if they don't immediately get you the answers you need.

On the Internet, look for files of Frequently Asked Questions (FAQs) to get answers to your questions. Want to know what topics are appropriate for a particular newsgroup? The newsgroup probably has a FAQ file, so look for it *before* you post a message asking everyone to tell you the topics. Wondering how to use a program that you just got via ftp? (ftp is the Internet's File Transfer Protocol, a program that lets you download files from many computers on the Internet. See

Chapter 9 for details.) Look in that ftp site for a FAQ file or other documentation relating to the program. Often the first thing you will see when you connect to a new service or site on the Internet is a FAQ or "README" file that will probably answer most of your initial questions. If you didn't read it when you first connected, you should definitely read it when you run into problems.

Finally, the on-line world is full of people whose expertise may be able to help you out of a jam. If you've exhausted the above possibilities, try posting a public message to a forum or message board where topics relating to your problem are discussed. To get the best responses, be sure to include a meaningful, precise subject line on your message, and describe your problem briefly, accurately, and politely. And make sure you've tried to help yourself before calling on others for assistance. You'll only irritate people by asking for help with something you could've resolved yourself by reading the manual or checking the FAQ file (if there is one).

Taking Security Precautions

When you go on line, should you worry about viruses infecting your hard drive, hackers breaking into your personal files, and the FBI reading your private e-mail? Probably not. Most responsible sysops scan files before putting them up on their bulletin board or commercial information service, so it's unlikely you'll download an infected file. Most would-be hackers will be more interested in your credit card number and its expiration date than in your private e-mail. And the FBI, conspiracy theories aside, can't possibly be monitoring everyone's e-mail—there is simply too much of it. But if you follow these simple principles, you will

greatly reduce the risk of damage from viruses and snoops:

> ▶ **Don't use easy-to-guess passwords.** *When choosing passwords for your on-line accounts—whether they're with a commercial information service or a private bulletin board—don't choose something that's easy to guess, such as your login name or a simple word like* password. *The best passwords are at least six to eight characters long and include a few numbers or punctuation marks, which are harder to guess.*

> ▶ **Don't tell anyone your password.** *Obviously, if you tell someone your password, they'll be able to log on and use your on-line account, just as if they were you. If your credit card information is part of the account, they may also be able to use that number to charge things to you.* Never give your password to anyone. *If someone claiming to be an employee of the on-line service asks you for your password for any reason, simply refuse—this is a common scam used by hackers to con passwords out of unsuspecting people.*

> ▶ **Get a virus scanner and use it.** *Get a virus-scanning program and use it on every file that you download from an online source. It's also a good idea to scan your entire hard disk periodically, just to make sure you didn't miss something. Because many viruses are set to do their damage on Fridays, make it a habit to scan your disk every Thursday.*

> ▶ **Remember that no e-mail system is completely secure.** *If you really need to keep your messages secret, you shouldn't be sending them over a commercial e-mail network or the Internet. Even the most secure systems can be cracked. Furthermore,*

many on-line services perform regular backups of their data—so even if you've deleted a message, there's a chance that it may be lingering on a backup tape somewhere. Anyone diligent enough may be able to locate it later. If privacy is a real issue for you, get a data-encryption program to scramble your messages before you mail them out. Only someone who has the same encryption program and knows the correct "key" will be able to unscramble your message.

If you follow these simple guidelines you'll reduce your security risks, whether from viruses or hackers, to almost nil.

Look It Up in Reference Resources

Do you want to find out more about a country or public figure in the news? Do you have to write a school report on one of the U.S. presidents? Or are you simply interested in increasing the breadth of your knowledge? An on-line encyclopedia may be the most convenient way to find out what you want to know. Many information services provide on-line general reference works for little or no cost. They're a valuable source of up-to-date information and are a good starting point for anyone's research—though they won't take the place of a trip to the library.

Someday encyclopedias printed on paper may be obsolete, replaced by electronic versions that are just as easy to use and provide just as much information as their printed counterparts. Unfortunately for the on-line traveler, however,

that day hasn't yet arrived. Don't expect electronic encyclopedias to replace the more extensive reference works you can find in your local library. References available on line vary greatly in quality, flexibility, and ease of use. However, even the best references don't provide the number of articles, the illustrations, or the extensive bibliographies that a traditional encyclopedia supplies. With on-line references, you're limited to plain text—and the general-purpose works are often aimed at a "lowest common denominator," so they're not suitable for finding detailed or obscure information. Still, for up-to-date general information, these encyclopedias are quite useful.

If you're looking for a good general-purpose on-line encyclopedia, *Grolier's Academic American Encyclopedia* is available on CompuServe (GO ENCYCLOPEDIA), Prodigy (Jump: ENCYCLOPEDIA), and Delphi (on the Reference menu). Grolier's contains over 33,000 entries. Some of the entries are detailed and lengthy, and include bibliographies for further reading; most, however, are short and to the point. And last but not least, entries are cross-referenced.

America Online offers *Compton's Encyclopedia* (keyword: ENCYCLOPEDIA). It has over 5,000 full-length articles and more than 26,000 abbreviated ("capsule") articles. Unfortunately, Compton's is not cross-referenced. This makes following a chain of ideas through the encyclopedia more difficult than using Grolier's.

For bibliographic references to articles and books, you can't beat CompuServe's *Knowledge Index* (GO KI), a combination of over 100 professional databases. Knowledge Index provides access to these databases for a lower hourly rate than is charged by comparable services such as IQuest or Dialog—and Knowledge Index is easier to use, too. Most of the databases provide bibliographic information only, but some include the full text of articles. Knowledge Index is available only in the evenings and on weekends.

Want to look up articles from popular and general-interest magazines? Check out *Magazine Database Plus*, available on CompuServe (GO MAGDB) and ZiffNet for CompuServe (GO ZNT:MAGDB). This database offers the full text of articles that appeared within the last five or so years, and it's a good place to find book and movie reviews, information about elections, news coverage, and interviews.

Consumer Reports is always a good source of product information, whether you're shopping for cars, cameras, or cookware, and both CompuServe (GO CONSUMER) and Prodigy (Jump: CONSUMER REPORTS) offer it on line. In both services you can view articles from the current issue or look up past articles relating to various subjects. *Consumer Reports* is free of surcharges on both CompuServe and Prodigy.

Getting the Most out of Shareware

One of the best reasons to go on line is to expand your software library by downloading programs. Need an inexpensive spreadsheet program? You can find one on line. Bored with the games you have? You can get better games on almost any information service. The on-line universe is packed with programs that are there simply for the taking.

But is it *free* software? Usually not. In most cases, programs available on line are *shareware*, which means you can "try before you buy." When you get a shareware program, use it and see if you like it. But if you continue to use it, you're expected to *register* the software by sending a fee to the program's original distributor or author. Registering a shareware program entitles you to

continue using it, and in many cases, you get additional benefits as well.

The idea behind shareware is that it's unfair to expect anyone to pay (sometimes a lot) for a program, only to find out that they don't like it or that it doesn't suit the task at hand. With shareware, you can try using the software, and if you don't like it, just delete it and forget about it. You only have to pay for programs you like and want to use.

Think of the shareware concept as a distribution strategy, ideally suited to nonprofessional programmers and small software companies who lack the funds for large-scale marketing and distribution. Anyone is free to copy and share a shareware program with anyone else (hence the name). Usually the only stipulation is that the original files aren't altered in any way and that the complete set of files is included in the shared copy.

To some extent, shareware operates on the honor system—which means nobody is getting rich writing these programs. On the other hand, you are in violation of a shareware program's copyright if you continue to use it beyond the tryout period without registering it. Besides, if no one registered his or her programs, shareware authors would no longer be able to continue writing. Registering the programs you like and keep is a way of making sure that there will be more quality shareware in the future.

How to Register

Shareware programs usually include text files that explain how long you're permitted to use the program, how much it costs to register it, and where to send your money. In some cases, the program itself has registration reminders coded into it. These reminders, which pop up when you start or shut down the program, are known as "nag screens."

Registration for shareware programs can cost anywhere from $1.00 to more than $100.00; most

are between $15.00 and $40.00. In nearly every case, shareware programs are considerably less expensive than comparable commercial products.

Human nature being what it is, shareware authors generally include extra incentives for you to register the programs they write. If a program has nag screens, registering it will get rid of them. Registration often entitles you to a manual, technical support, or free upgrades. In some cases, you'll get extra goodies by registering (sets of templates for word processors, higher levels for games, and so forth).

Related Terms

Not every program that you download is shareware. Some publicly available programs are freeware, which means they're free to anyone who wants to use them. A freeware program has no registration fee, so you're free to use it as long as you want to. A freeware program is, nonetheless, copyrighted, so you're not allowed to pass it off as your own, incorporate pieces of it into your own software, or sell it for profit.

Public domain software is both free and uncopyrighted. You can do whatever you want with it—including cutting it up, recycling its code, and reselling it. It goes without saying that public domain software generally comes "as is," without any guarantees about its performance.

Finally, *demo* programs are simply demonstrations of commercial software packages. A demo can be anything from a simple slide show to a working model of the software. What distinguishes demo software from shareware is that demo programs are "crippled"—they don't have the full functionality of the commercial version. For example, a database demo might have all the features of the database program, but will only allow you to enter ten records. Other than getting to see how the program looks and acts, you won't

get much use out of a demo. If you like it, you'll have to purchase the real program in a store.

Identifying Yourself On Line

What's in a name? Many people use *handles* or pseudonyms instead of their real names when posting messages to on-line discussion areas. A good number of people use handles simply because they feel more comfortable expressing themselves under an alias. Should you follow suit, and use a handle of your own? The answer depends partly on your preference and partly on what's customary in the area you're visiting.

Whether you can use a handle at all depends on the on-line service that you're using. In some, you can't change your on-line name; you're stuck with whatever user name or ID you started with. Others let you change your name in some places. For example, CompuServe's forums ask you for your name when you join, and there's nothing to prevent you from typing in whatever you want. Still other services, including America Online, let you choose whatever user name you want when you sign up, and that becomes the name by which you're known throughout all of the service's discussion areas.

A handle can be a way to create an alter ego. When you go on line, you have a great deal of freedom to present yourself just as you wish to be known. A handle like Hobbes or Merlin says something about you: It shapes someone's first impressions of you, and contributes to your on-line "image."

Should you use a handle? If the participants in the discussion area you're visiting seem to be using handles, then it's probably OK for you to do so, too. But be aware that handles are considered

impolite in some circles—for example, certain CompuServe forums require that you sign on with a real name. Using a handle in those forums is not only rude, but may get you a reprimand from the sysop. So pay attention to your surroundings, and when in Rome, do as the Romans do.

Future Travel on the Information Superhighway

The Clinton administration is actively involved in planning a National Information Infrastructure (NII), also known as the "information superhighway," that will greatly expand the on-line universe. Because it's still in the planning and research stages, the government, leading technology companies, and interested scientists and citizens are all still trying to define parameters for the NII—so it's difficult to say exactly what shape it will take.

The most recent statements from the administration call for an infrastructure of computers, networks, and consumer electronics that will integrate the capabilities of telephones, cable television, personal computers, and modems. According to these statements, someday you'll be able to use the same equipment and cables to get data, to call your friends on your video phone, or to download feature-length movies. It's an optimistic vision, not limited to what we now know as the on-line world: If even a fraction of these dreams are realized, it will substantially affect everyone's daily life.

The administration's plans call for private industry to play a significant role in the development and implementation of this infrastructure. It's a good bet that cable companies and telephone companies are going to be major forces in this field; experimental systems are already providing computer information via coaxial cable (the same kind used for your cable TV) instead of modems. What actually develops from these plans, however, will depend on many factors, and it's hard to predict at this point.

One development to watch for in the near future: In mid-1994, the U.S. government's funding of the Internet (through the National Science Foundation) will end. This will probably have a minimal effect on the actual operation of the network because most of the Internet is paid for by the various universities and institutions whose computers form the network itself. However, it's likely that commercialization of the Internet will increase. Many commercial interests, such as Internet access providers, are already changing the character of the network. And the number of people using the Internet is increasing at an astronomical rate. Within a year or two, there may be serious problems with the Internet's bandwidth (the amount of data that it can easily transmit). If commercial interests step in at that point and offer high-bandwidth extensions to the Internet, it could make room for many more people and companies—but it's also going to mean the end of the Internet as a free network.

What's really going to come of the Clinton administration's plans for the NII is anyone's guess. In the meantime, the administration has made some steps toward getting connected to the *existing* networks and "information highways." For example, you can send e-mail to the president or vice-president via Internet; their addresses are, respectively, PRESIDENT@WHITEHOUSE.GOV and VICE-PRESIDENT@WHITEHOUSE.GOV. On CompuServe, you can contact the administration by sending a message to ID 75300,3115. On MCI, send a message to White House or to MCI ID 589-5485. On GEnie, address your message to WHITEHOUSE. On America Online, send your letters to ClintonPZ. The likelihood of a message

sent to any of these addresses actually being read by a human being is quite slim. You'll probably receive a response from an automatic reply program, thanking you for your letter and telling you that the White House is working on ways to provide more personalized responses. Still, it's a start.

If you want to get the latest White House news, press releases, statements, and speeches, there are a variety of on-line sources. On Compu-Serve, GO WHITEHOUSE to visit the White House forum; its libraries contain everything released by the Press Office. On MCI, type VIEW WHITE HOUSE to see the same material. It's also available on America Online under the keyword WHITEHOUSE. On the Internet, you can find White House press releases in many locations. See Chapter 9 for details.

Check Out Special Interest On-line Services

This book covers the major on-line information services in the United States. Chances are that no matter what you're looking for, you'll be able to find it (or something like it) within one or more of these primary services. But they are by no means the only games in town. There are smaller, more specialized on-line services out there. You may want to check them out, particularly if you have special interests and aren't satisfied by what the big services offer. Following are descriptions of three of the most interesting ones: BIX, The WELL, and the ImagiNation Network.

BIX: the Byte Information Exchange

If you're a computer professional or hobbyist, you'll want to consider BIX. It is home to some of the most technically sophisticated and powerful members of the computer industry. BIX began in 1985 as a service for readers of *Byte* magazine, but it's grown to a respectable on-line service in its own right. You can still get the full text of all issues of *Byte* each month on BIX, and many *Byte* editors and authors are on line here. BIX is mostly a forum for those who want to discuss computers, high technology, programming, and similar issues. You'll find lots of industry movers and shakers on BIX—programmers, executives, and computer journalists. The discussions in BIX conferences are at a high level of technical knowledge, and "flames" are rare.

BIX has a text interface, but a Windows-based graphical interface is also available. There is full Internet access—including gophers, Usenet newsgroups, ftp, and more—as well as an e-mail service with a gateway to the Internet. (See Chapter 9 for details on the Internet.)

BIX has a monthly membership fee of $13.00. You're charged for connect-time depending on how you access BIX: Via SprintNet or TYMNET, it costs $9.00/hour during business hours, and $3.00/hour evenings, weekends, and holidays; Telnet access is $1.00/hour; and direct-dial connection to BIX's Boston phone lines (which support access speeds up to 9600 baud) costs $2.00/hour. To sign up for BIX, set your comm software to 8N1 and dial (800) 695-4882 or (617) 491-5410; hit the Return or Enter key once or twice and follow the instructions. Or, telnet to x25.bix.com. (For an explanation of telnet, the Internet's remote-access utility, see Chapter 9.) For customer service, call BIX at (800) 695-4775 (voice) or (617) 354-4137 (voice) between noon and 11:00 p.m. eastern standard time.

The WELL: Whole Earth 'Lectronic Link

Interested in the cutting edge of technology and computer culture? Look to The WELL, based in

Sausalito, California (near San Francisco). The WELL offers many public and private conferences (message boards), which are its main attractions. The WELL, one of the hippest on-line hangouts around, is home to a wide range of people and viewpoints. You'll find lively discussions on topics as diverse as cyberpunk, motorcycles, progressive politics, and music. The abundance of conferences carry some of the most intellectual arguments and disputations of any on-line service we've seen. But beware: WELL denizens can be long winded, too, so if your time is short, you may not be happy here.

The WELL is a UNIX-based system and sports full Internet access. It also gives users a great deal of flexibility to customize their own accounts. To sign up for the WELL or to request more information, set your comm software to 8N1 and dial (415) 332-6106. If you have Internet access, telnet to well.sf.ca.us. The WELL's voice number is 415-332-4335. WELL memberships cost $15.00/month, plus connect-time charges of $2.00/hour; the first five hours after you join are free. If you don't live in the 415 area code and don't have access to telnet, you can use the CompuServe Packet Network (CPN) to connect to the WELL for an extra $4.00/hour.

The ImagiNation Network

If you're just looking for a good time, try the Imagi-Nation Network—it has more on-line games than you can shake a stick at. Formerly called The Sierra Network (TSN), the ImagiNation Network lets you play board games, card games, and arcade games with players all across the country. Its colorful interface uses an amusement park metaphor, with a map of the park on your screen showing the various "lands" and buildings you can visit. SierraLand features arcade-style, shoot-'em-up games, including Red Baron, a flight simulator where you get into dogfights with other players. MedievaLand has

fantasy role-playing games, and in the ClubHouse you can play chess, checkers, hearts, or a number of other traditional games. LarryLand is the network's somewhat risqué casino, based on the popular "Leisure Suit Larry" games. Finally, there's a Mall where you can go shopping. One of the niftiest features of the ImagiNation Network is that you can design your own on-screen persona using the software's face-drawing program. This face is what other members see when they're playing games with you.

You can sign up for the ImagiNation Network by calling (800) IMAGIN1 or (800) 462-4461 by voice phone. The required software costs $4.95, and basic membership is $12.95/month, which gets you up to 30 hours of evening and weekend access. Additional hours cost $2.00/hour, or $7.00/hour during business hours.

If you're a Prodigy member, you can connect to the ImagiNation Network through Prodigy's Game Point (Jump: Game Point)— you'll have access to all of the ImagiNation Network's features except LarryLand and the Mall. There's no monthly fee for Game Point access, and the hourly rate is based on how much you use the service in a month: $4.80/hour for up to 3 hours of access; $4.20/hour for 3 to 6 hours; or $3.60/hour for more than 6 hours. Daytime rates for Game Point are an additional $3.00/hour.

Get On Board with Bulletin Board Systems

Bulletin boards are much smaller versions of the large on-line services. A major on-line service may have hundreds or thousands of modems and several large mainframes to handle

its vast quantity of information. In contrast, a bulletin board system (BBS) might have but one modem and be run by a humble personal computer sitting in somebody's home. And the distinction isn't just one of scale; there's a vast difference in character, too—anybody can start a BBS. All that's required is a computer, a modem, and BBS software, which means that BBSs are as varied and as quirky as their sysops (system operators). Successful bulletin boards can grow quite large, but for the most part, they are small, privately run ventures.

Bulletin boards can be found all over the world. New ones crop up all the time, as others disappear just as quickly. Some BBSs are free, and some charge an access fee. There are BBSs whose primary purpose is to serve as a discussion area or meeting place for people interested in a specific topic. Many BBSs carry large collections of files that you can download; often a BBS will specialize in a certain type of file (OS/2 software, Macintosh software, or graphics files, for instance). Still other BBSs are soapboxes for their sysops, who use the boards to express their views, to publish interesting or funny material, or to create on-line "worlds" that are novel, entertaining, or just interesting. An increasing number of BBSs are offering additional services, such as varying degrees of Internet access. (See Chapter 9 for details on the Internet.) And finally, there are technical support BBSs run by various computer companies; these boards generally offer good technical support and downloadable files (printer drivers, technical notes, and other related material), without any additional "frills."

Many BBSs are connected through an informal network called Fidonet. If you don't have access to an e-mail account on a major on-line service or on the Internet, you may be able to get a Fidonet e-mail address by joining a Fidonet BBS. Don't expect fast delivery times with Fidonet however. Because it's an informal network

and no one gets paid for maintaining it, your messages may take a day or two to arrive.

It's impossible to generalize very much about BBSs. Ultimately, the best way to find out what's available on one is to connect to it.

Getting Connected

Connecting to a bulletin board usually means a long-distance phone call, unless you're lucky enough to live in the same area code. Using a general-purpose comm program, set your software to 8N1 (unless you know ahead of time that the BBS requires other settings). When you connect, be prepared to give your name and other information about yourself. If it's a free BBS, you'll be able to sign on immediately; otherwise, you'll need to provide credit card information to get access. After you've connected, there is usually a self-explanatory menu system that you use to get around, read messages, and download files. Every BBS is different, but most are easy to figure out with a little experimentation.

How to Find Bulletin Boards

Because BBSs tend to come and go, the best sources for information about them are magazines, commercial on-line services, or other bulletin boards.

▶ BOARDWATCH Magazine *is the BBS world's publication of choice. It features lists of bulletin boards, news about the bulletin board world, advice for sysops, and more.*

▶ Computer Shopper *publishes a monthly list of BBSs that includes a brief description of each board; this is a good way to find out about the new and interesting ones.*

▶ *On line,* Computer Shopper's *list can be found in Windows .HLP file format,*

on the Computer Shopper forum in ZiffNet for CompuServe (GO ZNT:COMPSHOPPER).

▶ *A text file listing many BBSs, called The BBS List, is compiled by Sonya Chang; this list is distributed monthly on the Usenet newsgroup alt.bbs.lists, on America Online's Mac Communications forum (keyword: mcm), and CompuServe's IBM BBS and Mac Communications forums (GO IBMBBS and GO MACCOMM, respectively). You can also get a copy of the list by e-mailing a request to the Internet address lchang@uoft02.utoledo.edu or to the America Online address TheBBSLst.*

Many other BBS lists exist—a good place to look for these lists is in the forums just named and on BBSs in your area. And, of course, once you start connecting to some BBSs, you're bound to find out about others that you'll want to investigate. Have fun exploring!

CHAPTER 3

CompuServe

CompuServe is one of the oldest and largest of the major on-line information services. Started in 1979, CompuServe has grown from humble beginnings to a giant information company with over 1.5 million subscribers worldwide. The service offers hundreds of forums, dozens of databases, a large "virtual" shopping mall, a plethora of games, a real-time, global CB Simulator, a complete e-mail service with gateways to several other mail networks, and more. If you live in the U.S., you can probably connect to CompuServe with a local call—no matter where you live—because CompuServe has access numbers all over the world.

CompuServe's most popular offerings are its *forums*, which are file libraries and conference rooms all in one. There are over 500 forums on CompuServe, each dedicated to a specific area of interest, a product, or a company. Some of CompuServe's forums allow subscribers to discuss their careers and hobbies, share information, and make friends via message boards. Computer hardware and software companies use forums to provide technical support, answer questions, solve problems, and listen to suggestions from customers.

File libraries contain files relevant to the forum's area. For example, in a customer support forum's library you might find macros, valuable utilities, and text files containing answers to frequently asked questions. While visiting a forum, you can chat with anyone else who's in the forum at the same time, by using the *conference rooms* feature. On the other hand, this feature is not frequently used because the CB Simulator (item 3 on the map) is more efficient when you want live on-line interaction. Forums that do take advantage of the conference rooms feature do so only at scheduled group discussion times, which are announced in advance.

CompuServe also offers a rich array of reference and news resources—some cheap, some costing a pretty penny. From Associated Press Online to IQuest, you'll find a whole gamut of news and research resources on CompuServe. The Associated Press Online gives you the latest news and headlines each hour at no additional cost. IQuest provides simplified (though quite expensive) access to over 850 databases worldwide. Each surcharged resource clearly indicates its cost before you begin, so pay attention: It's easy to run up enormous CompuServe bills if you aren't careful. See the "Cutting Costs" section in Chapter 2 for some guidelines.

CompuServe's electronic mail service, or *e-mail*, is reliable and relatively easy to use. It also has gateways to a variety of other mail networks, including MCI and the Internet. You can send either a text message or a file. However, one shortcoming of CompuServe e-mail is you can't attach a file to a text message—a feature most other mail systems offer. For extra fees, you can even compose messages to be sent to a fax machine or printed out and mailed via the Postal Service.

In addition to the basic e-mail service, CompuServe offers the CompuServe Mail Hub, a wide-area message service designed for corporate network use. With the Mail Hub, you can transfer e-mail from one LAN (local area network) to another via modem dial-up connections to CompuServe.

A computer system or information service uses an *interface* to display information on your terminal and interpret your commands. The CompuServe interface is almost completely menu driven. It's one of the most basic among commercial on-line information services, consisting mostly of plain text without graphics

embellishments. At times this interface is extremely frustrating.

```
        Copyright (c) 1993
        CompuServe Incorporated
          All Rights Reserved

You have Electronic Mail waiting.


CompuServe    TOP

  1 Access Basic Services
  2 Member Assistance (FREE)
  3 Communications/Bulletin Bds.
  4 News/Weather/Sports
  5 Travel
  6 The Electronic MALL/Shopping
  7 Money Matters/Markets
  8 Entertainment/Games
  9 Hobbies/Lifestyles/Education
 10 Reference
 11 Computers/Technology
 12 Business/Other Interests

!
 ANSI    ONLINE   2400 7E1  [Alt+2]-Menu  FDX 8 LF X F D CP LG ↑ PR  00:00:51
```

CompuServe's text-based interface

Reading and replying to messages on forums, for instance, is difficult using the menus alone. To make CompuServe a little easier to deal with, there is a specialized interface program, the Compu-Serve Information Manager (CIM). As an optional front-end communications program, CIM puts a more graphical face on CompuServe. CIM is available in three flavors—DOS, Windows, and Macintosh—and it's included with the Compu-Serve membership package. If you're considering connecting to CompuServe or if you already subscribe, try CIM and see if you like it. Chances are it will save you a lot of headaches. CIM has menu-driven interfaces for CompuServe's menus, forums, and basic services, and it boasts an especially well designed interface for the CB Simulator.

CIM probably won't cut down on your connect-time charges, though. Just wandering around CompuServe's forums can cost you a lot in hourly fees. So if you're a heavy forum user, you'll want to try one of the many *off-line reader* comm programs available. For the Mac, Compu-Serve Inc. provides Navigator; the DOS programs TAPCIS (shareware, $79 registration) and OzCIS (freeware) are the best and most popular off-line

readers for the PC platform. (All three can be downloaded from CompuServe.) These programs let you specify ahead of time which forums you're interested in and what messages you'd like to read. The off-line reader program connects to CompuServe, retrieves all the messages you've selected, and disconnects. You're then free to read the messages off line at your leisure, without accumulating all those hourly fees. If you want to send a message, create it off line, and the reader will post it to the correct forum the next time you use the reader to connect to CompuServe.

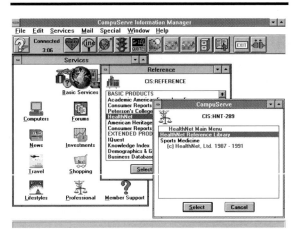

The CIM interface

CIM is probably the best comm program for you if

▶ *You use CompuServe mostly for its information or shopping resources*

▶ *You like to use CompuServe's CB feature*

▶ *You use the forums mostly for their libraries*

The graphical interface will simplify getting from one place to another. But remember—if you're interested in following or taking part in

forum discussions, you should use an off-line reader to keep your hourly charges to a minimum.

Despite rather steep rates and a rudimentary interface, CompuServe is unmatched in the sheer quantity of material and features that it offers. Almost anybody can connect to CompuServe and take advantage of its full range of features, regardless of the type of computer that is used. All you really need is a personal computer capable of displaying at least 40 columns of text, a modem, and a generic comm program to get connected.

Subscribing to CompuServe

To sign up for CompuServe, you need to purchase either a DOS, Windows, or Macintosh membership kit, which includes

▶ *Your member ID and password*

▶ *The CompuServe Information Manager (CIM) software*

▶ *A user's guide for the service and for the software*

▶ *$25.00 of connect-time credit.*

You'll also get phone numbers for local CompuServe access. CompuServe, Inc. often offers the membership kit at a discount, as do computer software retailers, so shop around. The kit's suggested retail price is $49.95. To order your membership kit directly from CompuServe, call toll-free 800-848-8199 (voice), or 614-457-0802 (voice).

Fees

CompuServe offers two pricing plans: the Standard Plan and the Alternate Plan. The Standard Pricing Plan is available for the monthly membership fee of $8.95, which covers membership and gets you unlimited access to CompuServe's Basic Services. You must pay connect-time charges for access to *extended* services, which are labeled with a + (plus sign) on CompuServe menus. You'll pay connect-time charges *plus* additional surcharges to use the *premium* services, which are identified with a $ (dollar sign). Premium Service surcharges vary, but are always clearly indicated.

The Alternate Pricing Plan has a monthly membership fee of only $2.50, but you'll pay higher hourly rates while connected to CompuServe, and these rates apply in every area of CompuServe except the Member Assistance area. For the premium services, you'll pay the hourly rate plus the service's surcharge. The Alternative Plan isn't cost effective if you spend more than an hour a month on CompuServe.

CompuServe Hourly Charges

Baud Rate	Hourly Charge
Standard Pricing Plan Connect-Time Charges (Extended and Premium Services):	
300	$ 4.80
1200 or 2400	$ 4.80
9600 or 14400	$9.60
Alternative Pricing Plan Connect-Time Charges (Basic, Extended, and Premium Services):	
300	$ 6.30
1200 or 2400	$12.80
9600 or 14400	$22.80

Gallery of Graphics

CompuServe is a rich source of all kinds of graphics. To explore some of its best offerings, enter the command GO GRAPHICS. (A GO-word consists of the command GO followed by the resource's name.) You'll find graphics support and development forums, as well as forums dedicated to collecting images. Bear in mind that CompuServe's Extended Service hourly rates apply while accessing any of these forums; only the Weather Maps service is free of connect-time charges. Here are some of the graphics file resources accessible from the Graphics menu, organized in the order in which they appear on the menu:

Graphics File Finder [GO GRAPHFF] Find graphics files and programs anywhere in CompuServe's graphics forums with this easily searched database of library file descriptions.

Quick Pictures Forum [GO QPICS] Smaller picture files, on all subjects, are featured here. No file has more than 32 colors or shades of gray, so your download time is shorter. The DTP/Clipart library specializes in clip art for desktop publishing.

Graphics Corner Forum [GO CORNER] These images are all rendered in more than 32 colors or shades, so their quality is high. You'll find grayscale photographs and 256-color images—from celebrities to cathedrals.

Graphics Plus Forum [GO GRAPHPLUS] These images are all in "high-color" or "true-color" formats and can contain literally millions of colors. This allows for rich, realistic images—but they're also the largest graphics files around, so be prepared.

Fine Art Forum [GO FINEART] An on-line art gallery featuring works by contemporary artists as well as old masters, this forum is a good resource for fine art in many styles, of various periods, and from many parts of the world.

Graphics Gallery Forum [GO GALLERY] This forum contains photographs from the Smithsonian Institute, NASA, the USDA's collection of National Forest images, and many local tourism bureaus throughout North America.

Glamour Graphics [GO GLAMOUR] Look here for images from the world of fashion. Haute couture styles, lingerie, and businesswear are some of the featured subjects.

Computer Art Forum [GO COMART] This forum contains images created using computer painting and drawing programs. You'll find a variety of material that shows some of the infinite possibilities for computer art.

Clip art from the Quick Pictures forum (Graphic courtesy of CompuServe, Inc.)

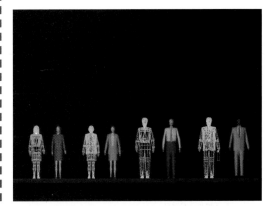

Sample images from the Autodesk Software forum (Copyright 1993, Rachel L. Rosenthal. Graphic courtesy of CompuServe, Inc.)

Gallery of Graphics (cont.)

Sight and Sound Forum [GO SSFORUM] A forum for people interested in both computer graphics and computer sounds, this forum contains many sound, MIDI, and graphics files.

Weather Maps [GO MAPS] The Accu-Weather Map service provides satellite photos, radar images, and weather maps for current, recent, and forecast conditions around the world.

Autodesk Software Forum [GO ASOFT] This forum is devoted to the support of Autodesk products. Its libraries contain animations and still images created by Autodesk Animator, Autodesk 3D Studio, and other programs.

Comics Forum [GO COMICS] The Comics forum's libraries are filled with images from comic books and animated movies, as well as original comic art uploaded by forum members.

Reuter News Pictures Forum [GO NEWSPICS] This library-only forum contains scores of current news photographs from around the world, with new pictures added each day. It also has historical images from the Bettman Archives that are of current interest.

Getting Around CompuServe

Though CompuServe is menu driven, you can also take shortcuts to any resource by typing its *GO-word* at any CompuServe prompt. Many member services are available through their GO-words.

The first table in this section shows you how to access member services. It's followed by tables of CompuServe commands, and forum commands, respectively.

GO-Words for Member Services

GO-Word	Result
BILLING	Get billing information and current rates
CIS-1	Go to the CompuServe main menu
COMMAND	Get summaries of CompuServe commands
GRAPHFF	Go to the Graphics File Finder and search for graphics files anywhere on CompuServe
IBMFF	Go to the IBM File Finder and search for IBM-compatible files anywhere on CompuServe
MACFF	Go to the Mac File Finder and search for Macintosh-compatible files anywhere on CompuServe
MEMBER	Go to the Membership Assistance area
PASSWORD	Change your password
PHONES	Find out CompuServe access numbers in your area
QUESTIONS	Access Customer Service
QUICK	Search for GO-words throughout CompuServe

Note You should be aware that the on-line world is a very dynamic place. It's a good practice to check with member services if you ever have any trouble accessing resources.

There are also many types of commands you can use anywhere within CompuServe. The Ctrl key commands can be used at any time. The other commands can be used at any CompuServe prompt. If the command is a single letter, you can type that letter alone or enter its full-word version in all caps.

CompuServe Commands

Command	Result
Ctrl-S	Pause text flow from CompuServe
Ctrl-Q	Resume text flow from CompuServe
Ctrl-C	Abort the current program
Ctrl-O	Stop text flow without aborting current program
Ctrl-U	Delete the line you're currently typing
H	Get HELP
T	Go to the topmost menu page (TOP)
M	Go to the previous MENU
R	RESEND a page
F	Go FORWARD one page
B	Go BACK one page
N	Display NEXT menu item
P	Display PREVIOUS menu item
S *item(s)*	SCROLL one or more menu *items* without pausing
FIND *topic*	FIND CompuServe resources relating to *topic*
OFF or BYE	Log off CompuServe
PER	Exit to Personal File area
QUOTE	Get current market quote on any ticker symbol (cost is $0.015/quote)
SET	SET terminal display option

You can use SET in two ways. If you enter SET on a line by itself, CompuServe will prompt you for an option and its setting. If you enter SET followed by the option and its setting, all on a single line. The following SET options are available:

PAG ON/OFF	Paged mode (CompuServe pauses after each screenful of information)
BRI ON/OFF	Brief mode (CompuServe prompts are shorter)
TTY *xxx*	Terminal type (VIDTEX, TELERAY, TELIDON, DUMCRT, TELETYPE, TRS80, VT100, or VT52)
WID *nnn*	Screen width (in columns, from 10–255)
LIN *nnn*	Screen length (in lines, from 10–255)

Additional commands apply only within CompuServe's forums, and are used for searching, selecting, and reading messages, finding files, and other activities. (Turn the page to see a list of these commands.) The first time you enter a forum, you will need to join the forum to get full access to it. Joining is free and is simply a matter of volunteering your name (real full names are encouraged). *Note:* If you use CIM, the CIM software provides menu options or buttons to perform all forum functions.

Forum Commands

Command	Result
ANNOUNCEMENTS	Read announcements from the sysop
CONFERENCE x	Go to conference room x
CONFERENCING	Go to forum Conference menu
DESCRIPTIONS	View descriptions of forum message sections and libraries
HELP	Get context-sensitive help
HIGH:n	Mark message number n as the last message read; the next time you visit the forum you'll see only those messages with numbers higher than n
INSTRUCTIONS	Access general forum instructions
JOIN	Initiate full access to a forum
LIBRARIES	Go to forum Libraries menu
MESSAGES	Go to forum Messages menu
NAME	Get a list of forum message sections, libraries, and conference rooms
OPTIONS	Go to Options menu (switch between command mode and menu-driven mode, plus other forum options)
ULOG	See who has visited the forum recently, and when
USTATUS	See who else is currently in the forum
WHO x	Display member ID

INSIDE COMPUSERVE

CompuServe boasts over 1,500 separate resources. The forums alone account for nearly 500 of those, while databases, news sources, services, and games make up the rest. Before you begin exploring, you should familiarize yourself with the three-page fold-out map of CompuServe at the back of this book. The map shows you all of CompuServe at a glance, and will help you find your way to what interests you most.

The following pages describe and evaluate the best and most popular of CompuServe's many resources. Each description is preceded by a number that you can use to find that resource on the map. Or, when you see a number on the map, you can look for that number among the resource descriptions. This listing not only gives you a sense of what's inside CompuServe, but it will also help you quickly find the best resources as they appear on the map.

For an estimation of the quality and usefulness of each resource described, just look for the following symbols:

▲▲▲▲   Outstanding—don't miss it!
▲▲▲   Excellent—worth going out of your way to see it.
▲▲   Very good—worth a look.
▲   Above average—stop by if it's on your way.
▼   Disappointing—don't bother.

You'll also find an indication of the cost of each described resource. The exact amount of surcharges, if any, are specified at the end of each description, and the dollar icons give you a general idea of how its price compares to other features inside CompuServe.

$$$ Steep—hang on to your wallet!
$$ Moderate—not a bargain, but reasonable
$ Cheap—a good value, easy on your pocketbook.
✛   Free—no surcharges or connect time charges!

If you need direct access, you'll also find the GO-word for each resource in the listing as well as on the map. Finally, each resource is classified by type. The types are News, Forum (which consists of a discussion area and a file library), Information, Entertainment, Help, Discussion, and Service, and are represented by the same symbols that appear on the map.

Basic Services *The Basic Services area (GO BASIC) collects in one place all of CompuServe's services that are not surcharged under the Standard Pricing Plan. If you stick to this menu and its submenus, you won't incur any charges beyond your standard monthly fee. All of the services here are also available elsewhere on CompuServe, so think of this menu as a way to avoid temptation. You don't have to come here, but you'll keep your CompuServe bills down if you do. Right next to Basic Services on the map is the Member Assistance area (GO HELP), which is also free.*

1. ACADEMIC AMERICAN ENCYCLOPEDIA   ▲▲   ✛
GO ENCYCLOPEDIA

When you need a quick brush-up on Mikhail Gorbachev's bio, or you want a short history of the telephone, Grolier's

Academic American Encyclopedia is the place to look. It's easy to use: Just type in the word you want to look up, and Grolier's gives you the article. Cross-referenced words are in all caps, making it easy for you to follow a train of ideas through the encyclopedia. You won't find lengthy essays here—this encyclopedia is the "short entry" type, but that's plenty for most reference needs.

Surcharges: None (hourly rates apply to members on the Alternative Pricing Plan)

2. PETERSON'S COLLEGE DATABASE   ▲▲▲   ✛
GO PETERSON

An on-line, searchable version of the printed Peterson's *Guide to Four-Year Colleges* and Peterson's *Guide to Two-Year Colleges*, this database lets you search up-to-date listings of over 3,400 colleges by name, location, size, majors offered, cost, and more. The database lists the colleges that meet your search criteria, and you can then view more information about any college on this list: address, admissions information, expenses, athletics, majors, and so on. Best of all, there's no surcharge! Required reading for anyone applying to college.

Surcharges: None (hourly rates apply to members on the Alternative Pricing Plan)

Communications *The Communications menu (GO COMMUNICATIO) provides access to all of CompuServe's communications services, including e-mail, the CB Simulator, the Convention Center, and forums. The forums appear elsewhere on CompuServe's menus under the relevant subject headings, but if you're especially interested in forums, then you can get directly to all of them through this menu.*

3. CB SIMULATOR   ▲▲ $
GO CB

Want to chat with people around the world? CompuServe's CB Simulator is a real-time discussion area where you "broadcast" your thoughts by typing them, while reading what other CBers are typing. It's organized into three bands of 36 channels each. The General band is for general-interest discussions, and it's rated PG. The Adult bands are rated R—they tend to be raunchy and none too sophisticated. Just as on a real CB, you can tune into whatever channel you want, use a "handle" to disguise your true identity, and pretend to be whomever you want to be. Or just listen in on conversations as they happen. But be careful—a lot of time can fly by while you're hanging out on line. Join the CB Club (GO CBCLUB) if you're a real devotee; you'll get discounts for your CB time.

Surcharges: CompuServe extended service hourly rates

4. CONGRESSGRAM   ▲▲▲   ✛
GO CONGRESS

🄢 What do you do when your congressperson commits yet another outrageous crime against the constituency? Let him or her know what you think! CompuServe's CONGRESSgram service lists the phone numbers and committee assignments of every senator and representative in the U.S. Congress, and throws in the president's and vice-president's addresses for good measure. All that, for free! Here's a bonus: For a fee, you can write a letter on line to the elected representative of your choice, and CompuServe will print it on paper, put it in an envelope, and mail it for you. It will usually arrive in the addressee's office the very next day.

The only way to access CONGRESSgram is by using its GO-word.

Surcharges: No surcharges to browse the service, but hourly rates apply to members on the Alternative Pricing Plan; $1 to send a letter.

News/Weather/Sports
The News/Weather/Sports menu (GO NEWS) provides a variety of comprehensive news and current-events sources, from the AP wire service to the latest in entertainment news and information.

5. ASSOCIATED PRESS ONLINE   ▲▲▲   ✛
GO APO

🄝 Get the latest AP stories here: New articles are added every hour, so you can follow the news as it unfolds. AP stories under the heading Latest News are short summaries of the top stories. You can also get the latest sports news; read more detailed news stories under the headings National, Washington, World, Political, Entertainment, and Business; check the latest Wall Street and Dow Jones news; or read current Science & Health stories. AP also offers weather around the U.S., as well as feature stories, including a daily Today In History piece. Everything a news junkie could want!

Surcharges: None (hourly rates apply to members on the Alternative Pricing Plan)

6. CITIBANK'S GLOBAL REPORT   ▲▲▲ $$$
GO GLOREP

🄝 Citibank's sophisticated news service, aimed at financial professionals, provides a quick, easy, and customizable way to get market quotes, news articles, calendars, and other data pertinent to many U.S. and international markets. Global Report brings together current news from a wide range of sources, saving you the trouble and time of hunting it down yourself. When you're in Global Report, you can get data about any company (including SEC filings, and news about the company from the last six months) by entering its ticker symbol. The Autosearch feature lets you customize your news reports, so you only see what you need to see. One nice feature of Global Report is that the latest headlines flash across the bottom of the screen as they're posted—so you won't miss anything while you're reading other items. This service carries

a steep surcharge, but if you need accurate, up-to-date news and quotes, the Global Report is probably worth every penny.

Surcharges: $60.00/hour during prime time (8:00 a.m. to 7:00 p.m. your time), $30.00/hour evenings and weekends; plus CompuServe Extended Service hourly rates

7. EXECUTIVE NEWS SERVICE   ▲▲▲▲ $$
GO ENS

🄝 This is one of the best news services available, and it's got smarts, too: Using the *folder* feature, you can specify the subjects you're interested in, and ENS will automatically clip relevant stories for you as they appear. ENS supplies current news stories from AP, UPI, Reuters, The Washington Post, and Deutsche Presse-Agentur. Public folders (with preset sorting criteria) simplify searching and browsing the news. In the Current News folder, you can browse current headlines or leads for items that interest you. When you're looking for news about specific companies, use the News By Company Ticker folder to search by ticker symbol. Or check out the special subject folders to see stories relating to a single news topic.

But the most powerful feature of ENS is that it lets you create one or more *private* folders to scan the news just for you. To create a private folder, you specify keywords, and ENS checks incoming stories for those words. The next time you visit ENS, your private folder will contain only stories that contain the keywords you designated. Although it requires a little experimentation, once you get the right keywords set up for your folder, it's a real timesaving feature!

Surcharges: $15.00/hour, plus CompuServe Extended Service hourly rates

8. WEATHER   ▲▲▲   ✛
GO WEATHER

🄝 Tired of your local TV station's so-called meteorologist? Find out the current weather and the forecast for any area of the U.S. or the world, right here on CompuServe. Download weather maps, radar maps, and current satellite photos, and get other weather and climate information. You get easy-to-use, reliable weather reports, at no extra cost—more weather information than you'll probably ever need.

Surcharges: None (hourly rates apply to members on the Alternative Pricing Plan)

Travel
CompuServe's Travel section (GO TRAVEL) brings you airline and hotel reservation systems that you can use free-of-charge (though you still have to pay for the tickets!). Get information about traveling abroad, U.S. State Department advisories to travelers, and more. Nearby are the Electronic Mall and other shopping services (GO SHOPPING) where you can buy all the things you'll need to take on your trip.

9. ABC WORLDWIDE HOTEL GUIDE ▲▲▲ $
GO ABC

The Hotel Guide contains detailed information about more than 60,000 hotels worldwide. Its listings include each hotel's street address, distance from the downtown area, telephone numbers, total number of rooms, facilities, business services, and credit cards accepted. Additional information is available for many hotels, including distance from the nearest airport, architectural style, and a description of its atmosphere. You can search the database by location, hotel chain, or type of services and hotel you want, and if your search turns up too many possibilities you can specify additional criteria to narrow the list. If you're going to be traveling and need to figure out which hotel to stay in, this is the place to look.

Surcharges: CompuServe Extended Service hourly rates

10. AIR INFO/RESERVATIONS ▲▲ +
GO FLIGHTS

The three services here—WORLDSPAN Travelshopper, EAASY SABRE, and the Official Airline Guide (OAG Electronic Edition)—all offer access to commercial airline flight information and fares, and let you make reservations on line for flights, car rentals, and hotels. WORLDSPAN Travelshopper is the CompuServe version of a global reservation system owned by TWA, Northwest Airlines, and Delta Airlines; EAASY SABRE is a similar service owned by American Airlines; and OAG is an independent global reservation system. All three of these systems offer similar services: You can search for the cheapest flights, book reservations, and arrange for delivery of tickets to you either by mail or through a travel agent. WORLDSPAN Travelshopper and EAASY SABRE are free and have both a standard interface and one customized for CIM users. OAG is surcharged and only has one interface option. There's a vast amount of information, and finding the right flight can sometimes be difficult. If you spend much time with any of these daunting systems, you'll soon learn to appreciate your travel agent.

Surcharges: For WORLDSPAN Travelshopper and EAASY SABRE, none (though hourly rates apply to members on the Alternative Pricing Plan); for OAG Electronic edition, $28.00/hour ($0.47/minute) during prime time/daytime hours, $10.00/hour ($0.17/minute) during evening hours, plus CompuServe Extended Service hourly rates

11. CONSUMER REPORTS ▲▲▲ +
GO CONSUMER

Consumer Reports articles and product ratings from the past two or three years are all here for your perusal. Just pick the category of product you're interested in, and select the article from the menu. There's a wealth of automobile-related information, of course, and a wide range of other topics, as well. This may be the easiest and cheapest way to get information and ratings about products you're thinking of buying.

Surcharges: None (hourly rates apply to members on the Alternative Pricing Plan)

12. ELECTRONIC MALL ▲▲ +
GO MALL

If you've ever been to a mall, the Electronic Mall will be familiar to you. Over a hundred merchants hawk their wares and catalogs here, and you can browse them all, free of connect-time. There are sales, special promotions, a shopper's discount club (Shopper's Advantage), and more. Many stores let you purchase products on line (billing to your credit card) or order more complete catalogs to be mailed to you. There are clothing stores, computer hardware and software merchants, bookstores, office supplies stores, and travel agents, to name a few. For an alphabetical listing of mall merchants, enter GO MALLDIRECT. If you want an index of products offered in the mall, enter GO INX. And hang on to your credit cards!

Surcharges: None (hourly rates apply to members on the Alternative Pricing Plan)

13. ZAGAT RESTAURANT SURVEY ▲ +
GO ZAGAT

This service gives a new meaning to the term *menu driven*. Zagat surveys restaurant patrons annually and compiles the results into a restaurant guide covering most major metropolitan areas of the U.S. You select the area of the country you're interested in and specify the criteria by which you want to screen restaurants: neighborhood, price range, cuisine, or perhaps the presence of celebrity patrons. You can then see Zagat's survey results displayed for any restaurants matching your criteria. It's a useful way to scan for some good restaurants in an area, but the "reviews" are too sketchy to be a reliable indicator of restaurant quality. Too often, basic information about a restaurant is missing. Still, it's free, so who's complaining?

Surcharges: None (hourly rates apply to members on the Alternative Pricing Plan)

Money Matters/Markets
The Money Matters and Markets menu (GO MONEY) is the doorway to vast quantities of current and historical market information, on-line brokerage services, business databases, and personal finance tools. The sheer quantity of information in this comprehensive array of services is staggering. It's one of CompuServe's strongest areas.

14. BUSINESS DATABASE PLUS ▲▲▲ $$
GO BUSDB

Here you can search over a million full-text articles for information pertaining to your business. Business Database Plus contains two collections: articles from business and trade journals over the past five years, and articles from industry newsletters over the past year. The former is better suited to coverage of products and companies, the latter to coverage of current industry events and analysis of market trends. Whatever your business, these databases contain valuable information. The search menus make it easy to construct searches based on titles, keywords, subjects, and publication information, and to gradually refine your search until you have a manageable number of titles.

Business Database Plus charges are much lower than many other information sources on CompuServe, but be aware that there's no display of a running total of accumulated surcharges.

Surcharges: $15.00/hour ($0.25/minute), $1.50 per article viewed or downloaded

15. E*TRADE STOCK MARKET GAME ▲▲▲ $
GO ETGAME

Here's your chance to make a killing in the stock market without risking a cent. You're given $100,000 of game money to invest as you choose, in stocks only, or in both stocks and options. Set up your portfolio any way you choose, using all of CompuServe's financial tools to help you make decisions, if you want to. You decide what to buy and when to sell, and the game adjusts your holdings based on actual market performance. The game is very realistic: Your transactions even include fees at the rate actually charged by E*TRADE, an electronic brokerage. At the end of the month, the player who has made the most money wins a cash prize of $50.00 (that's *real* money!) and a new game starts the next day. It's a great way to learn about the stock market without worrying about losing your shirt.

Surcharges: CompuServe Extended Service hourly rates

16. FUNDWATCH ONLINE ▲▲▲ ✦
GO MONEYMAG

FundWatch contains data on over 1,900 mutual funds. You can search this database for funds that match your investment philosophy and find out detailed information about those funds, including holdings, performance, and more. Search criteria include investment objective, fees, return, and performance and risk ratings. If you're looking for funds in which to invest, this is an easy way to quickly refine the list of possibilities. Each fund's description includes a contact phone number, so you can find out more information if you're interested. FundWatch Online is a service of *Money Magazine*.

Surcharges: None (hourly rates apply to members on the Alternative Pricing Plan)

17. INTERNATIONAL COMPANY INFORMATION ▲▲▲ $$
GO COINTL

There are a wide variety of databases under this heading, providing plenty of data on U.S. companies (GO COMPANY) as well as companies in Canada (GO COCAN), Europe, (GO COEURO), Germany (GO COGERMAN), the United Kingdom (GO COUK), and in Australia, New Zealand, and Pacific countries (GO ANZCOMPANY). You'll find extensive data on the largest companies in each country, their products, earnings, size, and more. U.S. company services include Standard & Poor's Online, Dun's Market Identifiers, TRW Business Credit Profiles, and others.

Surcharges: Various; CompuServe Extended Service hourly rates apply in most cases

18. MARKET QUOTES AND HIGHLIGHTS ▲▲▲ $
GO QUOTES

This menu provides a rich array of market information. Check the performance of your investments or research new ones. Look up ticker symbols and check current quotes for stock issues, funds, and commodities. Take a look at the current market snapshot, or check yesterday's market highlights. You can look up the past performance of any items and get an analysis of that performance. You can analyze your portfolio, screen companies or securities, and analyze returns. These services provide useful market information, but keep in mind that quotes are delayed 15 minutes or more, and that the surcharges for these services vary.

Surcharges: Various; CompuServe Extended Service hourly rates apply in most cases

Entertainment/Games
CompuServe's Entertainment and Games offerings (GO GAM) are rich and varied. You can find entertainment information here, as well as interactive games—from the most basic text adventure to sophisticated modem-to-modem arcade games. There are also forums for people who are interested in all sorts of games, computer and noncomputer.

19. GAME FORUMS ▲▲ $
GO GAMECON

The Electronic Gamer (GO TEG) offers reviews and "walkthroughs" (complete, step-by-step solutions) to many popular computer games. Just looking for a few hints, or want to talk about your favorite games? Go to the Gamers' Forum (GO GAMERS). This forum's libraries contain mostly tips files, but you'll also find shareware games to be downloaded. Eight more specialized gaming forums are also available from the Game Forums menu, including the Role-Playing Games Forum, the Modem Games Forum, the Flight Simulation Forum, and the Chess Forum.

Surcharges: CompuServe Extended Service hourly rates

20. ROGER EBERT'S MOVIE REVIEWS ▲▲▲ ✦
GO EBERT

It's just not the same without Gene Siskel, but Ebert is a pretty good movie reviewer on his own. Look here for reviews of recent major movies and film festival winners. The reviews are detailed and thoughtful and give you plenty of information about each movie without spoiling it for you. There are celebrity interviews, a glossary of movie terms, and the Movie Lover's Source List, a bibliography of film resources. You can also search the entire collection of reviews for specific movies, actors, or directors—whether recent or classic. And if you want to tell Roger what *you* think, there's even a Feedback section where you can send him a message. (Or stop by the ShowBiz forum, GO SHOWBIZ, and post your message in the "Ask Roger Ebert" section.)

Surcharges: None (hourly rates apply to members on the Alternative Pricing Plan)

21. ALL-MUSIC GUIDE FORUM ▲▲ $
GO AMGPOP

Although it's a forum, the emphasis here is not on messages, but rather the file library. The All-Music Guide aims to be a comprehensive guide to popular music, with discographies and reviews of every imaginable artist or group. Enter the library and search for a band you want to know about, and it's quite likely there will be a file detailing the band's recording history, evaluating each album, and listing the tracks on each record. The libraries also include MusicMaps that trace the history of any given instrument through the years and through a variety of musical styles. When we checked it out, the All-Music Guide had just been started and its libraries weren't complete. Nonetheless, this forum was pretty impressive even in a partially completed state, and its ambitions are high. Give it a look.

Surcharges: CompuServe Extended Service hourly rates

Hobbies/Lifestyles/Education
Under Hobbies/Lifestyles/Education (GO HOME) are tucked a large number of special-interest forums on topics from fish to foreign languages. There are also many health references here under the Health menu.

22. DEMOCRATIC FORUM ▲▲ $
GO DEMOCRATS

The *Democratic* here is for the Democratic Party, though the messages in this forum show that the party is by no means showing a unified front. There's a lot of lively debate going on here between people representing all points of the political spectrum, on every major current political topic. If you're interested in the workings of the Democratic Party, the libraries have plenty of files, press releases, and more to satisfy you. There's also a library with the latest White House news, including all the president's speeches. Step right up and voice your opinion!

Surcharges: CompuServe Extended Service hourly rates

23. EDUCATION FORUM ▲▲▲ $
GO EDFORUM

Here's where educators, students, and parents can discuss a wide range of educational issues. A lot of different people take part in these discussions, and you'll find plenty to interest you. The libraries contain directories of scholarships and financial aid sources, which alone justify a visit to this forum—but there's a lot more to be found. Look for information about courses available on line, colleges, educational materials, computers in education, even how to get money to support kids' gardening projects. Or take part in the discussions yourself!

Surcharges: CompuServe Extended Service hourly rates

24. GARDENING FORUM ▲▲ $
GO GARDENING

From landscaping to flower cultivation, herbal remedies to pest control, the Gardening forum's got the books,

references, graphics, and software you need. It's managed by the National Gardening Association, publishers of *National Gardening Magazine*, and the participants are knowledgeable and friendly. Some items to look for in the file libraries: The Secret Life of Potatoes, The Plant-Killer's Guide to Orchids, Kiwi's Big Adventure, and the Hot Pepper discussion. There are also bibliographies on almost every type of gardening.

Surcharges: CompuServe Extended Service hourly rates

25. HEALTH & FITNESS FORUM ▲▲ $
GO GOODHEALTH

The biggest discussion areas in this popular forum are Addiction & Recovery, Mental Health, and Martial Arts. Whether you want conversation, information, or support, there are lots of people here ready to share their experiences and knowledge. The forum sponsors 12-step on-line conferences several evenings a week: meetings of Alcoholics Anonymous, Overeaters Anonymous, and Narcotics Anonymous. See the sysop's announcement for scheduled meeting days.

Surcharges: CompuServe Extended Service hourly rates

26. HEALTH DATABASE PLUS ▲▲▲ $$
GO HLTDB

If you're researching any health, fitness, or nutrition issue, this is the place to turn. Health Database Plus is a compendium of articles from consumer and professional publications covering all aspects of health. Most of the information is not aimed at medical professionals; the core of the database comprises articles from magazines on general-interest health, medicine, nutrition, and fitness. There are also articles from more specialized publications and professional medical journals. (To find out what publications are included, enter GO ZIFFHELP and download the file HDPPUB.TXT from Library 10.) In most cases, the full text of the article is available, but some are abstracted.

Surcharges: $1.50 per full-text article read or downloaded, $1.00 per abstract viewed or downloaded, plus CompuServe Extended Service hourly rates

27. HUMAN SEXUALITY DATABANK AND FORUMS ▲▲▲ $
GO HUMAN

The Human Sexuality Databank is a combination of question-and-answer files, plus two discussion forums, all devoted to providing a safe, supportive context for bringing up questions and concerns about most aspects of human sexuality, and for getting information about sex topics. You can share feelings, opinions, and questions with others, learn from experts such as Dr. Joyce Brothers, or just observe what other people have asked and what responses they got. The Databank and its forums deal with sex frankly and honestly, and it's expected that all participants in the discussions will, too.

Surcharges: CompuServe Extended Service hourly rates

28. LITERARY FORUM ▲▲▲ $
GO LITFORUM

A quick trip to the Literary forum will disabuse you of any notions that poetry, literature, and fine writing are forgotten passions. The denizens of LitForum, as it is called, are enthusiastic readers and writers who will as eagerly debate Elizabethan metrics as postmodern novels. There's also a dedicated Writer's Workshop message section, where forum members carry on serious and focused critiques of one another's work. Many LitForum habitués have had their own novels or poetry published and are happy to offer advice about writing and getting published.

Surcharges: CompuServe Extended Service hourly rates

29. OUTDOORS FORUM ▲▲▲ $
GO OUTDOORS

People are flocking to the Outdoors forum. There are subject areas for most of your favorite outdoor pastimes: cycling, hiking, camping, scouting, fishing, hunting, canoeing, boating, snow sports, climbing, photography, RVing, and even naturism (nudism) and computing outdoors. When we checked, there were some huge discussions of guns and gun control laws going on. The libraries contain helpful tips, history, equipment advice, true tales of outdoor experiences, and of course a few fishing stories.

Surcharges: CompuServe Extended Service hourly rates

30. RELIGION FORUM ▲▲▲ $
GO RELIGION

This forum has a broad scope, with sections for the discussion of every major world religion. The most popular areas are those on Christianity, Judaism, and the Church of Latter Day Saints, but there's also a lot going on in the Free Thought, Ethics & Debates, and Pagan/Occult message sections. Each Thursday at 9:00 p.m. eastern time, the Religion forum sponsors a Bible study in Conference Room 2. The libraries here are a rich source of texts and materials, including journals, tracts, magazine articles, calendars, and graphics. For example, look for the hypertext New Testament for Windows in Library 2, a variety of Hebrew fonts in Library 3, the full text of the Koran (Library 5), a deck of Tarot card graphics (Library 8), and a shareware program, "Effective Action," designed to help you in making decisions and raising grassroots support for any issue (Library 15).

Surcharges: CompuServe Extended Service hourly rates

31. SPACE AND ASTRONOMY FORUMS ▲▲▲▲ $
GO SPACE

The Space menu is a rich resource for stargazers and astronomy aficionados, and a mother lode of source material and ideas for teachers. From this menu you get access to current bulletins from NASA, *Sky & Telescope* magazine, and the European Space Agency, plus up-to-date information about sunspots and astronomy in the classroom. Want to know the latest about the current space shuttle mission? Get the most recent Mission Control statement from the NASA menu (GO NASA). Find out what interesting celestial events are coming up from

Sky & Telescope (GO SKYTEL). Check out the Space forum and the Astronomy forum (also on this menu); their large collections of pictures ranges from comets to moons to space probes. The Astronomy forum's library also contains public-domain astronomy software for the PC and the Mac, plus plenty of informational text files for both amateurs and experienced astronomers. You can't go wrong with any of the offerings here.

Surcharges: CompuServe Extended Service hourly rates

32. WHITE HOUSE FORUM ▲▲ $
GO WHITEHOUSE

Here's where to find the most vigorous debates available on line about all aspects of the presidency and the current administration's policies. Message threads under headings ranging from "Boot Clinton Out Now" to "Great Job Mr. President" can be found in this forum, and you can be sure that everyone's got an opinion about every one of them. Whew! This is one of the best uses of cyberspace we've seen—if these folks were all together in one *physical* space, somebody might get hurt! The libraries contain White House press releases only, filed under a variety of topics.

Surcharges: CompuServe Extended Service hourly rates

33. WORKING FROM HOME FORUM ▲▲▲ $
GO WORK

This forum provides genuinely useful information for anyone working from home, telecommuting, or running their own business. Whether you're starting a flower business in your basement or going into the information brokerage business, you should stop by this forum to get valuable advice from other work-at-homers—about improving your business, dealing with legal and tax matters, and finding information. There are lots of useful files and software in the libraries. The forum doesn't have any organizational affiliations, and the people are friendly. Stop by the "I'm New & What I Do" message section to introduce yourself and get to know the regulars; they'll be happy to meet you.

Surcharges: CompuServe Extended Service hourly rates

References *CompuServe's range of reference services (GO REFERENCE) is large, and there are many excellent databases available. Some fine offerings come free of surcharges, but the majority of the reference products here do carry extra fees, some of them very steep. Read all the instructions before you access any surcharged service in the Reference section, and save yourself time and money by avoiding common errors.*

34. BIZ*FILE ▲ $$
GO BIZFILE

Biz*File is a national yellow pages that you can use to find a business anywhere in the country. You can search Biz*File by business category and geographic region to find what you want. It's pretty easy to use, but there's no provision for narrowing a search that turns up hundreds of entries. You just have to list them all and pick the ones you're interested in. For instance, if

you don't know an exact zip code, that means wading through all the florists in the New York metropolitan area just to find one on Long Island.

Surcharges: $15.00/hour ($0.25/minute), plus CompuServe Extended Service hourly rates

35. CENDATA ▲▲ $
GO CENDATA

This is the U.S. Census Bureau's data, on line. There's a wealth of information, from the most recent census all the way back to the first one in 1790. CENDATA's menu-driven structure doesn't make it easy to zero in on specific data for any particular area, but if you're interested in the big picture, you'll get it here. You can read a report of how the U.S.'s population grew over the last 200 years, find out how to order a CD-ROM containing all of your state's census data, or examine changes in home ownership statistics from 1980 to 1993. There's a lot of data! With no surcharges other than CompuServe's hourly rates, CENDATA is a good value.

Surcharges: CompuServe Extended Service hourly rates

36. INFORMATION USA ▲▲ $
GO INFOUSA

Matthew Lesko's reference book on finding free information is available on line. Want to know about state and federal grants for which you may qualify? Looking for sources of insurance information? Trying to determine whether there's a market for your product? Check out Information USA—if it can't produce a phone number or address for you to contact, it's probably got a suggestion for finding the information you need. Information USA is essentially a big grab bag of information about how to get information. Unfortunately, there's no way to search the text for a particular term or subject; you just have to work through the menus.

Surcharges: CompuServe Extended Service hourly rates

37. IQUEST ▲▲▲ $$$
GO IQUEST

IQuest offers simplified access to more databases than any other service on CompuServe: over 850 bibliographic and full-text databases in all. IQuest is particularly strong in business and financial databases, but you'll also find categories such as Art, Literature, and Entertainment; News (U.S., by state, and international); Law and Patents; Medicine; Science and Technology; Philosophy and Religion; Social Sciences; and General Reference. Unfortunately, IQuest's comprehensiveness comes at a steep price. At $9.00 per search, plus database surcharges, it's easy to run up three-figure charges in no time at all. *Tip:* If you don't know which database to search, perform a SmartSCAN first for $5.00. IQuest will list the databases that contain references to your search term, from which you can pick a promising database and run your search on it. If you want help searching, type SOS for online help from a real, live person.

Surcharges: $9.00 per search, $5.00 per SmartSCAN, $3.00 per abstract, $1.00 per search that retrieves no titles. Additional surcharges run from $2.00 to $75.00 per database. Each search includes up to ten references (in full-text databases, you get 15 references plus one article). In addition, CompuServe Extended Service hourly rates apply while you're in IQuest.

38. KNOWLEDGE INDEX ▲▲▲▲ $$
GO KI

The Knowledge Index is one of the best database values on CompuServe. It offers discounted access to over 100 professional-quality databases, covering topics ranging from agriculture and books to science and technology. Many of these databases are exactly the same as those found in the more expensive IQuest service; some of them are also available elsewhere in CompuServe, for varying rates. Knowledge Index brings them all together for a flat $24.00/hour fee. The catch? You can only access Knowledge Index between 6:00 p.m. and 5:00 a.m. (your time) Monday through Thursday, or on weekends from 6:00 p.m. Friday until 5:00 a.m. Monday. For students, educators, people working at home and those staying late at the office, Knowledge Index is a good value.

Surcharges: $24.00/hour ($0.40/minute), plus CompuServe Extended Service hourly rates

39. SUPERSITE ▲ $$$
GO SUPERSITE

This service offers an easy way to get organized 1990 census data by state, country, zip code, Arbitron TV Market, Nielsen TV Market, and other regional designations. You can specify any area or combination of areas, and SUPERSITE will compile the data. You then decide which reports for the selected area you want to purchase. These reports are neatly presented, easy to read, and extremely detailed, but they're also quite specific and you'll probably need to purchase several of them to get a complete picture. At up to $45.00 a report, that can add up pretty quickly. If you need a lot of information, you'd better have deep pockets.

Surcharges: $25.00 to $45.00 per report, plus CompuServe Extended Service hourly rates

Computers and Technology *The Computers and Technology menu (GO COMPUTER) is CompuServe's strongest area. You'll find nearly 200 technical support forums, run by many different vendors, providing customer support and product information for a substantial number of products. It's impossible for us to list them all here, so we've described some of the items of more general interest. If you want to know whether technical support for a product is available in this CompuServe area, check with the product's manufacturer or with CompuServe. Or, if you're already a CompuServe subscriber, you can look on the Hardware and Software menus (GO HARDWARE and GO SOFTWARE).*

40. CDROM FORUM   ▲ $
GO CDROM

To help you keep abreast of the latest CD-ROM titles or recent developments in CD technology, this forum is devoted to the discussion and sharing of information about CD-ROMs, CD-ROM readers, and multimedia. The libraries contain reviews of recent products and a few samples thereof. You'll also find information about upcoming conferences and shows.

Surcharges: CompuServe Extended Service hourly rates

41. DESKTOP PUBLISHING FORUMS   ▲▲▲ $
GO DTP

Here you'll find a menu that collects all of CompuServe's DTP-related forums in one place. Looking for some nifty new headline fonts or clip art to spice up a newsletter? Try the libraries of the Desktop Publishing Forum (GO DTPFORUM). There's a vital community of desktop publishing professionals as well as nonprofessional users in this forum. Its libraries contain a lot of useful resources for both Mac and PC users, including utilities, templates, news, and technical tips, in addition to clip art and fonts. The DTP menu also offers access to about two dozen vendor forums, where you can get additional materials and technical support for many hardware and software products.

Surcharges: CompuServe Extended Service hourly rates

42. ELECTRONIC FRONTIER FOUNDATION   ▲ $
GO EFFSIG

The Electronic Frontier Foundation (EFF) is an organization devoted to "homesteading" the boundaries of cyberspace; this organization is actively involved with e-mail privacy issues. Unfortunately, their CompuServe forum is less dynamic than their home base on The Well (see Chapter 2)—perhaps the EFF's strong Internet emphasis reduces their activity here on CompuServe. Still, if you have a question about the Internet or about electronic privacy, you can ask it here. Also, the forum's libraries contain many fine electronic journals, many of which can't be found anywhere else outside of the Internet, plus guides and manuals for those interested in the Internet.

Surcharges: CompuServe Extended Service hourly rates

43. ZENITH FORUM   ▲▲▲▲ $
GO ZENITH

In addition to being a technical support forum for Zenith computer users, this is one of the best sources of DOS and Windows shareware and freeware. The Zenith forum folks keep its libraries updated with the latest and greatest indispensable utilities, editors, productivity programs, games, fonts…you name it. If you've got a PC-compatible of any description, be sure to browse through the DOS Utilities, DOS Applications, DOS Fun & Games, and Windows libraries. Of course, you also get a great source of technical support for your Zenith Data Systems product.

Surcharges: CompuServe Extended Service hourly rates

Business/Other Interests *Under Business/Other Interests (GO BUSINESS), you'll find a variety of professional forums and services, grouped under headings such as Business Management, Entrepreneurial/Small Business, Health Professionals, and Legal Services.*

44. PAPERCHASE   ▲▲▲ $$
GO PCH

Here's where to get access to MEDLINE, an enormous database of medical and biomedical literature maintained by the National Library of Medicine, as well as to the HEALTH, AIDSLINE, and CANCERLIT databases, also from the NLM. The MEDLINE database alone contains over 7 million references to articles in more than 4,000 journals. In many cases, abstracts as well as bibliographic references are available. PaperChase boasts a remarkably easy-to-use interface that lets you select articles you want to print from several search sessions, and then print them all together at the end of your PaperChase session. PaperChase is most useful for medical professionals, but health care consumers will also find helpful, pertinent information.

Surcharges: $24.00/hour from 8:00 a.m. to 7:00 p.m. (your time) on weekdays, $18.00/hour from 7:00 p.m. to 8:00 a.m. weekdays and anytime on weekends; plus CompuServe Extended Service hourly rates

45. TRADEMARKSCAN   ▲ $$
GO TRD-1

If you need to find out whether a term is trademarked, you might want to check out TRADEMARKSCAN before you call a lawyer. TRADEMARKSCAN lets you search for words or phrases that appear in all federal- or state-registered trademarks, and you can get details on any trademarks that match your query. Since a trademark may be legal without being registered, however, TRADEMARKSCAN can't provide you with the final, legal word: You must consult a lawyer to confirm whether a trademark is available.

Surcharges: $10.00 per search (up to five record titles), $10.00 per additional five titles, $5.00 per full trademark record, $1.00 for a search that retrieves no trademark records; plus CompuServe Extended Service hourly rates

CHAPTER 4

ZiffNet for CompuServe

ZiffNet is the on-line information service of Ziff Communications Company, publisher of many computer magazines, including *PC Magazine*, *PC/Computing*, and *PC Week*. ZiffNet is dedicated to providing computer industry information and news, as well as software, technical advice, and lots of computer product data. Most Ziff magazines have their own forums on ZiffNet, where you can get in touch with editors and authors, download utilities, read tips and news, and talk to other readers.

ZiffNet offers databases, buying advice, and technical support. ZiffNet is also a useful and economical resource for PC or Macintosh information. If you're in the market for a new computer, software, or peripherals, ZiffNet will provide market information, product reviews and comparisons, and a chance to hear what other users have to say about the products you're thinking of buying. You'll also be able to find technical experts to give you advice on getting the most out of your hardware and software. Though not a complete information service by itself, ZiffNet is an excellent source of computer information.

You can access CompuServe's e-mail system with ZiffNet because ZiffNet resides on CompuServe's computers. You use the same access numbers used for CompuServe—which means it's available via a local call from almost everywhere in North America, and many places internationally. Its interface and organization are the same as CompuServe's, so you can use all of the CompuServe interface programs (CIM, Navigator, TAPCIS, OzCIS, and others) to access ZiffNet—or you can use a standard communications program. ZiffNet's text-based, menu-driven interface is easy enough to negotiate; but if you use its forums very much, you'll probably want one of the specialized interface programs. (See Chapter 3 for a discussion of CompuServe interface programs and forums.)

The ZiffNet for CompuServe menu

Although you don't have to be a CompuServe member to use ZiffNet, you'll probably want to join CompuServe too, in order to take advantage of CompuServe's much wider range of services and forums. You'll also have lower connect-time rates on ZiffNet if you join CompuServe on the Standard Pricing Plan. If you're already a CompuServe member, an additional $2.95 per month gives you full access to all of ZiffNet's services.

Many ZiffNet resources are included free with the monthly membership fee, while others (including most of the forums) carry additional connect-time charges. Some features carry connect-time charges plus additional surcharges—for example, the databases Computer Library, Business Database Plus, Magazine Database Plus, and Health Database Plus. Note that these four databases are also available on CompuServe at the same rates, so you don't need ZiffNet just to access them.

Subscribing to ZiffNet

If you're already a CompuServe member, simply log on to CompuServe and type **GO ZIFFNET** to enter ZiffNet and sign up. If you don't belong

to CompuServe, you can sign up for ZiffNet by modem. Just follow these instructions:

1. Set your comm program to 7 data bits, even parity, and 1 stop bit; and select your modem speed (1200, 2400, or 9600 bps).

2. Find your local ZiffNet access number: By modem, dial (800) 346-3247. At the "Host ID" prompt, type **PHONES** and follow the instructions. Or, by phone, dial (800) 635-6225 or (614) 457-8650, and follow the instructions for finding a local access number. Write down the number and hang up.

3. Dial your local ZiffNet access number.

4. At the Host Name prompt, type **CIS**.

5. At the User ID prompt, type **177000,5555**.

6. At the User Password prompt, type **ZIFF*NET**.

7. Enter the agreement number: **ZDPRESS**.

8. Register your name and credit card number.

9. When you're finished registering, ZiffNet will assign you a personal User ID and temporary password. Write them down and use them whenever you log on over the next ten days; within this time, you will get a replacement password by mail to confirm your membership.

If you want more information on signing up for ZiffNet, call their customer service number at (800) 666-0330 (voice).

Fees

ZiffNet's monthly membership fee is $2.95. If you're a CompuServe member, this is added to your monthly CompuServe membership fee. The monthly fee gives you access to ZiffNet's basic services, including the Buyers' Market, the latest *PC Magazine* and *MacUser* utilities, the Product Reviews Index, weekly news, and other features.

Most services in ZiffNet carry additional connect-time surcharges, however. If you're not a CompuServe member, or if you're a CompuServe member on the Alternate Pricing Plan, you'll pay these hourly charges for any extended services in ZiffNet (as well as in CompuServe).

ZiffNet Connect-Time Surcharges for Non-CompuServe Members and CompuServe Alternate Pricing Plan Members

Baud Rate	Hourly Charge
300	$6.30
1200 or 2400	$12.80
9600 or 14400	$22.80

If you're a CompuServe member on the Standard Pricing Plan, the following connect-time charges apply for surcharged services in ZiffNet, just as they do in CompuServe.

ZiffNet Connect-Time Surcharges for CompuServe Standard Pricing Plan Members

Baud Rate	Hourly Charge
300	$4.80
1200 or 2400	$4.80
9600 or 14400	$9.60

If you use ZiffNet at 1200 baud or higher for more than about two hours per month, you'll save money by signing up for CompuServe on the Standard Pricing Plan, because the connect-time charges are lower—which more than offsets the additional $8.95 per month you'll pay for a CompuServe membership. The Standard Plan also gets you lower e-mail rates.

The Interchange Online Network

As of this writing, ZiffNet's on-line resources were limited to ZiffNet for CompuServe and ZiffNet for Prodigy (see Chapter 5). However, in late 1994, a new on-line service, operated by Ziff Communications, will begin nationwide service. Called The Interchange Online Network, it will be a sophisticated on-line service in its own right, with a Windows-based interface, refined hypertext and multimedia features, and the ability to multitask (so you can download files while you read an article, for example). At first, Interchange will specialize in providing information and files pertaining to the computer industry, but other areas of interest are planned. Interchange aims at being not merely an on-line service, but an electronic "publishing platform," which publishers and companies can use to distribute information in a highly interactive way. Look for it to make some big waves in the on-line world.

If you use a public data network such as telnet or TYMNET to connect to ZiffNet, you'll pay hourly rates to that network in addition to your ZiffNet fees.

Getting Around ZiffNet

ZiffNet, like CompuServe, is menu driven, but you can take shortcuts to most resources by typing the command **GO** followed by the service's name (its *GO-word*). If you're already in CompuServe, you'll need to add the prefix **ZNT:** to the GO-word for any ZiffNet resource. For example, to get to the ZiffNet Speakeasy Forum, you'd type

GO ZNT:SPEAKEASY

If the item you want is on ZiffNet/Mac, use the prefix **ZMC:** instead. (See the ZiffNet/Mac sidebar at the end of the chapter for details.) If you're already in ZiffNet, you don't need to use the prefix. However, if you want to return to a resource in CompuServe, you'll need to add the prefix **CIS:** to get back to the CompuServe Information Service.

You should be aware that the on-line world is a very dynamic place. It's a good practice to check with member services if you ever have any trouble accessing resources.

Many ZiffNet member-assistance services are available through GO-words. Most of these are free of connect-time surcharges.

GO-Words for Member Services

GO-Word	Result
BILLING	Access ZiffNet billing information
CHARGE	Review your billing charges
COMMANDS	Access helpful commands to navigate through ZiffNet
OPTION	Change your terminal parameters
PASSWORD	Change your password

PHONE	Find out ZiffNet access numbers in your area
QUICK	Obtain quick reference to ZiffNet services and GO-words
ZIFFMEM	Access ZiffNet membership information
ZNTFF	Access the ZiffNet File Finder to search for files anywhere on ZiffNet

FIND topic	FIND all references to topic in ZiffNet
OFF or BYE	Log off ZiffNet
PER	Exit to Personal File Area
SET	Set terminal display option

ZiffNet recognizes the same set of commands that CompuServe does. The Ctrl-key commands can be used at any time. The other commands can be used at any ZiffNet prompt. If the command is a single letter, you can type that letter alone or enter the full word (in all caps).

ZiffNet Commands

Command	Result
Ctrl-C	Abort the current program
Ctrl-O	Stop text flow without aborting current program
Ctrl-Q	Resume text flow from ZiffNet
Ctrl-S	Pause text flow from ZiffNet
Ctrl-U	Delete the line you're currently typing
B	Go BACK one page
F	Go FORWARD one page
H	Get HELP
M	Go to the previous MENU
N	Display NEXT menu item
P	Display PREVIOUS menu item
R	RESEND a page
S item(s)	SCROLL specified menu items without pausing
T	Go to the topmost menu page (TOP)

You can enter SET on a line by itself, and ZiffNet will prompt you to enter the option and setting you want. Or, enter SET followed by the option and the setting you want, all on a single line.

SET Option	Definition
PAG ON/OFF	Paged mode
BRI ON/OFF	Brief mode
TTY	Set terminal type (VIDTEX, TELERAY, TELIDON, DUMCRT, TELETYPE, TRS80, VT100, or VT52)
WID nnn	Screen width (columns), from 10 to 255
LIN nnn	Screen length (lines), from 10 to 255

ZiffNet forums work just like CompuServe forums. There are special commands for searching, selecting, and reading messages, finding files, and other forum activities. These commands apply only within the forums.

The first time you enter a forum, you will need to *JOIN* the forum to get full access to it. Joining is free and is simply a matter of volunteering your name (real full names are encouraged). *Note:* If you use CIM, the CIM software provides menu options or buttons to perform all forum functions.

Forum Commands

Command	*Result*
ANNOUNCEMENTS	Read announcements from the sysop
CONFERENCE *x*	Go to conference room *x*
CONFERENCING	Go to forum Conference menu
DESCRIPTIONS	View descriptions of forum message sections and libraries
HELP	Get context-sensitive help
HIGH:*n*	Mark message number *n* as the last message read; the next time you visit the forum you'll see only those messages with numbers higher than *n*
INSTRUCTIONS	View general forum instructions
JOIN	Initiate full access to a forum
LIBRARIES	Go to forum Libraries menu
MESSAGES	Go to forum Messages menu
NAME	Display a list of forum message sections, libraries, and conference rooms
OPTIONS	Go to Options menu (switch between command mode and menu-driven mode; access other forum options)
ULOG	See who has visited the forum recently, and when
USTATUS	See who else is currently in the forum
WHO *x*	Display information about member ID *x*

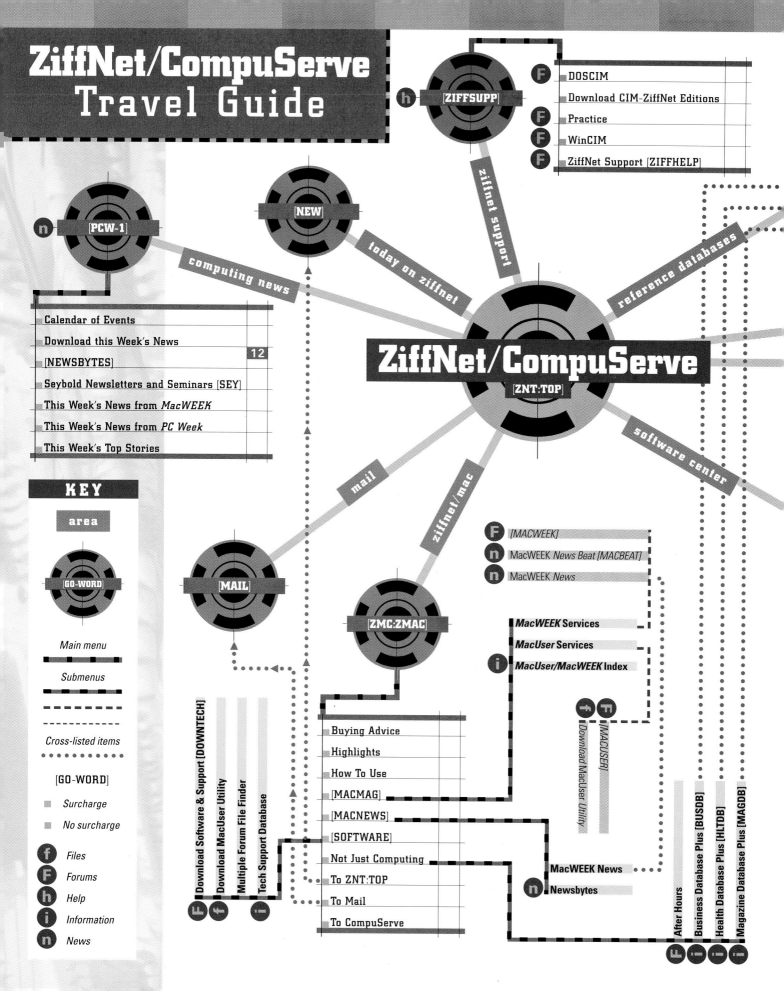

ZiffNet/CompuServe Travel Guide

[ZIFFSUPP] h

- F DOSCIM
- Download CIM-ZiffNet Editions
- F Practice
- F WinCIM
- F ZiffNet Support [ZIFFHELP]

[PCW-1] n

computing news

- Calendar of Events
- Download this Week's News [NEWSBYTES]
- Seybold Newsletters and Seminars [SEY]
- This Week's News from *MacWEEK*
- This Week's News from *PC Week*
- This Week's Top Stories

12

[NEW]

today on ziffnet

ziffnet support

reference databases

ZiffNet/CompuServe

[ZNT:TOP]

software center

mail

ziffnet/mac

KEY

area

[GO-WORD]

Main menu

Submenus

- - - - -

Cross-listed items

• • • • • • •

[GO-WORD]

- Surcharge
- No surcharge

- f Files
- F Forums
- h Help
- i Information
- n News

[MAIL]

[ZMC:ZMAC]

- F [MACWEEK]
- n MacWEEK *News Beat [MACBEAT]*
- n MacWEEK *News*

MacWEEK Services
MacUser Services
i *MacUser/MacWEEK* Index

f F

Download MacUser Utility
[MACUSER]

Download Software & Support [DOWNTECH]
Download MacUser Utility
Multiple Forum File Finder
Tech Support Database

- Buying Advice
- Highlights
- How To Use
- [MACMAG]
- [MACNEWS]
- [SOFTWARE]
- Not Just Computing
- To ZNT:TOP
- To Mail
- To CompuServe

L f i

MacWEEK News
n Newsbytes

After Hours
Business Database Plus [BUSDB]
Health Database Plus [HLTDB]
Magazine Database Plus [MAGDB]

F i i i

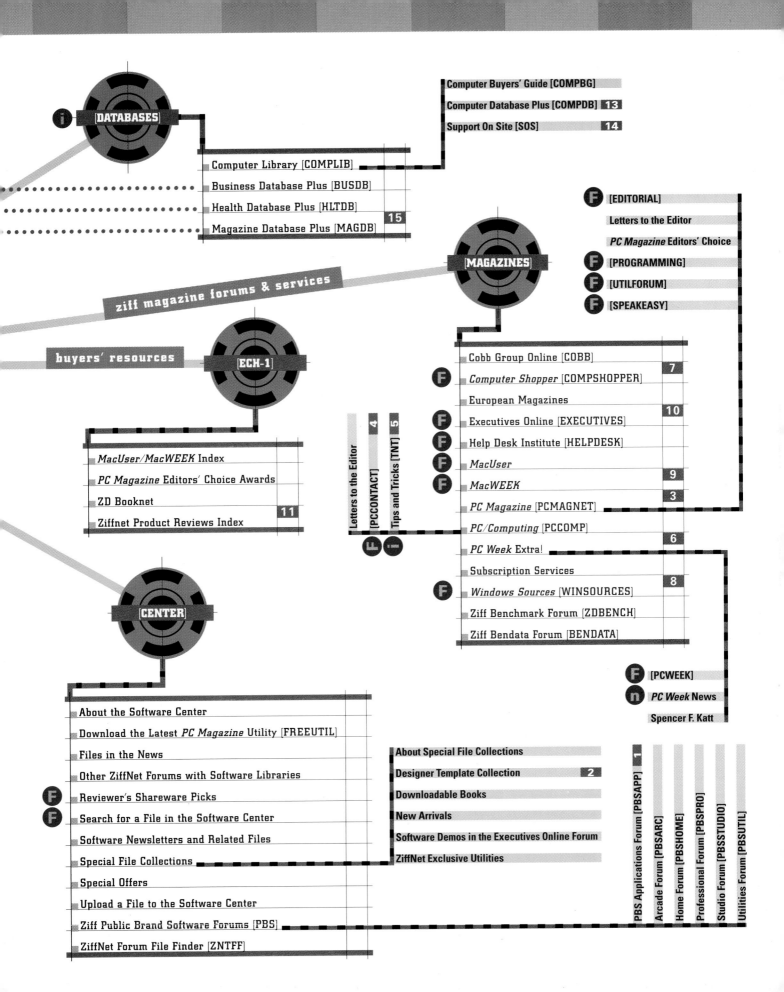

[DATABASES]

Computer Buyers' Guide [COMPBG]
Computer Database Plus [COMPDB] **13**
Support On Site [SOS] **14**

Computer Library [COMPLIB]
Business Database Plus [BUSDB]
Health Database Plus [HLTDB]
Magazine Database Plus [MAGDB] **15**

ziff magazine forums & services

[MAGAZINES]

F [EDITORIAL]
Letters to the Editor
PC Magazine Editors' Choice
F [PROGRAMMING]
F [UTILFORUM]
F [SPEAKEASY]

buyers' resources

[ECH-1]

MacUser/MacWEEK Index
PC Magazine Editors' Choice Awards
ZD Booknet
Ziffnet Product Reviews Index **11**

Letters to the Editor
[PCCONTACT] **4**
Tips and Tricks [TNT] **5**

Cobb Group Online [COBB]
F *Computer Shopper* [COMPSHOPPER] **7**
European Magazines
F Executives Online [EXECUTIVES] **10**
F Help Desk Institute [HELPDESK]
F *MacUser*
F *MacWEEK* **9**
PC Magazine [PCMAGNET] **3**
PC/Computing [PCCOMP]
PC Week Extra! **6**
Subscription Services
F *Windows Sources* [WINSOURCES] **8**
Ziff Benchmark Forum [ZDBENCH]
Ziff Bendata Forum [BENDATA]

F [PCWEEK]
n *PC Week* News
Spencer F. Katt

[CENTER]

About the Software Center
Download the Latest *PC Magazine* Utility [FREEUTIL]
Files in the News
Other ZiffNet Forums with Software Libraries
F Reviewer's Shareware Picks
F Search for a File in the Software Center
Software Newsletters and Related Files
Special File Collections
Special Offers
Upload a File to the Software Center
Ziff Public Brand Software Forums [PBS]
ZiffNet Forum File Finder [ZNTFF]

About Special File Collections
Designer Template Collection **2**
Downloadable Books
New Arrivals
Software Demos in the Executives Online Forum
ZiffNet Exclusive Utilities

PBS Applications Forum [PBSAPP] **1**
Arcade Forum [PBSARC]
Home Forum [PBSHOME]
Professional Forum [PBSPRO]
Studio Forum [PBSSTUDIO]
Utilities Forum [PBSUTIL]

INSIDE ZIFFNET FOR COMPUSERVE

You'll find the best of ZiffNet for CompuServe listed in the following pages. From databases to technical support, ZiffNet provides some of the best computer-related information available on line. And, of course, it's also the home of Ziff's many magazines, where you can get in touch with authors, editors, and other readers. Read on to find out what's inside ZiffNet.

The following pages describe and evaluate the best and most popular of ZiffNet for CompuServe's many resources. Each description is preceded by a number that you can use to find that resource on the map. Or, when you see a number on the map, you can look for that number among the resource descriptions. This listing not only gives you a sense of what's inside ZiffNet for CompuServe, but it will also help you quickly find the best resources as they appear on the map.

For an estimation of the quality and usefulness of each resource described, look for the following symbols:

▲▲▲▲   Outstanding—don't miss it!
▲▲▲   Excellent—worth going out of your way to see it.
▲▲   Very good—worth a look.
▲   Above average—stop by if it's on your way.
▼   Disappointing—don't bother.

You'll also find an indication of the cost of each described resource. The exact amount of surcharges, if any, are specified at the end of each description, and the dollar icons give you a general idea of how its price compares to other features inside ZiffNet for CompuServe.

$$$ Steep—hang on to your wallet!
$$ Moderate—not a bargain, but reasonable.
$ Cheap—a good value, easy on your pocketbook.
✦   Free—no surcharges or connect time charges!

If you need direct access, you'll find the GO-word for each resource in the listing as well as on the map. Finally, each resource is classified by type. The types are News, Forum (which consists of a discussion area and a file library), Information, Help, and Files, and are represented by the same type symbols that appear on the map.

Software Center *The Software Center is where you'll find several large collections of shareware and freeware programs and files. It includes the vast collections of Public Brand Software, as well as more specialized collections of shareware. This is also where you go to get the latest PC Magazine or MacUser utilities (GO FREEUTIL).*

1. PUBLIC BRAND SOFTWARE APPLICATIONS FORUM ▲▲▲▲ $
GO PBSAPPS

Public Brand Software (PBS) is a clearinghouse for shareware programs. PBS was a mail-order business for years before coming on line in ZiffNet, and they've accumulated a huge collection of shareware. You'll find almost everything under the shareware sun here, from word processors and spreadsheets to horse-breeding databases and lottery odds-calculating systems. It's no exaggeration to say that if you can imagine it, there's probably a shareware program for it on this forum somewhere. Although some of these programs are free, most are shareware—which means you can download them for free (except for connect-time charges), but if you continue to use the program, you must pay a registration fee to the program's author. For games and entertainment programs, check out the PBS Arcade Forum next door (GO ZNT:PBSARC).

Surcharges: ZiffNet hourly connect-time rates.

2. DESIGNER TEMPLATE COLLECTION ▲▲ $$
GO FORMS

Designed by KMT Software, Inc., the Designer Template Collection comprises word-processing and spreadsheet templates for common business uses. The word-processing templates include cover letter forms, envelope forms, calendars, and planners. Spreadsheet templates include forms for calculating home mortgages, small business forms, expense sheets, and finance forms. Many popular PC and Mac word-processing and spreadsheet programs are represented. The forms are professionally designed and look sharp, and each collection includes between 6 and 12 related templates. If you want to see what the forms look like, download the sample templates collections, which are free except for connect-time surcharges.

Surcharges: $9.95 per template collection, plus ZiffNet hourly connect-time rates

Ziff Magazines Online *Each Ziff magazine has a forum here on ZiffNet, where you can download tips and utilities, talk with the people who make the magazine, and get expert advice. Some magazines, such as PC Magazine, boast more than just a forum—they're rich resources of information in their own right, offering news, free utilities, and other services.*

3. *PC MAGAZINE* ▲▲▲ $
GO PCMAGNET

PC Magazine has a variety of on-line services here on PC MagNet. You can write letters to the editors, get the latest *PC Magazine* utility (free of connect-time charges), or look up the CompuServe IDs of various magazine staff members. There are also four forums where you can get advice from experts, including *PC Magazine* authors and editors, or just hang out with computer enthusiasts and professionals:

▶ The Utilities/Tips Forum (GO ZNT:UTILFORUM) is where to go for technical advice. Its libraries contain past PC Magazine utilities, tips from the Solutions department of the magazine, and more.

▶ To discuss PC Magazine feature articles and columns, go to the Editorial Forum (GO ZNT:EDITORIAL).

▶ Check out the Programming forum (GO ZNT:PROGRAMMING) if you're interested in PC programming issues.

▶ The Speakeasy Forum (GO ZNT:SPEAKEASY) is where ZiffNetters go to discuss everything not computer-related. Here you'll find people engaged in political debates, discussing science fiction, or simply offering their observations on the state of the world.

Surcharges: ZiffNet hourly connect-time rates, except when downloading the latest *PC Magazine* utility or when taking the *PC Magazine* Survey

4. PC/CONTACT   ▲▲▲ $
GO PCCONTACT

PC/Contact is *PC/Computing* magazine's online forum. You can contact the magazine's editors and quite a few other computing experts here, so it's a good place to visit if you're looking for information, technical advice, or if you just want to express your opinion about an article in the magazine. Check out the forum's libraries—they're chock full of useful utilities. Strangers are welcome on PC/Contact, and you'll find everyone generally very friendly and helpful. There's less traffic and fewer visitors than in similar forums, so for better or worse, you won't see many large-scale debates.

If you want to write a letter or submit an article to *PC/Computing*, GO ZNT:PCCOMP for *PC/Computing*'s full range of on-line services.

Surcharges: ZiffNet hourly connect-time rates

5. TIPS AND TRICKS FROM *PC/COMPUTING*   ▼ $
GO TNT

A potentially rich source of useful information for most PC users, Tips and Tricks puts *PC/Computing*'s Help section on line. In these detailed how-to's, you'll find answers that aren't in the manuals, and solutions to problems you didn't realize you had. Tips are diligently tested by *PC/Computing*'s editors and have all appeared in the pages of the magazine. Unfortunately, these postings are somewhat out-of-date (seven months behind the current issue, when we checked). Also, there's no way to search through the tips, so you're limited to the menus provided. These drawbacks make getting to the tips frustrating, and limit the usefulness of this resource.

Surcharges: ZiffNet hourly connect-time rates

6. *PC WEEK* EXTRA!   ▲▲   ✦
GO PCW-115

Want to know who's announcing new products, who's planning layoffs, and all the latest from the computer business world? Check out *PC Week* Extra! *PC Week* is a weekly computer news magazine that you can't subscribe to unless you're in charge of buying computers for a big corporation. But you *can* get *PC Week*'s top stories, for free and on line: Just GO ZNT:PCWNEWS. The stories appear as early as Friday evening— and since the paper doesn't get delivered until Monday or Tuesday, that's a big advantage.

You can also check out *PC Week*'s rumor column, Spencer F. Katt (GO ZNT:KATT). And the *PC Week* Forum (GO ZNT:PCWEEK) is the magazine's discussion forum, where you can talk about the news or ask questions of the magazine's reporters and editors. The libraries contain some genuinely helpful materials, as well.

Surcharges: None, except in the *PC Week* Forum, where ZiffNet hourly connect-time rates apply

7. *COMPUTER SHOPPER* FORUM   ▲▲▲ $
GO COMPSHOPPER

If the magazine *Computer Shopper* seems overwhelming to you (it's an enormous, fat book), try this unintimidating forum instead. Lots of knowledgeable folks discuss the ins and outs of buying computers and every possible component and peripheral. If you are looking for something in particular, the shopper's guides, found in the libraries, will be especially helpful. If you have a question, post a message to "Ask Dr. John," or look in the library for past columns. You can learn a lot here, and you won't have to carry around that heavy magazine!

Although you'll miss out on the many advertisements in the pages of Computer Shopper (one of the reasons many people buy the magazine), you can visit the Computer Buyers' Guide (GO ZNT: COMPBG), to get company phone numbers and product listings.

Surcharges: ZiffNet hourly connect-time rates

8. *WINDOWS SOURCES* FORUM   ▲▲ $
GO WINSOURCES

This is a mixed bag—*Windows Sources* is a relatively new magazine, and they haven't had a lot of time to accumulate large quantities of files, nor do their message sections yet have a substantial following. However, the files that *are* there in the libraries are of consistently high quality, and the people posting messages are friendly and helpful. The sysops are always ready to answer technical questions or provide advice about Windows and Windows programs. Check out the "Simon's Picks" library, where Windows Sources author Barry Simon posts utilities and his favorite shareware programs.

Surcharges: ZiffNet hourly connect-time rates

9. *MACWEEK* FORUM   ▲▲ $
GO MACWEEK

All the Mac news you could want is here in this forum dedicated to the weekly news magazine covering the Macintosh world. Discussion is brisk in the message area, concerning topics such as the merits and shortcomings of a variety of products, and the future of Apple products. The libraries contain almost exclusively news and reviews, although there are also some utilities and quite a few files for the Newton.

Surcharges: ZiffNet hourly connect-time rates

10. EXECUTIVES ONLINE FORUM ▲▲ $
GO EXECUTIVES

The Executives Online Forum hosts scheduled guest appearances by luminaries of the computer world. Each guest appearance lasts about one week, during which a computer company executive, technology expert, or celebrity is the guest of honor in one of the message sections. You can post questions and see the guest's answers, usually within the same day. Drop in during someone's guest appearance and find out about his or her company's plans, right from the horse's mouth. To see who's scheduled for upcoming weeks, check out ZiffNet's calendar (GO ZNT:CALENDAR).

Executives Online is also the home of the Women Online section (section 17). This section is a message area for the discussion of issues and problems that concern women using on-line services.

Surcharges: ZiffNet hourly connect-time rates

11. ZIFFNET PRODUCT REVIEWS INDEX ▲▲▲   ✦
GO INDEX

Can't remember in which issue, or in what magazine, you saw that great review of WidgetPerfect 2.0? Looking for some references to reviews of hard drives? Come to the Product Reviews Index, where you can scan back issues of Ziff magazines for reviews—by subject, product name, company name, or date. You can't get article abstracts or text here—for that you'll have to go to Computer Database Plus (GO COMPDB), which is covered in item 13 of this chapter. But you'll be able to save time and money if you do your searching here (for free), note the article numbers your search turns up, and then go to Computer Database Plus to retrieve the articles you want.

Surcharges: None

News *ZiffNet's news resources give you computer company news, announcements about new products, and analyses of major trends. You can view or download the week's news from PC Week or MacWEEK, read daily computer headlines, and find out about upcoming conferences and seminars from the Seybold Corporation. Special offers offered jointly by ZiffNet and various software vendors also appear frequently on this menu.*

12. NEWSBYTES ▲▲▲   ✦
GO NEWSBYTES

Newsbytes is a daily computer and telecommunications industry newswire. It provides up-to-date stories, written by its own staff of reporters, covering most major happenings in the computer industry. You can search the past week's news for any topics of interest to you. Newsbytes is a convenient complement to more general newswires—you don't have to sort through all the headlines to get computer industry news, and you can read articles written by specialists in the computer field. New articles are posted each day by 5:00 p.m. eastern time, Monday through Friday.

Surcharges: None

Databases *ZiffNet's family of databases is one of the service's best features. Demand for these databases is so high that most of them are also available on CompuServe at the same rates. (For descriptions of Business Database Plus and Health Database Plus, see Chapter 2.) To make the most of these databases without incurring excessive surcharges, be sure to read the searching instructions on the opening menus of each resource.*

The heart of the database menu is Computer Library, a collection of three databases: Computer Database Plus (computer-related articles), Computer Buyers' Guide (computer product specifications), and Support On Site (technical questions and answers). The other databases provide additional information on noncomputer topics, such as health and business.

13. COMPUTER DATABASE PLUS ▲▲▲▲ $$
GO COMPDB

For computer industry information, this database can't be beat. It's a compendium of full-text articles and abstracts culled from over 230 magazines, journals, and newspapers, including *PC Magazine, PC/Computing, PC Week,* and *InfoWorld.* The database is updated frequently (as often as weekly) and contains articles from as far back as 1987. The menu-driven search engine is easy to use, so you can quickly build complex searches based on keywords, subject headings, and publication date. If you're looking for news or reviews of computer products, this is the place to start. *Note:* There's no running total of your charges, but you can determine them from the search menu at any time.

Surcharges: $15.00/hour ($0.25/minute); $2.50 per article read or downloaded ($1.50 if no abstract is present); $1 per abstract read or downloaded; plus ZiffNet hourly connect-time rates

14. SUPPORT ON SITE ▲▲ $$
GO SOS

Support On Site is a searchable database of articles on technical support for many computer products. It's a convenient, one-stop way to answer many technical support questions. Software support dominates here, with coverage of products from Aldus, Borland, Claris, Lotus, Microsoft, Symantec, and WordPerfect, among others. But there's also support for printers and scanners from Epson, Hewlett-Packard, IBM, and other companies. Be sure to check the list of supported products *before* you begin your search. The articles, culled from the customer support files of each vendor, usually address a specific problem and detail its solution.

Surcharges: $15.00/hour ($0.25/minute), plus ZiffNet hourly connect-time rates

15. MAGAZINE DATABASE PLUS ▲▲ $$
GO MAGDB

Magazine Database Plus includes the full text of articles from many general-interest national magazines, written since 1986. Magazines covered include *Car and Driver, Cosmopolitan, The Nation, The New Republic,* and about 130 others. (For

a complete list, GO ZIFFHELP and download the file MDPPUB.TXT from library 11. It's a free forum, so you won't be charged for connect-time while you're there.) Magazine Database Plus is updated as often as weekly, but you won't find much in it that's less than a month or two old—so it's not suitable for finding up-to-the-minute information. The database is easy to use, however, and it's a good resource for tracking down a specific article, stories about a person or event, or book reviews.

Surcharges: $1.50 per article read or downloaded, plus ZiffNet hourly connect-time rates

ZiffNet/Mac

ZiffNet isn't just for PC users: It's got many offerings for Macintosh users under the ZiffNet/Mac heading. To get there, just type GO ZMAC.

Like ZiffNet, ZiffNet/Mac resides on the CompuServe computers, but access to it isn't included in the basic CompuServe fees. You need to sign up for ZiffNet to get access to ZiffNet/Mac. When you use the GO command while in ZiffNet or CompuServe, put the prefix ZMC: before any ZiffNet/Mac page to which you want to go. Once you're in ZiffNet/Mac, use the prefix ZNT: to get to a ZiffNet page, or CIS: to go to a CompuServe page. ZiffNet/Mac works just like CompuServe and ZiffNet: It has the same types of menus, the same forum structure, and the same text-based interface. In fact, many of the items found on ZiffNet/Mac are identical to items accessible through ZiffNet proper.

Following are highlights of ZiffNet/Mac. Most of these features—except the *MacUser* and *MacWEEK* Forums and *MacWEEK* News—are unique to ZiffNet/Mac and are only accessible through the ZMC: prefix.

▶ Download Software & Support Forum (GO ZMC:DOWNTECH): Stop in at this busy forum to ask the experts for technical advice on your Mac problems, or to download shareware, graphics, and fun files from the libraries.

▶ MacUser Services, including

 ▶ The MacUser *Forum (GO ZMC:MACUSER): Get in touch with MacUser's editors, chat with other Mac users about products, or download software—including Newton software—from the forum libraries.*

 ▶ Download MacUser *Utility (GO ZMC:POWERTOOLS): Download the latest MacUser utility, free of connect-time surcharges.*

 ▶ MacUser *Ultimate Buyers' Guide (GO ZMC:GUIDE): Search through the MacUser editors' recommendations for the best products in any category, or look up a product by name and read a capsule review of it.*

▶ MacUser/MacWEEK *Index (GO ZMC:INDEX): This index, free of connect-time surcharges, lets you search for any article or review from past issues of MacUser and*

MacWEEK. If you don't have the back issues on hand, use the article reference numbers to retrieve them from Computer Library (GO ZNT:COMPDB).

▶ *MacWEEK* Services, including

 ▶ *The* MacWEEK *Forum (GO ZMC:MACWEEK): See item 9, earlier in this chapter.*

 ▶ MacWEEK *News: Every Friday, the week's top stories from MacWEEK magazine are uploaded here. You can read or download these stories free of connect-time surcharges.*

 ▶ MacWEEK *News Beat (GO ZMC:MACBEAT): More news headlines from MacWEEK.*

▶ Multiple Forum File Finder (GO ZMC:FILEFINDER): Search through all of ZiffNet/Mac for files, by specifying keywords, file names, file types, and more.

▶ Tech Support Database (GO ZMC:TIPS): Use the menus to find tips, technical notes, and solutions to common problems for many Mac products.

▶ ZiffNet/Mac Map (GO ZMC:MAP): See an outline overview of the entire ZiffNet/Mac service.

CHAPTER 5

Prodigy

Prodigy enjoys a carefully guarded reputation as a "family" service. It is one of the largest information services in the U.S., though CompuServe is comparable in size. With over a million accounts and an average of 2.4 people using each account, there are more people connected to Prodigy than to any other commercial information service. It is also one of the best deals among on-line services, with low or no connect-time fees for most features.

The first thing that you'll notice about Prodigy is its unique look. It is colorful, graphical, and even animated—a far cry from the monotony of plain white text on a black backround! Prodigy uses a graphical interface designed to be flexible and fast without requiring high-resolution video or lots of computing power. As a result of the limitations imposed by this interface, Prodigy's display may seem unsophisticated to some people. On the other hand, Prodigy will run on just about any personal computer—all you need is the software, which is available in DOS, Windows, and Macintosh flavors. And, to be fair, it's often remarkable what visual effects can be achieved even within the limitations of the Prodigy display.

Note You can't connect to Prodigy using a general-purpose comm program.

Prodigy excels at providing information. Its news, business, and family offerings are its strongest areas, with a rich array of material available in each of those categories. Every screen on Prodigy is well designed and easy to use. Graphs and photos combine with text in a format that packs a lot of information into an accessible, readable format. Color-coded buttons, icons, and a variety of display styles make it easy to see at a glance where you are and where you're going. And many of Prodigy's resources are provided at no additional cost beyond the monthly fee; even the Plus features only cost you $3.60 an hour.

There are no exorbitantly priced databases on Prodigy. (See the "Fees" section.)

Although Prodigy is an outstanding information resource, it doesn't fare so well as a medium for communication and discussion. There are only about three dozen bulletin boards on Prodigy altogether (compared with the hundreds of discussion areas on CompuServe), but those boards carry a lot of message traffic. Furthermore, Prodigy's bulletin boards are awkward to use and aren't conducive to long messages or sustained debates; this reality tends to limit the discussions within them. Prodigy also lacks the real-time "chat" areas common to many other information services (although there are plans to add a chat feature by mid-1994), and there are no libraries where you can upload your own files for public perusal. For all these reasons, some people consider it less than ideal as an on-line hangout.

Prodigy's graphical interface

Prodigy's graphical interface is unlike that of any other information service. Color-coded buttons and a toolbar make navigation a simple matter.

Prodigy's e-mail is adequate, though it lacks some features present in other e-mail systems, such as message receipt acknowledgement. You can use the Prodigy Mail Manager program to read and compose messages off line, to send

messages to addresses on the Internet, to write messages up to 60,000 characters in length, and to send files. If you choose to read and compose your messages while on line (that is, without using Mail Manager), your maximum message length is 2,800 characters, and you can't send files or write to Internet addresses. These are frustrating limitations because it can be inconvenient to go off line just to deal with your e-mail.

Prodigy's e-mail is expensive: $0.25 per message if you write your messages on line; $.10 per message "block" (up to 6,000 characters per block) if you write your messages with the Mail Manager. For an additional fee, you can use Prodigy to have messages sent to a fax machine or printed on paper and mailed via the U.S. Postal Service.

If you're looking for shareware on Prodigy, ZiffNet is the place to go. ZiffNet for Prodigy offers computer industry news and technical advice, and boasts a sizeable collection of fine shareware programs. ZiffNet is the only place on Prodigy where you can download files (with the exception of some software "stores" in the main section of Prodigy). However, these stores don't have nearly as many files to choose from as ZiffNet.

There's no way for ZiffNet members to upload files they want to contribute, which sharply limits the range of choices you have when searching for files. You only have access to the uniformly high-quality programs ZiffNet picks for you. Lastly, you won't find electronic magazines, scanned photos, stories, macros, or archived discussion threads within ZiffNet for Prodigy's files. These resources are more typical of bulletin boards or more "open" commercial information services.

The advertisements that periodically appear at the bottom of the screen are a conspicuous feature of Prodigy. There's even "junk mail": advertisements that appear in your mailbox whether you want them or not. Much as newspapers and

television stations do, Prodigy sells space for advertisers to hawk their wares. These ads don't get in the way of what you're doing; you may not even notice them after a few hours on line. But they're ads, nevertheless, and some purists may object to that. On the other hand, you may like the idea of window shopping as you browse the news or the latest encyclopedia entry. If you're interested in an ad, just click on it to see more information. Often you can make a purchase or sign up for a service right then and there, if you're so inclined.

On-screen advertisements

Prodigy's graphical look has a distracting element: advertisements that flash across the bottom of almost every screen.

You can connect to Prodigy through a local phone number almost anywhere in the United States. You'll probably want to connect at 9600 baud if your modem supports it, since Prodigy's graphics are slow at 2400 baud. Fortunately, Prodigy doesn't charge extra for 9600 access, and it's available almost everywhere.

As of this writing, Prodigy had just completed a major "look and feel" reorganization, and more changes are planned for the near future. By the time you read this, there will be a program available for reading and responding to bulletin board messages off line, and other improvements

are in the works. Prodigy adds to or reorganizes elements on its pages and menus far more often than other commercial information services do, which can be disorienting at times. For the most part, however, it's easy to find your way around, and the interface is forgiving enough that you can't ever get really lost.

Subscribing to Prodigy

You must obtain the Prodigy software before you can connect to the service. You can buy the membership package (DOS, Windows, or Mac versions) in stores that sell computers or software. Or you can call Prodigy directly at (800) PRODIGY, or (800) 776-3449, to sign up and have the membership kit mailed to you; you'll be charged $4.95. The Prodigy Mail Manager software can be ordered or downloaded from Prodigy; it costs an additional $4.95. There are no additional sign-up fees other than the cost of the software.

When you sign up for Prodigy, you get a "family" account that allows as many as six separate users to sign on, each with his or her own member ID. You can give these subsidiary accounts to anyone, friends or family, at no additional cost. All bills go to the primary member, however.

Once you get the software, you're ready to connect. The software takes care of the communications settings, dialing the phone, and so forth, so you have little to worry about. With its easy-to-follow setup routine, you'll have no problems getting on line.

Prodigy is available from 7:00 a.m. to 4:00 a.m. eastern time, seven days a week.

Fees

Prodigy offers several pricing plans, which affect how much you pay for *Core* features and *Plus* features. Core features include all of Prodigy's basics: news, weather, sports, and entertainment offerings. Plus services are the "extras," including bulletin boards, some stock-market quote services, the Company News feature, and the EAASY SABRE airline reservations system.

The Value Plan costs $14.95 a month and gives you unlimited access to Core features, two free hours of access to Plus features, and an e-mail allotment of 30 messages per month. Additional access to Plus features is charged at $3.60/hour.

The Alternate Plan costs $7.95 a month and gives you two hours of access to either Core or Plus features. After your two hours are used up, you're charged for access to Core and Plus features at $3.60/hour. There's no free allotment of e-mail messages.

Prodigy also offers Alternate Plans that provide larger allotments of access to Core and Plus features. One of these plans, aimed at bulletin board users, offers a large quantity of connect time (necessary for bulletin boards) at a relatively low price. Here's a summary of Prodigy's pricing plans:

Prodigy Pricing Plans

Plan	Monthly Fee	Monthly Services	Hourly Cost (After Allotment)
Value Plan	$14.95	Unlimited Core access, 2 hours Plus access, 30 e-mail messages	$3.60
Alternate Plan	$7.95	2 hours Core or Plus access	$3.60
Alternate Plan 2	$19.95	8 hours Core or Plus access	$3.60
Bulletin Board Plan	$29.95	25 hours Core or Plus access	$3.60

In addition to the Core and Plus areas, some features of Prodigy have their own rates. You'll get plenty of warning before entering one of these areas, however—and the standard Prodigy rates don't apply in them. Prodigy's Custom Choices—for instance, ZiffNet for Prodigy and games such as Baseball Manager—are special features that require an additional sign-up and fee before you can access them.

Getting Around Prodigy

Navigating in Prodigy is simple. Most screens have one or more buttons that you can click to take you to other screens. If you're using the keyboard, press the arrow keys to select the button you want, and then press Enter to "push" the button.

Screens with many buttons are, in effect, graphical menus. We've arranged the Prodigy map to reflect the organization of these menus. The core of the menu structure are the *Highlights screens*. There is a main Highlights screen that you see when you first log on, as well as ten subject Highlights screens. Each Highlights screen has color-coded buttons along the right side: dark blue for News, bright red for Computers, and so forth. A small box at the lower-right tells you whether the feature you're currently using is Core, Plus, or if it is charged at a special rate, in which case the box shows four asterisks (****). Just click on this box to get more information about the fees you're incurring by using this feature.

The toolbar at the bottom of each screen gives you access to most of the commands you'll need to get around and do things in Prodigy. If a particular command isn't applicable to the current screen, it will be grayed out (dimmed) and clicking on it won't do anything. Each toolbar button also has a corresponding keyboard shortcut you can use instead of pushing the button on screen. The keyboard shortcuts listed here are those used in the Windows version of the Prodigy software.

Prodigy Toolbar Buttons

Button	Keyboard Shortcut	Command	What It Does
	N/A	New Mail	If you have new mail, takes you to the mail service
	F5	Highlights	Takes you to the main Highlights screen
◀	PgUp	Back	Returns you to the previous page in a series
▶	PgDn	Next	Takes you to the next page in a series
M	Ctrl-M, F9	Menu	Returns you to the previous menu; can usually be used to "back up" through your last few selections
J	Ctrl-J, F6	Jump To:	Takes you directly to the page you specify
P	F4	Path	Goes to the next feature on your PathList (list of favorite features)
A-Z	Ctrl-I, F7	Index	Displays a searchable index of all Prodigy jump-words
X	F8	X-Ref	Displays a list of cross-references (features related to the one you're in)

Button	Keyboard Shortcut	Command	What It Does
Z	Ctrl-Shift-Z	Zip	When an ad appears at the bottom of the screen, you press the Look button if you want to see more about the ad. Zip returns you to where you were before you pressed Look.
A	F2	Action	Takes an action; used when making an order or purchase
Pr	Ctrl-P	Print	Prints or copies the current page
T	Ctrl-T	Tools	Lets you customize the way you use Prodigy
E	Alt-F4	Exit	Displays the Exit window, where you can disconnect or allow another member to sign on

AUTOLOGON	Set up your software to log you on to Prodigy automatically, without prompting you for an account number or password
CHANGE PATH	Make or alter a list of your favorite features to be accessed with the Path command
CHANGE HIGHLIGHTS	Pick the Highlights screen you want to appear first when you log on
CHANGE COLORS	Pick the text colors you want to see; affects only the Mail service, bulletin boards, and the Encyclopedia
HELP HUB	Get help on using Prodigy
MEMBER ACCESS	Add or remove household member IDs; restrict access to parts of Prodigy
PASSWORD	Change your password
PERSONAL INFO	Change your personal information, billing address, and other billing information
PHONES	Look up local access numbers

You can jump directly to any feature on Prodigy if you know its *jump-word*. Just push the J button on the toolbar or type Ctrl-J, and enter the name of the service you want in the Jump window. You'll go directly to it. If you don't know the exact jump-word or you've mistyped it, don't worry— Prodigy will ask you to pick the service you want from a list of close matches.

Many member assistance services are available through their jump-words. Here are some of the most useful:

Member Assistance Jump-Words

Jump-Word	Result
ACCOUNT STATEMENTS	See information about your account bills

You should be aware that the on-line world is a very dynamic place. It's a good practice to check member services if you ever have any trouble accessing resources.

Prodigy Travel Guide

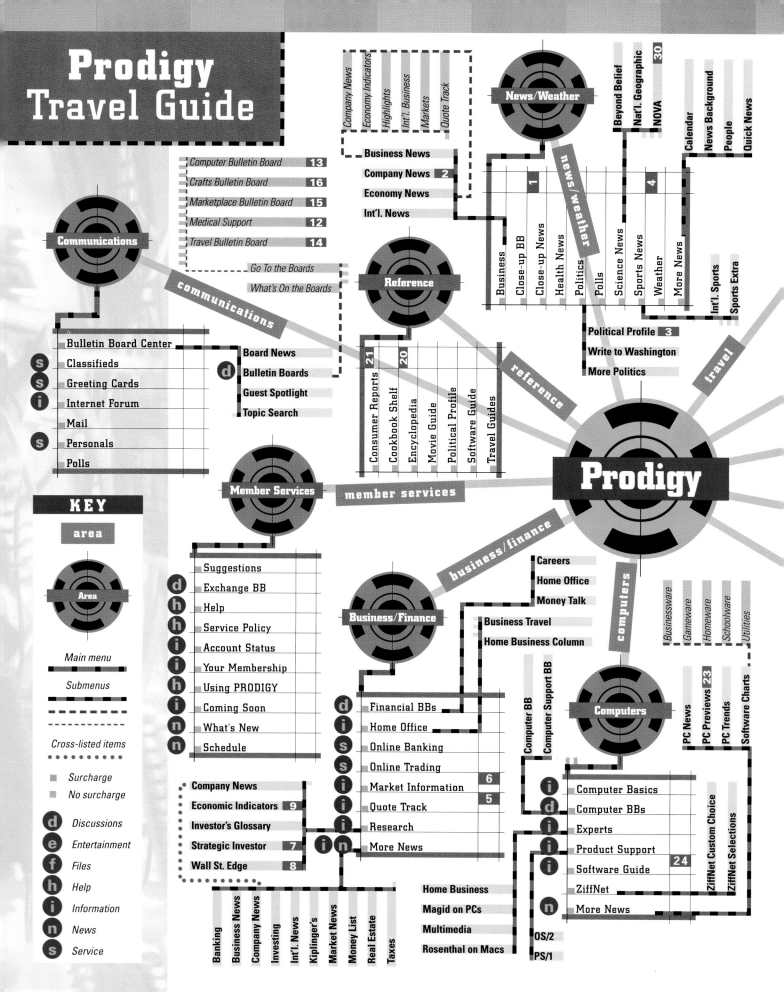

Communications

- Computer Bulletin Board — 13
- Crafts Bulletin Board — 16
- Marketplace Bulletin Board — 15
- Medical Support — 12
- Travel Bulletin Board — 14
- Go To the Boards
- What's On the Boards

- (s) Bulletin Board Center
- (s) Classifieds
- (s) Greeting Cards
- (i) Internet Forum
- Mail
- (s) Personals
- Polls

- Board News
- (d) Bulletin Boards
- Guest Spotlight
- Topic Search

News/Weather

- Company News
- Economy Indicators
- Highlights
- Int'l. Business
- Markets
- Quote Track

- Business News
- Company News — 2
- Economy News
- Int'l. News

- Business
- Close-up BB
- Close-up News
- Health News
- Politics
- Polls
- Science News
- Sports News
- Weather
- More News — 1 / 4

- Beyond Belief
- Nat'l. Geographic
- NOVA — 30
- Calendar
- News Background
- People
- Quick News

- Int'l. Sports
- Sports Extra

- Political Profile — 3
- Write to Washington
- More Politics

Reference

- Consumer Reports — 21
- Cookbook Shelf
- Encyclopedia
- Movie Guide
- Political Profile — 20
- Software Guide
- Travel Guides

Prodigy

Member Services

- (d) Suggestions
- (h) Exchange BB
- (h) Help
- (i) Service Policy
- (i) Account Status
- (h) Your Membership
- (i) Using PRODIGY
- (n) Coming Soon
- (n) What's New
- Schedule

Business/Finance

- Careers
- Home Office
- Money Talk
- Business Travel
- Home Business Column

- Company News
- Economic Indicators — 9
- Investor's Glossary
- Strategic Investor — 7
- Wall St. Edge — 8

- (d) Financial BBs
- (i) Home Office
- (s) Online Banking
- (s) Online Trading
- (i) Market Information — 6
- (i) Quote Track — 5
- (i) Research
- (n) More News

- Banking
- Business News
- Company News
- Investing
- Int'l. News
- Kiplinger's
- Market News
- Money List
- Real Estate
- Taxes

- Home Business
- Magid on PCs
- Multimedia
- Rosenthal on Macs
- OS/2
- PS/1

Computers

- Businessware
- Gameware
- Homeware
- Schoolware
- Utilities

- Computer BB
- Computer Support BB
- PC News
- PC Previews — 23
- PC Trends
- Software Charts

- (i) Computer Basics
- (d) Computer BBs
- (i) Experts
- (i) Product Support
- (i) Software Guide — 24
- ZiffNet
- (n) More News

- ZiffNet Custom Choice
- ZiffNet Selections

KEY

- area
- Area

- Main menu
- Submenus
- Cross-listed items

- ■ Surcharge
- No surcharge

- (d) Discussions
- (e) Entertainment
- (f) Files
- (h) Help
- (i) Information
- (n) News
- (s) Service

Labels on connecting lines: communications, news/weather, reference, travel, member services, business/finance, computers

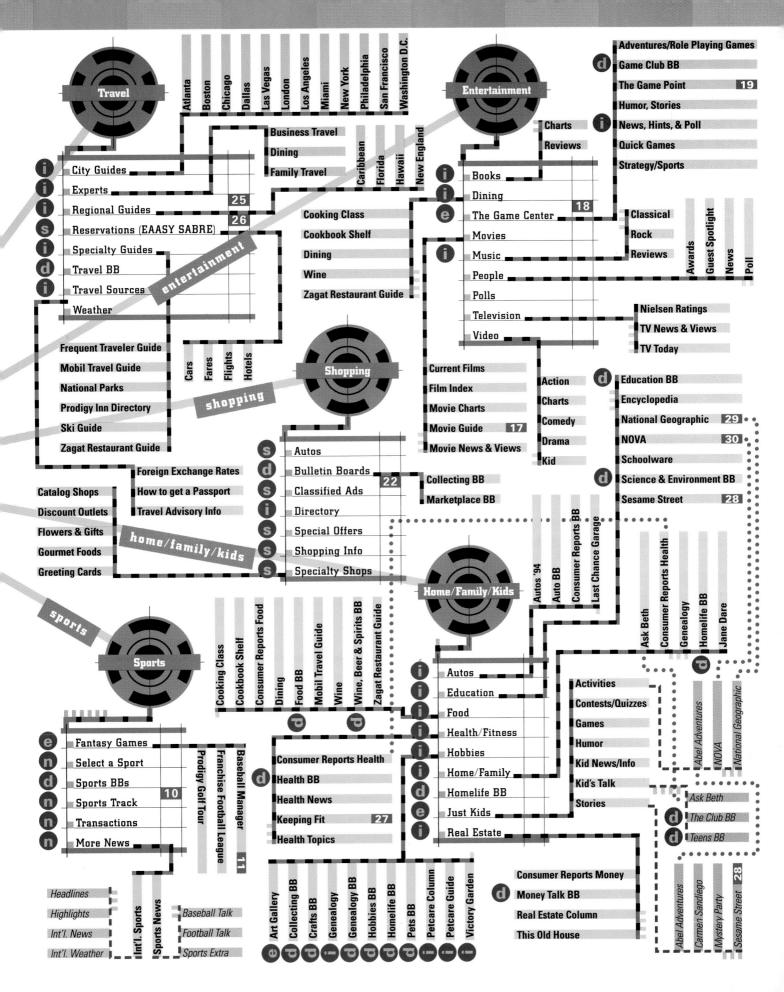

INSIDE PRODIGY

Prodigy is one of the most colorful and exciting on-line services. But the resources it offers aren't just for show; there's a lot of valuable information here. If you're looking for news, financial information, educational resources, or background on current events, Prodigy is the place to look. And, of course, it's a good place to go shopping, too!

The following pages describe and evaluate the best and most popular of Prodigy's many resources. Each description is preceded by a number that you can use to find that resource on the map. Or, when you see a number on the map, you can look for that number among the resource descriptions. This listing not only gives you a sense of what's inside Prodigy, but it will also help you quickly find the best resources as they appear on the map.

For an estimation of the quality and usefulness of each resource described, look for the following symbols:

▲▲▲▲▲   Outstanding—don't miss it!
▲▲▲▲   Excellent—worth going out of your way to see it.
▲▲▲   Very good—worth a look.
▲   Above average—stop by if it's on your way.
▼   Disappointing—don't bother.

You'll also find an indication of the cost of each described resource. The exact amount of surcharges, if any, are specified at the end of each description, and the dollar icons give you a general idea of how its price compares to other features inside Prodigy.

$$$ Steep—hang on to your wallet!
$$ Moderate—not a bargain, but reasonable
$ Cheap—a good value, easy on your pocketbook.
✦   Free—no surcharges or connect time charges!

If you need direct access, you'll find the jump-word for each resource in the listing. Finally, each resource is classified by type. The types for Prodigy are News, Files, Information, Help, Discussion, Entertainment, and Service and are represented by the same symbols that appear on the map.

News/Weather *Prodigy's News/Weather menu gives you access to all kinds of news: general-interest, business, sports, and more. New stories from Reuters and other newswires are added throughout the day. Often, you can follow developments in the news almost as they happen. The cross-reference feature is especially useful for getting related and background information on news stories.*

1. CLOSE-UP NEWS   ▲ $
Jump: CLOSE-UP

The Close-Up News screen gives you access to detailed news articles on topics of current news interest. Each article has a Topics button that you click to get a dialog box showing places on Prodigy where you can get related information. Depending on the topic, that may be a bulletin board, more news stories, a poll, or encyclopedia articles. Unfortunately, there's usually not more than one or two options per topic—you're not going to

become an expert through this feature, but you'll learn more than you would just scanning the headlines. Every day, a new topic is added to the Close-Up board, and five are visible at any time. You can also go to the Close-Up Bulletin Board from this menu.

Surcharges: None for Value Plan members; $3.60/hour on other plans, after monthly connect-time allotment

2. COMPANY NEWS   ▲▲ $$
Jump: COMPANY NEWS

Search the newswires for stories relating to any company; you can specify the company name or ticker symbol, or an industry or news category you're interested in. Prodigy returns all the stories relating to that topic, which you can read one at a time; or click on the Headlines button to see a list of selected stories' headlines. The stories are culled from the Dow Jones News Retrieval Service and are updated continuously during every business day. This is a fast, easy way to zero in on current news that's relevant to you—but the stories only go back about a week, so it's not a source of historical information.

Surcharges: $3.60/hour, after monthly connect-time allotment

3. POLITICAL PROFILE   ▲▲▲▲ $
Jump: POLITICAL PROFILE

Want to find out what your elected representatives are up to? What they did before they got elected, and who contributed money to their campaigns? Check out Political Profile, where you can look up detailed information about any member of the U.S. Senate or House of Representatives. The amount of information you can find here is truly impressive, and it's very well organized. Political Profile is easy to use: You just specify the state, congressional district, or zip code; or search through the profiles by name, party, or using other categories. Each profile includes a detailed biography, the committees on which the congressperson sits, how they voted on key issues, previous election results, and campaign financial information. This last item includes an exhaustive breakdown of PAC (Political Action Committee) contributions by category, with comparisons to average PAC contributions throughout Congress. A state or congressional district profile is also available for each Senator or Representative. Truly an excellent resource.

Surcharges: None for Value Plan members; $3.60/hour on other plans, after monthly connect-time allotment

4. WEATHER   ▲▲ $
Jump: WEATHER

Prodigy's weather forecasts and maps are convenient and easy to understand. If you want to know whether to expect sun or snow, Prodigy's weather services will do the trick, and you can also find some additional information on high- and low-pressure zones and jet streams. From the Weather menu, you can select a map (Jump: WEATHER MAP) that shows weather all across the

48 contiguous United States. From the main map, you can zoom in on regional maps comprising a few states. Want to read the forecast for your area? Choose US City Weather from the main Weather menu, pick a city, and see its forecast. You can also jump directly to your city's forecast; for example, Jump: NEW YORK WEATHER or Jump: W NEW YORK will take you directly to the weather forecasts for the Big Apple.

Surcharges: None for Value Plan members; $3.60/hour on other plans, after monthly connect-time allotment

---

Business/Finance *Prodigy's business services are aimed at the private investor, rather than the professional broker or financial professional. You'll find lots of information here, much of it presented in striking, easy-to-read graphs and tables.*

5. QUOTE TRACK ▲▲▲ $
Jump: QUOTE TRACK

Quote Track is a clever securities-tracking system that lets you follow your entire portfolio at a glance. Rather than looking up one quote at a time, you enter your current holdings (security, quantity, and purchase price), and Quote Track provides you with continuous information about how your portfolio is performing. The table it constructs shows each security's current market price (there's a 15-minute delay built-in during market hours), the current market value of your holdings, and the amount your investment has gained or lost. Further details are available for each security, including related company news. Jump directly to Strategic Investor for more information, or to the PC Financial Network if you can't wait to take action and want to buy or sell on line. You can also download your current track information. Prodigy will save the information you specify for two separate tracks containing up to 24 securities each; if you want to create additional tracks, you can save them on your local computer.

Surcharges: During market hours (weekdays 9:40 a.m. to 4:20 p.m. eastern time): $3.60/hour for all members, after monthly connect-time allotment. After market hours: no surcharges for Value Plan members; $3.60/hour on other plans, after monthly connect-time allotment.

6. MARKET INFORMATION ▲▲ $
Jump: MARKETS

Here's Prodigy's central source for market information of all kinds—presented quickly, graphically, and intuitively. The opening screen has four graphs showing the performance of key indexes. Buttons on the right take you directly to more information on the latest market news, U.S. and world stock markets, gold prices, the U.S. dollar's performance, and the state of the market when it last closed. All of the data is presented in graphs and readable tables, with green text for gainers and red text for losers. Quote Check feature (Jump: QUOTE CHECK) lets you look up the current value of any stock, money market fund, or other security. You won't find a great depth of historical or detailed information here, but for the essential features of the market, as well as the current status of any security, Prodigy's basic market information is a good value.

Surcharges: None for Value Plan members; $3.60/hour on other plans, after monthly connect-time allotment

7. STRATEGIC INVESTOR ▲▲▲ $$$
Jump: STRATEGIC

If you want more market news and information than is provided by Prodigy's standard fare, Strategic Investor may be just the ticket. You get access to market news, columns, and charts from *Investor's Business Daily.* The Stock Analyst feature provides detailed information about any stock's continuing performance, dividends, and financial strength, as well as figures from the company's balance sheet. Its data is updated once a week. You can use Stock Analyst to search for stocks that meet criteria you specify. The Stock Hunter feature lets you apply more sophisticated searching options to the Stock Analyst database, so you can locate prospective investments even more accurately. The Mutual Fund Analyst offers detailed data on any fund. Throughout Strategic Investor, glossary definitions of terms used are always available. The only shortcoming to this wealth of information is the lack of graphs, but if you really want graphs you can download the data in spreadsheet format and do it yourself.

Surcharges: Custom Choice, $14.95 per month

8. WALL ST. EDGE ▲▲ $$$
Jump: WALL ST EDGE

Wall St. Edge is a digest of columns, newsletter articles, and analysts' predictions about various markets. It is published the evening before each business day, so you can read up on what the experts think is going to happen in the markets tomorrow. Get the scoop on what stocks are hot, what companies are planning expansions or layoffs—even what major brokerage firms are *about* to recommend, before they actually do so. Wall St. Edge emphasizes "street talk" and recommendations based on expert opinions; it doesn't provide lots of data or quotes. It's a good complement to the raw data available elsewhere on Prodigy.

Surcharges: Custom Choice, $19.95 for a month-long subscription, or $1.95 for a single issue

9. ECONOMIC INDICATORS ▲▲ $
Jump: ECONOMIC INDICATORS

Check out the economy's current health, based on ten key economic indicators: unemployment, consumer inflation, consumer confidence, retail sales, housing starts, home sales, factory orders, the purchasing index, the government's Index of Leading Indicators, and the trade deficit. Each indicator is introduced by a graph showing changes over the past year. The graph is accompanied by an article explaining the most recent data; this story usually includes several tables of figures. Prodigy's Economic Indicators service is updated monthly, or whenever the latest statistics are released. One shortcoming: There's no glossary of definitions, which means this feature is more useful to experienced economy-watchers than to amateurs or students.

Surcharges: None for Value Plan members; $3.60/hour on other plans, after monthly connect-time allotment

Sports
Prodigy has a special section devoted to sports news, scores, and games. Sports fans, Prodigy loves ya!

10. SPORTS TRACK ▲ $
Jump: SPORTS TRACK

Sports Track collects your favorite teams' scores and schedules in one place. You specify the teams you want to follow, and whether you want scores, schedules, or both. Sports Track saves your personal profile, and automatically collects the latest scores and informs you of upcoming games for the teams you've requested. Each item on the scoreboard has a button that provides more information: a story about the game or a list of all the coming events. Sports fans will probably wish for statistics along with their news, but Sports Track doesn't offer that. Also, you are limited to a maximum of ten items in your personal profile.

Surcharges: None for Value Plan members; $3.60/hour on other plans, after monthly connect-time allotment

11. BASEBALL MANAGER ▲▲ $$$
Jump: BBM

If you've always wanted to manage a major-league baseball team, you're in luck: Baseball Manager, a high-tech rotisserie league, makes it possible. Bid against other Baseball Manager players to get major-league players on your "team," make crucial management decisions the day before each game, and then see who won the game. Winners are determined by the actual statistics of your team's players, and by the decisions you made the night before. This game has it all—there's even a "managers only" bulletin board, the Diamond Club, where you can meet the other people playing Baseball Manager. Baseball Manager's one-time sign-up fee is steep, but you get to play for the duration of the actual baseball season. Because you can only sign up for Baseball Manager between July 14 and July 31, we didn't get to experience the thrill ourselves—but we know many baseball fans who are devoted players.

Surcharges: Classic version, $69.95 per season; Lightning (a faster-playing version), $49.95 per season. The Diamond Club bulletin board has an additional surcharge of $6.00/hour; the first two hours are free.

Communications
Prodigy's Communications center includes its e-mail service and bulletin boards. Go to the Bulletin Board Center (Jump: BB CENTER) to see what's on the boards. You can look through the boards by name, or view a list of all the topics on all bulletin boards—then jump directly to the board that has the topic you're interested in. The bulletin boards are among Prodigy's most popular features, though they can be difficult to use and it's easy to run up large connect-time charges. When we visited the boards, many people there were still disgruntled about price hikes a few months before, which had apparently led many users to stop using bulletin boards altogether. Nevertheless, the boards seemed pretty active!

12. MEDICAL SUPPORT BULLETIN BOARD ▲▲▲ $$
Jump: MEDICAL SUPPORT

This bulletin board houses discussion and support relating to medical conditions. Topics include AIDS, alcohol abuse, cancer, infertility, and smoking, among others. The board is well moderated, so it functions well as a forum for people who genuinely want to share their thoughts, feelings, and questions. And the people who use the board are sincere about communicating with and providing support for one another. Access to this bulletin board is restricted—you must agree to certain ground rules before you can get in—and fees are charged at a different rate than most bulletin boards.

For discussions about fitness, nutrition, alternative medicine, and other health topics, see the Health & Fitness Bulletin Board (Jump: HEALTH & FITNESS).

Surcharges: $2.40 per hour; the first 5 hours are free

13. COMPUTER BULLETIN BOARD ▲▲ $$
Jump: COMPUTER BB

Here you can get technical information, advice on computing problems, or just discuss computer technology. A wealth of topics cover every major area of the personal computing industry, and lots of people take part in discussions on subjects ranging from modems and monitors to the best deals among on-line services. Although computer product vendors don't generally participate here, there's a good chance that if you have a technical question, somebody on this board will be able to answer it. The message volume is much higher than on the Computer Support Bulletin Board (Jump: COMPUTER SUPPORT BB), and the participants seem much more eager to talk, help out, or debate a point.

Surcharges: $3.60/hour, after monthly connect-time allotment

14. TRAVEL BULLETIN BOARD ▲▲ $$
Jump: TRAVEL BB

Do you know the best hotel in Hong Kong? What is there to do in Buffalo, after you've seen the Falls? How do you find the best package tour deals? For answers to these and other questions, stop by the Travel Bulletin Board. Most of the people who spend time here are seasoned veterans of tours all over the U.S. and the rest of the world, and you can tap into their experience for travel tips before you set out on your own journeys. Or, if you just want to talk about other states and countries you've seen or want to visit, that's OK too—you'll find plenty of people willing to chat.

Surcharges: $3.60/hour, after monthly connect-time allotment

15. MARKETPLACE BULLETIN BOARD ▲ $$
Jump: MARKETPLACE

Although it's a bulletin board, the Marketplace supplies more than a discussion. More often, it's a place where you can find buyers, sellers, or traders—just by posting a message. There are topics for cars, books, computer equipment, video tapes, and more. You'll find a lot of messages here, offering things for sale and looking for things to buy. Stop in before you go to the

Classifieds (item 25 on the map)—you might save yourself the cost of an ad! On the other hand, since most replies are by private e-mail, it's hard to know if the Marketplace is actually an *effective* place to sell your old jalopy, but hey, it's worth a try.

Surcharges: $3.60/hour, after monthly connect-time allotment

16. CRAFTS BULLETIN BOARD   ▲▲▲ $$
Jump: CRAFTS BB

This is a lively forum where artisans of all types talk about their crafts, share patterns, discuss techniques, or just visit. There are many topics here, but Quilting is by far the most active, with Crochet, Knitting, and Sewing coming in close behind. If this board is any indication, the village quilting bees of yesteryear have become today's on-line communities of quilters. They share ideas, use the U.S. Postal Service to swap fabrics and patterns, and chat over an electronic "back fence."

Surcharges: $3.60/hour, after monthly connect-time allotment

Entertainment *The Entertainment menu includes resources for people interested in film, music, videos, and TV; it also covers Prodigy's games. If you're worried about connect-time charges, be careful how much time you spend here having fun!*

17. MOVIE GUIDE   ▲▲▲▲ $
Jump: MOVIE GUIDE

Magill's Survey of Cinema provides the information behind this marvelous database of over 3,000 reviews and more than 11,000 movie synopses. It's a convenient way to look up almost any movie's director, cast, year made, and plot summary. And for the movies that have full reviews, the Movie Guide is a formidable educational resource. The reviews are well written and substantial and provide just the right mix of critical distance and fond appreciation. The detailed reports also list the movie's cast, awards won, and production credits; there are also citations to newspaper or magazine reviews of the film. It's a simple matter to zero in on the movies you want by specifying a title or by searching the database for a specific genre, star, director, or year. In short, the Movie Guide is an excellent companion for moviegoers and video-renters alike.

Surcharges: None for Value Plan members; $3.60/hour on other plans, after monthly connect-time allotment

18. THE GAME CENTER   ▲▲ $
Jump: GAME CENTER

The Game Center gives you access to dozens of interactive games and diversions, most of which are Core features, and some of which cost extra. Most of these games are pretty entertaining, and some are exceptional. But be careful if your pricing plan includes hourly fees for Core features: It's easy to while away the hours here, accumulating lots of connect-time charges.

The Game Center is divided into four categories, which you select by pushing the appropriate button.

▶ Under Adventure and Role Playing Games, you'll find a wonderful version of Where in the World Is Carmen Sandiego? (Jump: CARMEN), an entertaining educational game in which you use your knowledge of geography to track down a criminal.

▶ The Strategy and Sports section includes Prodigy's sports simulations (Baseball Manager, Fantasy Football, and Golf Tour—all Custom Choices), as well as CEO, a fantasy game in which you play the head of a major corporation. There's also a chess center (Jump: CHESS) where you can see move-by-move coverage of major international matches, look up historic games, and learn more about chess. You can't *play* chess here, however—for that you'll have to sign up for the Game Point (item 19 on the map).

▶ Prodigy's Quick Games section includes a trivia game, word-guessing games, a Mastermind-like game called Thinker, and Police Artist, in which you're shown a face and then you try to reconstruct it by putting together various noses, eyes, and mouths.

▶ Finally, the Humor, Stories, and Other Amusements button takes you to Prodigy's jokes library, several interactive stories, and a special kids' menu.

When you're done playing games here, stop in at the Games Bulletin Board (Jump: GAMES BB) and talk with other Prodigy game-players. This board has topics for discussing Star Trek, science fiction, fantasy role-playing games, modem-to-modem games, card games, chess, and flight simulators.

Surcharges: None for Value Plan members; $3.60/hour on other plans, after monthly connect-time allotment. Some games have additional fees.

19. THE GAME POINT   ▲▲ $$
Jump: GAME POINT

Prodigy members can access The ImagiNation Network (formerly TSN) through the Game Point on Prodigy. The ImagiNation Network is Sierra On-Line's "virtual amusement park," an information service devoted to games alone. The Game Point is a subset of the ImagiNation Network accessible to Prodigy subscribers. It's got several "lands," including SierraLand, where you can play arcade-style games; MedievaLand, which houses a fantasy role-playing game; and the Clubhouse, where you can play chess, checkers, and a variety of other board games with folks across the country. You need special software to access the Game Point, because you're actually leaving Prodigy to connect to The ImagiNation Network. If you play on-line games a lot, you may want to sign up for the ImagiNation Network directly, since you'll get lower hourly rates than when accessing it through Prodigy.

Surcharges: Rates are based on how much you use the Game Point in a month. Evenings and weekends, you pay $4.80/hr for up to 3 hours, $4.20/hour for 3 to 6 hours of access, or $3.60/hour for more than 6 hours in a month. Daytime fees are an additional $3/hour.

Reference *Prodigy does not boast large or sophisticated research databases, but focuses instead on a few solid features aimed at the general user. The Encyclopedia and Consumer Reports are the high points of the Reference section, and they are substantial sources of general and consumer information.*

20. ACADEMIC AMERICAN ENCYCLOPEDIA   ▲▲ $
Jump: ENCYCLOPEDIA

Grolier's provides the text for this large encyclopedia, which contains over ten million words in 33,000 articles. It's updated frequently, making it a good resource for background information on issues of current interest. (Jump: BACKGROUND to see a Prodigy service that provides background information from the Encyclopedia on three news topics each week.) Most articles are short "capsule" articles, but there are many longer, in-depth articles as well. Although the Encyclopedia has no true hypertext features, cross-referenced words are capitalized in the text, and you can jump to another article quickly by clicking the Cross-References button and typing in an article name. Surprisingly, the encyclopedia doesn't feature graphics of any kind. Nonetheless, it is a good source of information, and it's a real bargain at Core rates.

Surcharges: None for Value Plan members; $3.60/hour on other plans, after monthly connect-time allotment

21. CONSUMER REPORTS   ▲▲▲ $
Jump: CONSUMER REPORTS

Every month, when the latest issue of *Consumer Reports* hits the newsstands, the articles from that issue also appear on Prodigy. You can read the current issue's articles as well as those from the past six months, or go to the Consumer Reports Library for reviews from as far back as 1988 in any of a dozen major product categories. In some ways it's even better than reading the magazine, because articles are organized by menus that let you focus on just what you want, whether it's the ratings tables, recommendations, background information, or guides to shopping for a particular product. Of course, *Consumer Reports* excels in providing automobile and appliance data, but there's a lot more here, too. It's truly a gold mine of valuable consumer information.

Surcharges: None for Value Plan members; $3.60/hour on other plans, after monthly connect-time allotment

Shopping   *Prodigy's advertisements are the most conspicuous commercial feature on the service. In the Shopping section all the vendors are gathered in one place, where you can go shopping on line just as you do in a mall. The Shopping center also includes classified and personal ads.*

22. CLASSIFIED ADS   ▲   ✚
Jump: CLASSIFIEDS

Prodigy's classified ads are, like classified ads anywhere, a mixed bag. The majority are in the Business Opportunities category, with "make big money at home" opportunities making up the bulk of these. The other categories just don't have many ads at any given time, though you may still be able to find a good deal among them. Personal ads (Jump: PERSONAL ADS) are another matter: There are literally hundreds to choose from. But will you find what you're looking for? That's a question we cannot answer for you.

Surcharges: Free to browse. Placing an ad costs between $45.00 and $75.00 for a short classified ad with a 2-week run. Personals cost about $35.00 for two weeks.

Computers   *Prodigy's Computers section offers a variety of resources for new and sophisticated computer users. There are features to help you learn how to use your computer, as well as product reviews and the Computer Bulletin Board (Jump: COMPUTER BB).*

23. PC PREVIEWS   ▲ $
Jump: PC PREVIEW

Computer journalist John Edwards writes this weekly review of computer products. Each week, Edwards describes a new software package, peripheral, game, or multimedia product. His reviews are clear and fair, but not especially technical. You can look up past reviews by category. Since it's just a weekly column, PC Previews is hardly a comprehensive database of computer product information. Still, the reviews are a useful resource and will help you make informed decisions when you're shopping the computer stores or mail-order ads.

Surcharges: None for Value Plan members; $3.60/hour on other plans, after monthly connect-time allotment

24. SOFTWARE GUIDE   ▲ $
Jump: SOFTWARE GUIDE

This resource is a database of software reviews from *Home-Office Computing Magazine*. It's easy enough to find the review you want: You can specify a product by title, or search for one according to the platform it runs on, its category, or rating. The reviews help you find out the minimum system requirements for a program, what it costs, and how to contact the manufacturer; you can also use the category search to scan the market for the best available program in a specific class. Unfortunately, the reviews here are short and somewhat superficial, and you'll probably find yourself wanting more information. Also, some of the reviews are several years old, making them nearly useless.

Surcharges: None for Value Plan members; $3.60/hour on other plans, after monthly connect-time allotment

Travel   *Prodigy has several services for the traveler, most aimed at vacation travel and leisure activities. EAASY SABRE is also useful for business travel.*

25. REGIONAL AND CITY GUIDES   ▲▲ $
Jump: TRAVEL GUIDES

The Prodigy regional and city guides are fine introductions to regions such as Florida, Hawaii, New England, and the Caribbean, as well as major U.S. cities. Each guide has an interactive map; you click on the areas about which you want more information. The travel guides all include plenty of advice on getting around, what to see, what to do, and more. They're compiled and written largely by professional travel writers, but are heavily salted with comments and opinions from actual Prodigy members, so they are unique. Prodigy's travel guides aren't substitutes for actual maps and guides (the interactive maps aren't detailed enough to provide more than a general overview), but they're a great way to find out about a city or region you're thinking of visiting.

Surcharges: None for Value Plan members; $3.60/hour on other plans, after monthly connect-time allotment

26. EAASY SABRE   ▲▲▲ $$
Jump: EAASY SABRE

S EAASY SABRE is the American Airlines electronic reservation system, and on Prodigy it's got a friendly, usable interface. You just specify your point of origin, your destination, and when you want to fly, and EAASY SABRE gives you a list of flights that match those criteria on all airlines. Detailed fare information is available for each flight, and it's a simple matter to check out several different itineraries to see how and where you can find the lowest fares. Once you've found the flight you want, you can purchase tickets on line. EAASY SABRE also lets you make rental car and hotel reservations at your destination, if you like.

Surcharges: $3.60/hour, after monthly connect-time allotment

Home/Family/Kids
The Home/Family/Kids section of Prodigy is where you'll find Prodigy's best and most comprehensive features. It's got subsections on Health, Hobbies, Education, Autos, and more. This section is perhaps the best argument for joining Prodigy: Your whole family probably will find something of interest here.

27. KEEPING FIT   ▲▲ $
Jump: KEEPING FIT

i This menu brings together many articles of current interest in the fields of health, nutrition, and fitness. It's a good way to educate yourself about how to stay healthy, and stay on top of the fast-changing and complicated world of personal health care. Get answers to questions such as "How can I reduce stress?" and "How much sleep is enough?", as well as more general advice on exercise, diet, and the like. There's even a section called "Your Body: An Owner's Manual," which contains invaluable information on a variety of topics—weight, exercise, skin care, medical checkups, and more. The Health Bulletin Board (Jump: HEALTH BB) covers related topics.

Surcharges: None for Value Plan members; $3.60/hour on other plans, after monthly connect-time allotment

28. SESAME STREET   ▲▲▲▲ $
Jump: SESAME

e Sesame Street is an example of just how cool an interactive, on-line, educational resource can be. It is a fun way to introduce small children to computers. They'll see their friends from the *Sesame Street* program appearing in short, interactive stories and games featuring the numbers and letters for the day. There are mazes, "one-of-these-things-is-not-like-the-other" puzzles, and games in which you get to count along with the Count. The animated storybooks that let you choose what happens are a real treat. Sesame Street even has a "mail" service: Twice a week you receive mail—with your name on it—from Muppet characters in many different places. Sesame Street is fun, and uses simplified controls so that small children can get used to making things happen with the mouse or arrow keys. Children who don't read yet may be frustrated by parts of this service, so parental participation is encouraged. Another bonus: Sesame Street is commercial-free, just like the real thing.

Surcharges: None for Value Plan members; $3.60/hour on other plans, after monthly connect-time allotment

29. NATIONAL GEOGRAPHIC   ▲ $
Jump: NATIONAL GEO

i An educational resource aimed at older children, National Geographic features a new topic every few months, covering a current event, exploration, or adventure in great detail. When we were on line, Antarctic explorer Norman Vaughan was climbing a mountain near the South Pole, and there were almost daily updates from Norman himself about the status of his expedition. Nifty! There's also a library of past National Geographic features: From a world map you select the continent you're interested in, and then pick from a list of the features in that part of the world. Each feature is a basic introduction to its topic, including opportunities to learn more or read related topics as you go along. You won't find in-depth information here, but it might encourage you or your kids to learn more.

Surcharges: None for Value Plan members; $3.60/hour on other plans, after monthly connect-time allotment

30. NOVA   ▲▲▲▲ $
Jump: NOVA

i Highly recommended! Another interactive educational feature, Nova teaches science to grade-school and older children. It makes great use of Prodigy's graphics to illustrate scientific principles, show how to perform experiments, and encourage students to figure things out for themselves. Each week there's a new installment, which gives you enough time between lessons to do the experiments and think about the related science. It's a Mr. Wizard for the on-line computer age! You can look up past features in the library, too—some of which are real gems. For example, check out "Cosmic Cruise" to visit some exotic deep-space attractions, or choose "A Good Night's Rest" for a fine introduction to theories about dreaming. Each Nova feature also includes a list of books for further reading, which means it's ideal as a classroom activity. A related feature, Beyond Belief (Jump: BEYOND), is a weekly column by science writer Ethan Herberman, which focuses on unusual, interesting, or simply strange phenomena and scientific trends. Herberman is an engaging and entertaining writer, and an excellent complement to Nova's more interactive features.

Surcharges: None for Value Plan members; $3.60/hour on other plans, after monthly connect-time allotment

---

ZiffNet for Prodigy
ZiffNet for Prodigy (Jump: ZIFFNET) is the only place on Prodigy where you can download shareware programs, and it's also got the best computer news and reviews available through Prodigy.

ZiffNet is a Custom Choice, costing $7.50 a month for one hour of use (plus $7.80/hour beyond the first hour), or $14.95 a month for up to three hours of use (plus $6.00/hour for additional time). If you want to stay up-to-date on current trends and technologies, if you want to stuff your hard disk with top-quality shareware, or if you're looking for useful software tips and tricks, ZiffNet is well worth the membership fee. For only

occasional use, however, it may be overpriced. If all you want is to download software, check out ZiffNet Selections in Prodigy's Computers area (Jump: ZIFFNET SELECTIONS). There you'll find a library of selected shareware programs—and you don't have to join ZiffNet for Prodigy or pay a monthly fee (although you do pay a few dollars for each program you download from ZiffNet Selections).

ZiffNet's features don't have jump-words; instead, you get to them from ZiffNet's main menu, which is a special dialog box with buttons for each feature. Most ZiffNet screens have a ZIFFNET button that calls up this menu, from which you can get to anywhere else in the service.

ZiffNet for Prodigy has a strong bias toward IBM-compatibles. You'll find very little news about the Mac world, and there are no Mac programs or technical tips at all. If you don't have an IBM-compatible PC, ZiffNet for Prodigy is not for you.

The next page shows a special detail map of ZiffNet for Prodigy. The following resource descriptions are keyed to that map.

31. SOFTWARE LIBRARY   ▲▲▲ $$

The Software Library is an impressive collection of all kinds of programs—mostly shareware, but some freeware and public-domain programs, too. You can be fairly confident of the quality of these programs; the ZiffNet editors generally post only high-quality programs, whether they're slick games or indispensable utilities. Each program is accompanied by a fairly detailed description, including system requirements, file size, and estimated download time, so you have plenty of help deciding whether to download the program. To find something specific, you can browse any of the library's sections, including Newest Titles, Top 10's, and Special Collections. If you like, you can also search the library for a specific title or for all the titles in any given category. One nice feature for beginners is the ZiffNet Download Manager, a program that simplifies the process of downloading and decompressing the compressed program files in the library.

Surcharges: ZiffNet hourly rates

32. NEWSBYTES   ▲▲ $$

Select Today's News from the ZiffNet menu to get to Newsbytes, a reliable source of computer industry news and information. Today's headlines appear first, and you can click on the More News button to look up Newsbytes stories from the past week. Newsbytes is an independent news service covering many aspects of the computer and telecommunications world. You'll find timely, accurate stories about companies, trends, and technologies. There are only about seven stories per day, however, which means that even though the major stories are covered, there's a lot left out. Also, only a week's worth of stories are on file—if more were stored and available, Newsbytes would be a useful research tool.

Surcharges: ZiffNet hourly rates

33. PC WEEK AND MACWEEK NEWS   ▲ $$

When you want more in-depth news from the two leading weekly computer industry newspapers, check out *PC Week* and *MacWEEK* News for the week's top stories. Both of these publications emphasize company news, announcements, and new technologies, so perusing this compilation is a good way to stay on top of the PC-compatible and Mac worlds, respectively. Between this topic and Newsbytes, you will be well informed about the happenings in the computer industry.

Surcharges: ZiffNet hourly rates

34. BUYING ADVICE   ▲▲▲ $$

The Buying Advice section of ZiffNet offers three choices: First Looks, Hardware Reviews, and Software Reviews. Each contains a variety of excellent product reviews drawn from the pages of Ziff Communications publications, such as *PC Magazine*, *PC/Computing*, and *PC Week* (Macintosh product reviews are conspicuously absent). First Looks is updated each week with reviews of five new products, so look here first if you're interested in a new software package or piece of hardware. Software Reviews and Hardware Reviews are both libraries of past reviews and are great resources for making buying decisions. The reviews in the Buying Advice section are often lengthy, characterized by detailed product descriptions and in-depth evaluations of performance and usability. One minor quibble: The reviews don't always include information about how to contact the manufacturer of a product.

Surcharges: ZiffNet hourly rates

35. COMPUTING TIPS   ▲▲ $$

Check out these timesaving and problem-solving software tips and tricks. You'll come away with techniques that will make life easier in the programs you use every day. The tips are divided into seven categories: DOS, Windows, Databases, Desktop Publishing/Graphics, Spreadsheets, Utilities, and Word Processors. Choose a category, and then pick the product or subcategory you're interested in. You'll get a list of useful tips taken from the pages of *PC/Computing* and *PC Magazine*. The selection of DOS tips is especially comprehensive, but all the categories offer substantial valuable advice. *Note:* There are no tips on software for the Macintosh or other non–IBM-compatible platforms.

Surcharges: ZiffNet hourly rates

36. ZIFFNET FOR PRODIGY BULLETIN BOARD   ▼ $$

ZiffNet for Prodigy's bulletin board is, in contrast to the rest of the service, disappointing. You may be able to get some good technical advice by posting a message in "New Computer Users," but there's not much going on in the other topics. Messages are few and far between, and it seems that not many users spend much time here. Perhaps the problem is that this board is separate from the rest of Prodigy's bulletin boards, and doesn't show up on any jump-word lists. Or maybe the hourly fees discourage much use. Either way, if you're looking for computer discussions, you're better off stopping in at item 14 on the main Prodigy map, the Computer Bulletin Board (Jump: COMPUTER).

Surcharges: ZiffNet hourly rates

ZiffNet for Prodigy
Travel Guide

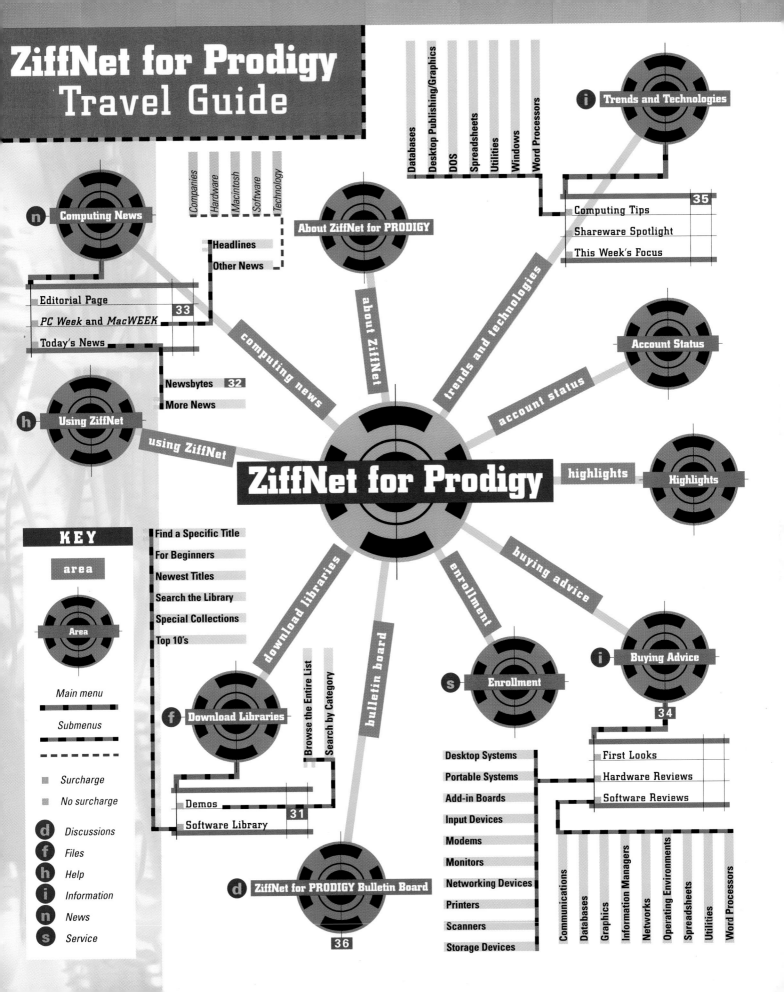

Databases
Desktop Publishing/Graphics
DOS
Spreadsheets
Utilities
Windows
Word Processors

i Trends and Technologies

Computing Tips | 35
Shareware Spotlight
This Week's Focus

Companies
Hardware
Macintosh
Software
Technology

n Computing News

Headlines
Other News

About ZiffNet for PRODIGY

Editorial Page | 33
PC Week and *MacWEEK*
Today's News

Newsbytes | 32
More News

h Using ZiffNet

computing news
about ZiffNet
trends and technologies
account status

Account Status

using ZiffNet

ZiffNet for Prodigy

highlights | **Highlights**

KEY

area

Area

Main menu

Submenus

- - - - - -

Surcharge

No surcharge

d Discussions
f Files
h Help
i Information
n News
s Service

Find a Specific Title
For Beginners
Newest Titles
Search the Library
Special Collections
Top 10's

download libraries
enrollment
buying advice

bulletin board

Browse the Entire List
Search by Category

f Download Libraries

Demos | 31
Software Library

s Enrollment

i Buying Advice | 34

First Looks
Hardware Reviews
Software Reviews

Desktop Systems
Portable Systems
Add-in Boards
Input Devices
Modems
Monitors
Networking Devices
Printers
Scanners
Storage Devices

Communications
Databases
Graphics
Information Managers
Networks
Operating Environments
Spreadsheets
Utilities
Word Processors

d ZiffNet for PRODIGY Bulletin Board | 36

CHAPTER 6

America Online

America Online (AOL) is growing fast. Started in 1989, AOL now has more than 600,000 subscribers, with over 300,000 of those joining since the introduction of AOL's Windows-based front-end in mid-1993. The interface is one of the best-designed and easiest to use of all the on-line services, which no doubt has a lot to do with AOL's growing popularity. Plus, it is overflowing with useful, entertaining, and interesting resources, and its rates are reasonable.

To connect to AOL, you need its front-end software; a general-purpose comm program won't work. This software is available in Windows, Macintosh, DOS, and Apple II versions, and using it is a snap. All of AOL's menus and information are presented in windows: You select what you're interested in by clicking on icons or double-clicking items in list boxes. Scroll bars let you see the text that won't fit in the current window. You can have many windows open at once, and you can minimize, resize, and arrange windows as needed, which provides a lot of flexibility for finding and viewing information from a variety of sources at once.

AOL has an excellent selection of news and reference materials. AOL has actively pursued relationships with magazines and newspapers, and carries news stories and other articles from more sources than most other on-line services. In addition to UPI news, you can read stories from the *San Jose Mercury News*, the *Chicago Tribune*, *Time*, *The Atlantic Monthly*, *The New Republic*, and more. The weekly columns of many editorial and advice columnists appear here, also. AOL's reference resources include Compton's Encyclopedia, as well as special educational services from the Smithsonian Institution, the Library of Congress, *National Geographic*, C-SPAN, National Public Radio, and *Omni* magazine, to name a few. You don't get access to serious research databases such as Dialog or IQuest, however; AOL concentrates

on entertaining and educational material, rather than professional reference resources.

AOL has dozens of special-interest forums where you can discuss everything under the sun with people who share your interests and hobbies. The heart of the forums are the message boards; thanks to AOL's simple interface, reading and replying to messages is a breeze. Forums also feature news and announcements. There are libraries of files you can download, and you can upload files you want to contribute to a forum's library.

Note AOL enforces a policy of not allowing any vulgar, discriminatory, or disruptive language or pictures in its forums, libraries, and public conferences. AOL is more restrictive than other on-line services in this respect, but on the other hand, it means that almost all areas of the service are suitable for all ages and sensibilities.

AOL's Window-based Interface

This interface is easy to use: Just click on a button or list box item, and a window appears with the information or menu you requested. Here, the News & Finance department window is on top.

AOL's *conferences*, where you can talk in real-time with other members, are easier to use than any other on-line service's chat program. The conferences are widely used, too—at any

given time you'll probably find dozens of members in the many rooms. There are also lectures in the Center Stage, AOL's auditorium, where you can listen to a public speaker while chatting with other members who are sitting in the same "row" as you, or you can pose questions to the lecturer. Despite the presence of guides who enforce AOL's "terms of service," the conversations in some conference rooms can get a little racy at times. And in the private rooms, anything goes—so parents may want to restrict their children's access to these features.

An increasing number of computer companies are providing technical support on AOL. The Industry Connection section under the heading "Computing and Software" later in this chapter gives you access to forums for dozens of vendors of hardware and software for both PC and Macintosh computers. Unlike many other on-line services, AOL doesn't have a strong bias towards the DOS and Windows platforms; its PC and Mac offerings are roughly equal. This is probably because AOL, when it first started, was available only for the Macintosh and for Geoworks-equipped PCs. Now that PC users can also get access to AOL, there are resources for them, too. Like the special-interest forums, each company's forum has a message board, where you can ask the company's support staff for answers to your technical questions, and a library of useful files, updates, and product information. Some companies' forums also boast a live conference area, plus folders containing additional information about their products, answers to frequently asked questions, and solutions to common technical problems.

For travelers, AOL offers access to EAASY SABRE, an on-line reservation system where you can find information about flights, book your own reservations, and even make hotel and rental car arrangements. There's also the Travel Forum, and a variety of on-line stores catering to travelers as well as stay-at-home shoppers. Although other on-line services offer more in the way of shopping services, AOL does have some merchants that you can patronize: there's a flower shop, AOL's own catalog of T-shirts and knickknacks, and AutoVantage, where you can get information about new car models. There are quite a few Classified ads, too.

Finally, AOL has a respectable Games & Entertainment section. There are several forums and conference areas for gamers, and several information libraries and newsletters on gaming topics. The available interactive games include a Dungeons and Dragons adventure and a casino. For film and TV buffs, AOL has reviews, movie guides, and soap opera summaries.

If you do much downloading from AOL, you'll wish 9600-baud access were more widely available than it is. When we were on line, AOL was just starting to offer 9600-baud access (for no extra charge) in selected areas—but most members were still limited to 2400 baud. With luck, that will change in the near future. Fortunately, AOL's Download Manager offsets the slow access speeds by making downloading as convenient as possible. With the Download Manager, you mark the files you're interested in and download them later, at the end of your AOL session. Because you can tell the Download Manager to sign off after it's received the batch of files you marked, you can leave your computer without fear of incurring extra connect-time charges.

Another problem we encountered when using AOL was periodic delays, especially during AOL's peak hours in the early evening. Due to AOL's rapid growth in late 1993 and early 1994, their computers had some difficulties handling the large number of subscribers attempting to use the service at the same time. While AOL is taking steps to correct this problem, customers were still experiencing some delays and occasional difficulty connecting to the service at the time this book went to press.

AOL lacks comprehensive Internet access. It does have an e-mail gateway to the Internet, but it doesn't offer access to gophers, Usenet newsgroups, WAIS, or ftp. (See Chapter 9 for details on these and other Internet utilities.) Newsgroup access, using a specially designed interface, was planned for early 1994, but we hadn't seen it as of this writing.

Despite a few shortcomings, AOL is a truly impressive service. Its interface is remarkably friendly and well designed—as a result, it's quite fun to use! But AOL is not just a pretty face: It boasts an excellent selection of resources in almost every area, and serves as a meeting place for thousands of people around the world.

Subscribing to America Online

To sign up for AOL, just call their customer service number at (800) 827-6364, or (703) 448-8700—both are voice numbers. There's no sign-up fee, and the software is free—it will be sent to you by mail. You'll need to specify whether you want the DOS, Windows, Macintosh, or Apple II version of the software. (The DOS and Apple versions use a graphical interface based on the Geoworks environment, but you don't need to have Geoworks to use AOL.)

When you sign up for AOL, you receive a master account, and you can create up to four auxiliary accounts, each with their own screen names (member IDs), e-mail boxes, and passwords. The person holding the master account is responsible for the charges incurred on any auxiliary accounts, but can also place restrictions on those accounts if necessary.

When you first run the AOL software, the program asks you to choose a screen name and password. Then it dials an 800 number to find a local access number for you, connects to that number, and signs you on to AOL. You get ten free hours of connect-time with your membership; after that, you're billed at the usual rate.

Fees

AOL's monthly membership fee is $9.95, which includes up to five free hours of connect-time each month. After that, connect-time is billed at $3.50/hour. There are no other pricing plans, and no surcharges for using any of AOL's resources (although some third-party services do carry their own additional fees).

Note that AOL has no "free" or "basic services" areas; you're charged for every minute you're on line. The only exception is their Members' Online Support area, which is free of connect-time charges during evenings and weekends. (AOL uses SprintNet and TYMNET to connect you to their central service, so you'll still be charged SprintNet or TYMNET fees during business hours, even when you're in the Members' Online Support area.)

Getting Around America Online

When you sign on to AOL, the welcome screen appears. This screen has buttons that take you to the day's highlights, a Mail button (grayed out if you have no mail), a Discover AOL button that takes you to additional highlights on AOL, and a Departments button.

Click on the Departments button to open a window displaying buttons for each of AOL's major departments: News & Finance, People Connection, Lifestyles & Interests, Travel & Shopping, Computing & Software, Games & Entertainment, Learning & Reference, and Members' Online Support. Each of these department buttons opens a window showing a menu of the department's resources. The Members' Online Support button takes you to the free member support area; while you're there, all other windows are closed or hidden.

AOL has a straightforward interface: To select something, click on a button or double-click on the item in a list box. A new window will open, displaying more buttons and list box items or showing text. If there's more text than will fit in a window or list box, use the scroll bar or arrow keys to scroll up or down. Although the mouse pointer changes to an hourglass while your modem is receiving information, you can still use it to scroll or resize the current window.

To stop your modem from receiving information before it's received all of the text for that window, Windows users press Esc; Mac users hold down the Apple key while pressing the period key; DOS users press Ctrl-X.

When you're finished with a window, close it by double-clicking on its control bar (in the upper-left corner). Or, if you want to be able to quickly retrieve the window later, minimize it.

To move directly to an item, use its keyword: Select Keyword from the Go To: menu or, in the Windows version, press the Keyword button. Type the keyword and press Enter to jump directly to that item. If you don't know the exact keyword, click on Keyword List. You'll see a list of AOL's departments (except for Members' Online Support). To see all the keywords in that department, double-click on the department name.

The Windows version of the AOL software has a Flashbar of quick-access buttons along the top of the screen. These buttons take you directly to various parts of AOL. For an explanation of what each button does, choose Contents from the Help menu, and select the Flashbar option under Getting Around Online.

To look up AOL resources by topic, use the Directory of Services (keyword: *dirofservices*), which is an index to most of AOL's resources. Or, the keyword *discover* will give you access to some of AOL's highlights.

Note You should be aware that the on-line world is a very dynamic place. It's a good practice to check the Member Assistance area if you ever have any trouble accessing resources.

America Online Travel Guide

America Online

Lifestyles & Interests

Astronomy Club · Aviation Club · Baby Boomers · Better Health & Medical Forum · Business Strategies · Cooking Club · disABILITIES · Environmental Club · The Exchange · Express Yourself · Gay & Lesbian Forum · Kodak Photography Forum · Military & Vets Club · National Space Society · Network Earth · Pet Care Forum · Rocklink · Science Fiction & Fantasy · SeniorNet · Student Access Online · Star Trek Club · Writers' Club

8 **9**

Members' Online Support

- **h** Accounts & Billing
- **h** Downloading Help
- **h** E-Mail, Chat & Message Help
- **h** Getting Around on AOL
- **h** Members Helping Members
- **h** Tech Help Live!
- **h** Technical & Connect Help

online support

Advice & Tips Boards
Ask Anita and Bob
Ask the Lawyer
The Crystal Ball
Tommy's Tips

lifestyles/interests

learning/reference

Learning & Reference

- **i** Academic Assistance Center
- **i** Apple II Education Software
- **i** Barron's Booknotes
- **i** Career Center
- CNN NEWSROOM
- **i** College Board
- **i** Compton's Encyclopedia **17**
- **i** Dictionary of Computer Terms
- **s** Electronic University Network
- **s** Int'l. Correspondence Schools
- **i** Library of Congress Online **18**
- **i** Mac Education Software
- **i** National Geographic
- **i** National Public Radio
- **i** NEA Public Forum
- **i** Omni Magazine
- **i** The Online Campus
- **i** Parents' Info Network
- **i** PC-MS/DOS Education Software
- **i** Scholastic Forum **16**
- **i** Smithsonian Online
- **i** Student Access Online
- **i** Teachers' Info Network

i Advice & Tips
AOL Tour
e Cartoons
The Gallery
gRaFfltl, the Que, and PC Clubs
What's Happening This Week

gRaFfltl
The Quantum Que
Teen Scene
Trivia Forum

The Box Office
Enter Center Stage
Transcripts

people

entertainment

Computoon
Dilbert
McHumor
Modern Wonder
Mike Keefe
Your Cartoons
Toon Talk

People Connection

- **d** Center Stage **7**
- **d** List rooms
- PC Studio

Critics' Choice **15**
Hollywood Online
Video Guide

C-SPAN
Educational TV Database
The Geraldo Show
Soap Summaries

Games & Entertainment

- **e** AD&D Neverwinter Nights
- **i** Book Bestsellers
- **e** Broderbund's Masterword
- **e** Bulls & Bears Game
- Check for Live Discussions
- **i** Disney Adventures Magazine
- Horoscopes
- **d** LaPub
- **i** Movie Reviews & News
- **i** Movies
- **d** Online Gaming Forums
- **i** Television
- **e** Rabbit Jack's Casino
- **i** Rocklink
- **i** Warner/Reprise Records Online

KEY

area

Area

- ▬ Main menu
- ▬ Submenus
- --- Cross-listed items
- ⬛ Surcharge
- ⬜ No surcharge
- **d** Discussions
- **e** Entertainment
- **f** Files
- **h** Help
- **i** Information
- **n** News
- **s** Service

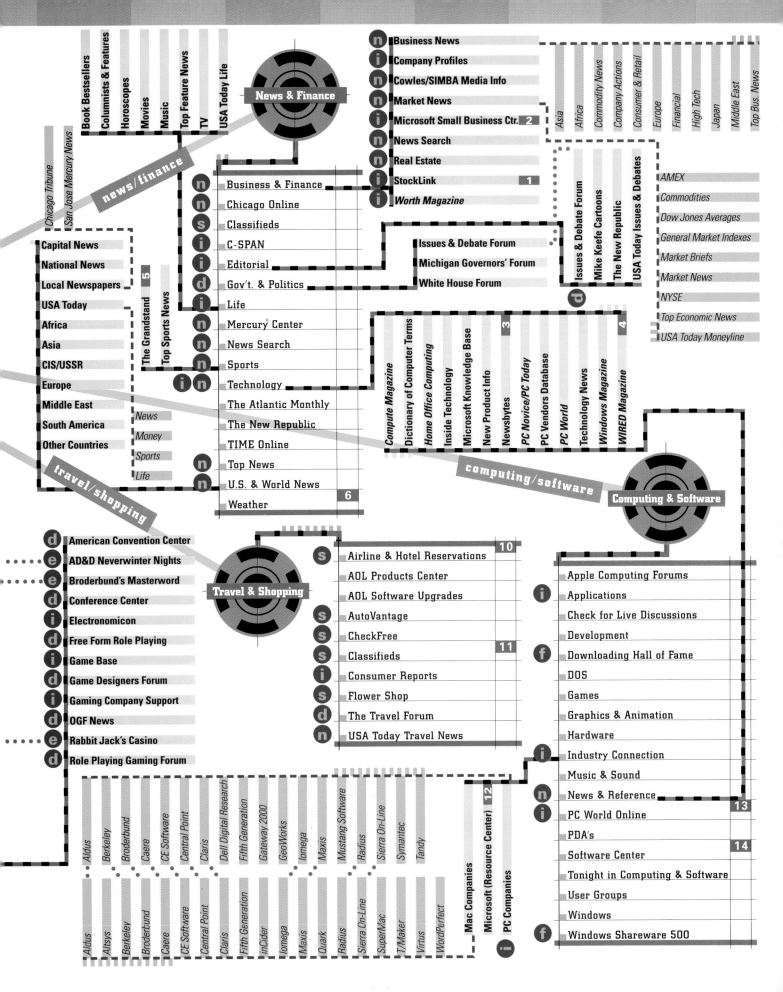

News & Finance

Book Bestsellers · Columnists & Features · Horoscopes · Movies · Music · Top Feature News · TV · USA Today Life

Chicago Tribune · San Jose Mercury News

news/finance

- Business News (n)
- Company Profiles (i)
- Cowles/SIMBA Media Info (n)
- Market News (n)
- Microsoft Small Business Ctr. (i) [2]
- News Search (n)
- Real Estate (n)
- StockLink (i) [1]
- *Worth Magazine* (i)

Asia · Africa · Commodity News · Company Actions · Consumer & Retail · Europe · Financial · High Tech · Japan · Middle East · Top Bus. News

- Business & Finance (n)
- Chicago Online (n)
- Classifieds (s)
- C-SPAN (i)
- Editorial (i)
- Gov't. & Politics (d)
- Life (i)
- Mercury Center (n)
- News Search (n)
- Sports (n)
- Technology (i)(n)
- The Atlantic Monthly
- The New Republic
- TIME Online
- Top News (n)
- U.S. & World News (n)
- Weather [6]

Issues & Debate Forum · Michigan Governors' Forum · White House Forum

Issues & Debate Forum · Mike Keefe Cartoons · The New Republic · USA Today Issues & Debates (d)

AMEX · Commodities · Dow Jones Averages · General Market Indexes · Market Briefs · Market News · NYSE · Top Economic News · USA Today Moneyline

Capital News · National News · Local Newspapers · USA Today · Africa · Asia · CIS/USSR · Europe · Middle East · South America · Other Countries

The Grandstand · Top Sports News [5]

News · Money · Sports · Life

travel/shopping

computing/software

Compute Magazine · Dictionary of Computer Terms · Home Office Computing · Inside Technology · Microsoft Knowledge Base · New Product Info · Newsbytes · PC Novice/PC Today · PC Vendors Database · PC World · Technology News · Windows Magazine · WIRED Magazine [3] [4]

Travel & Shopping

- American Convention Center (d)
- AD&D Neverwinter Nights (e)
- Broderbund's Masterword (e)
- Conference Center (d)
- Electronomicon (i)
- Free Form Role Playing (d)
- Game Base (i)
- Game Designers Forum (d)
- Gaming Company Support (i)
- OGF News (d)
- Rabbit Jack's Casino (e)
- Role Playing Gaming Forum (d)

- Airline & Hotel Reservations (s) [10]
- AOL Products Center
- AOL Software Upgrades
- AutoVantage (s)
- CheckFree (s)
- Classifieds (s) [11]
- Consumer Reports (i)
- Flower Shop (s)
- The Travel Forum (d)
- USA Today Travel News (n)

Computing & Software

- Apple Computing Forums
- Applications (i)
- Check for Live Discussions
- Development
- Downloading Hall of Fame (f)
- DOS
- Games
- Graphics & Animation
- Hardware
- Industry Connection (i)
- Music & Sound
- News & Reference (n)
- PC World Online (i) [13]
- PDA's
- Software Center [14]
- Tonight in Computing & Software
- User Groups
- Windows
- Windows Shareware 500 (f)

Aldus · Berkeley · Broderbund · Caere · CE Software · Central Point · Claris · Dell Digital Research · Fifth Generation · Gateway 2000 · GeoWorks · Iomega · Maxis · Mustang Software · Radius · Sierra On-Line · Symantec · Tandy

Aldus · Altsys · Berkeley · Broderbund · Caere · CE Software · Central Point · Claris · Fifth Generation · InCider · Iomega · Maxis · Quark · Radius · Sierra On-Line · SuperMac · T/Maker · Virtus · WordPerfect

Mac Companies · Microsoft (Resource Center) [12] · PC Companies (i)

INSIDE AMERICA ONLINE

AOL is filled with interesting, informative, and entertaining re-sources, from news and magazines to games and special-interest forums. The map on the preceding pages shows all of AOL, and will keep you from getting lost when exploring AOL's many resources. Use it to find the resources that interest you the most, or simply to see at a glance what AOL offers.

The following pages describe and evaluate the best and most pop-ular of AOL's many resources. Each description is preceded by a number that you can use to find that resource on the map. Or, when you see a number on the map, you can look for that number among the resource descriptions. This listing not only gives you a sense of what's inside AOL, but it will also help you quickly find the best resources as they appear on the map.

For an estimation of the quality and usefulness of each resource described, look for the following symbols:

▲▲▲▲   Outstanding—don't miss it!
▲▲▲   Excellent—worth going out of your way to see it.
▲▲   Very good—worth a look.
▲   Above average—stop by if it's on your way.
▼   Disappointing—don't bother.

You'll also find an indication of the cost of each described re-source. The exact amount of surcharges, if any, are specified at the end of each description, and the dollar icons give you a gen-eral idea of how its price compares to other features inside AOL.

$$$ Steep—hang on to your wallet!
$$ Moderate—not a bargain, but reasonable.
$ Cheap—a good value, easy on your pocketbook.
✛   Free—no surcharges or connect time charges!

If you need direct access, you'll find the keyword for each re-source in the listing as well as on the map. Finally, each resource is classified by type. The types for AOL are News, Files, Informa-tion, Help, Discussion, and Service and are represented by the same type symbols that appear on the map.

News & Finance *AOL's News & Finance department is one of its largest sections, offering a broad array of news, business, and mar-ket information. You can get the text of articles from many national magazines here, as well as stories from the* San Jose Mercury News *and* Chicago Tribune. *Plus, there's a wealth of information for market-watchers. The US & World News menu provides headlines from a vari-ety of sources, including a large number of UPI wire stories. Unfortunately, these headlines are not always clearly attributed, so it's sometimes hard to tell what news service, newspaper, or writer con-tributed the stories. Also, we encountered a surprising number of glar-ing typographical errors and data "garbage" in many of the national and international wire stories.*

1. STOCKLINK   ▲▲ $
KEYWORD: STOCKS

Here's where to get up-to-date stock quotes on any pub-licly traded corporation. Just enter the ticker symbol, and StockLink gives you the latest price (delayed 15 minutes if the stock market is open), changes, high and low prices for the day, volume, and other statistics. If you like, you can add the stock to a portfolio that AOL keeps for you. You can also specify your pur-chase price and quantity, and StockLink will automatically calcu-late the current value of your holdings. To see how your stocks are doing, just select the Display Portfolio button. Want more informa-tion on a particular company? Look in Company Profiles (keyword: company), a database providing detailed fiscal and historical in-formation about hundreds of public corporations.

2. MICROSOFT SMALL BUSINESS CENTER   ▲▲▲ $
KEYWORD: SMALL BUSINESS

If you own a small business or you're thinking of starting one, be sure to stop by the Small Business Center for some valuable advice. Microsoft and AOL have worked with over 20 companies and associations, including the U.S. Small Business Administration, *Dun & Bradstreet, Inc.*, and SCORE (the Service Corps of Retired Executives), to put together this rich supply of in-formation and tips for the small-business owner. You'll find articles discussing tax issues, how to incorporate, legal matters, market-ing, and sexual harassment in the workplace. There's a library of business software, and templates for spreadsheets and word processors. And there's a message board where you can post your questions, get advice, and network with other small business own-ers. The Small Business Center is well organized and brings a lot of valuable material together in one place—check it out!

3. NEWSBYTES   ▲▲▲ $
KEYWORD: NEWSBYTES

Newsbytes is an independent wire service covering the computer and high-tech industries. The stories collected here give you detailed information on new trends, company ac-tions, technologies, and products. It's a great source when you need to stay on top of such issues or if you're simply interested in recent developments in the market. News categories include Apple, IBM, UNIX, Business, Government, and Telecommunica-tions; there's also a selection of editorials on various topics. You can search through the database of recent articles by topic or product, or you can download all the stories for any day in the last month.

4. *WIRED* MAGAZINE   ▲▲▲▲ $
KEYWORD: WIRED

If you like *WIRED* magazine but find it hard to read the novel layouts (which feature such innovations as yellow type on red backgrounds), check out the magazine's on-line folders here on

AOL. You can get the full text of all past issues of *WIRED*, filed by department, or you can search through all issues for topics that interest you. And the articles are displayed on your screen in nice, crisp, ordinary text! There's also a file library containing extra files and longer articles from the magazine; and a message board where readers talk, debate, and speculate about the future of electronic communications. Even if you haven't read the magazine, you'll want to drop in here and read some of the stories—it's one of the most interesting and exciting technology magazines around.

5. THE GRANDSTAND ▲▲ $
KEYWORD: GRANDSTAND

A gold mine for the sports fan, The Grandstand is AOL's sports club, where you can meet people and argue about your favorite sports and teams: baseball, football, basketball, hockey, golf, and even auto racing. You'll find a message board and a conference area for each sport, and the file libraries include plenty of programs and stats for serious sports enthusiasts. The conference rooms have packed schedules, with many meetings every night of the week. You can also get the latest sports scores here, of course. There's an overwhelming amount of material in The Grandstand, but it's organized so that getting to the parts you're interested in is an easy task.

6. WEATHER ▼ $
KEYWORD: WEATHER

AOL's weather forecasts are harder to use and understand than those of any other on-line service. To find the forecast for a U.S. city, you have to select U.S. Cities Forecasts, then open another folder, and then open the file for your state—an awkward process that has about two steps more than should be necessary. What you get when you open the file for your state is a column of numbers and two-letter codes representing the forecasted highs, lows, and general conditions for all cities in your state for the next week. There are no written descriptions of current and coming weather, nor long-range forecasts. Weather maps are available, but you can't view them on line; you have to download them and look at them with GIF image viewer. In short, AOL's weather service is awkward and more difficult to use than it should be.

People Connection
When you first enter the People Connection, you're placed in a special conference room lobby. If there are other users there, you can start chatting with them right away. To see what other conference rooms are currently open and who's in them, click on the List Rooms button. To go to other, nonconference attractions in People Connection, click on the PC Studio button. Note: If you're a real information jockey, you can keep a conference window open while you browse other parts of AOL—the conversation will keep scrolling as long as the conference window is open. The only limitation is your ability to concentrate on more than one thing at once! You can't be in more than one conference room at a time, however.

7. CENTER STAGE ▲▲ $
KEYWORD: SHOWS

Center Stage is AOL's "auditorium," where celebrities make live appearances and AOL hosts game shows and contests. The auditorium, unlike the conference rooms, can accommodate a large number of people (the audience), but during the presentation, an audience member can talk only to the seven other people in the same "row." If you want to pose a question, you can add it to a queue of messages that the on-line host will pose to the lecturer. Most nights, the Center Stage hosts games and competitions of various sorts. Occasionally there are lectures and Q&A sessions from celebrities—past lecturers include evangelist Billy Graham, rock star Melissa Etheridge, and the band Depeche Mode. Check the Box Office for upcoming events. The library of Center Stage transcripts will tell you what happened at past events.

Lifestyles & Interests
This department is home to dozens of special-interest forums, clubs, and meeting places. Almost every forum has message boards, file libraries, and a live conferencing area. Most also have folders full of additional information relating to their subject. Whether you're interested in astronomy, cooking, health, or anything else, you'll probably find people to share that interest with you. For a complete list of these clubs and forums, click on the Special Interests Keywords button.

8. BETTER HEALTH AND MEDICAL FORUM ▲▲▲▲ $
KEYWORD: HEALTH

This forum is a reference of great value—you'll find hundreds of articles on all kinds of health, fitness, and wellness issues. Many of these articles describe a disease or a condition in great detail; others talk about ways to keep healthy, understanding health insurance, and other topics. The Home Medical Guide supplements this information with a menu-driven database of articles on symptoms, diseases, and treatments. A separate Search Health Forum button lets you search all of the forum's many articles. There is a truly amazing quantity of information here, and it's all presented in friendly, nontechnical language. The forum also boasts its own live chat area and a message board.

9. THE EXCHANGE ▲ $
KEYWORD: THE EXCHANGE

Nothing but discussion here—on just about any topic you can think of. This is AOL's "grab bag" for debate and chatter. There are message boards here for cars, crafts, the outdoors, philosophy and politics, gardening, people in their twenties and thirties, water sports, and much more. Debate and arguments abound in some topics; others are more advice oriented. If you can't find a specific club for your favorite special interest on AOL, check out The Exchange—there's likely to be a place for you here.

Travel & Shopping *Although not as large and diverse as the shopping services offered by other on-line services, AOL's Travel & Shopping department has several useful resources. You can make your own flight reservations with EAASY SABRE, and there are on-line stores where you can buy gifts or software, or learn more about new car models. You may want to sign up for CheckFree, an electronic bill-paying service that saves you the trouble of writing out checks every month.*

10. AIRLINE & HOTEL RESERVATIONS ▲ $
KEYWORD: SABRE

This is where you get access to EAASY SABRE, the American Airlines reservations and ticketing system. You can find out about all the flights from any city to any other, and easily try several different combinations of departure and arrival times, airlines, and destinations until you find the flight that's least expensive. Then you can make your own reservations and have the tickets mailed to you. You can also arrange hotel and rental car reservations.

EAASY SABRE uses a text-based menu system—unusual for AOL and unlike any other resources on AOL. A window-based interface like the rest of AOL would be better, but fortunately the text menus aren't too hard to use. There are no surcharges for using EAASY SABRE, though of course you have to pay for any tickets you buy.

11. CLASSIFIEDS ▲▲▲ $
KEYWORD: CLASSIFIEDS

AOL's classified ads are free! This resource is a plain-and-simple message board that works like any other in AOL, and it has topics for many types of computer equipment, as well as home items, cars, and employment. Just post your message or browse everybody else's. AOL helpfully provides a couple of files giving you warnings and pointers about buying items through the Classifieds: how to ship products, how to pay, and what to do if you bought something that doesn't work. It's good advice, and you should read it before ordering or selling anything through these ads.

Computing & Software *The Computing & Software department boasts many useful resources, such as software and hardware tips and a collection of shareware programs you can download. But its star is the Industry Connection, where you'll find a panoply of hardware and software vendors' forums matched only by CompuServe's. Go to these vendor forums for technical support, advice, and customer service. Each forum has a format similar to that used for the special-interest clubs: Message boards and file libraries are the focal points, and sometimes you'll also find folders containing additional information.*

12. MICROSOFT RESOURCE CENTER ▲▲ $
KEYWORD: MICROSOFT

The Microsoft Resource Center includes two databases of information: the Small Business Center (see item 2 on the map), and the Microsoft Knowledge Base. The Knowledge Base is a vast collection of technical notes, solutions to problems, and tips

for optimizing the performance of Microsoft products. You can browse the database by selecting a category and application, or search for keywords. Much of the information is highly technical in nature, and you might spend some time wading through articles that don't solve your particular problem. But a patient search often pays off, yielding little-known secrets and tricks that will improve your computer's performance.

13. *PC WORLD* ONLINE ▲▲▲ $
KEYWORD: PC WORLD

PC World Online is more than the usual magazine forum for discussion and files—this is truly an interactive, on-line magazine in its own right. You can get the full text of *PC World* articles, search back issues for topics of interest, check out product comparisons and reviews, and read up on current trends, technology, and terms. Articles and reviews from *PC World* appear here at about the same time as the magazine hits the newsstands. Check out "The Adventures of Lone Wolf Scientific" in Online Exclusive; it's an entertaining computer column by Michy Peshota, found on bulletin boards across the country but not in the printed version of *PC World*.

One shortcoming of *PC World* Online is that you can't see graphs or tables of data from the articles; all you can get is text. There is a software library, but it contains mostly shareware, utilities, and batch files mentioned in the magazine.

Of course, there's also a message board for getting in touch with the editors.

14. SOFTWARE CENTER ▲▲ $
KEYWORD: SOFTWARE

Need a shareware virus scanner? Looking for a good addition to your collection of adventure games? The Software Center collects tens of thousands of files from many different forums' libraries. You can search for files by category (games, utilities, applications, and so forth) or search the entire database. Although the Software Center doesn't have *everything* that can be found in AOL's many download libraries, there's a vast quantity of useful material here, and it's worth exploring if you are looking for a particular shareware program or if you just want to get an idea of what's available. Unfortunately, there's no way to search all of AOL's forum libraries from one place, but this is a good start.

Note There are separate Software Centers for PC and Macintosh versions of AOL.

Games & Entertainment *Come here to play games, discuss them, or just to find out about the newest movies and Hollywood gossip. AOL has several on-line games, including a Dungeons & Dragons game called Neverwinter Nights, and RabbitJack's Casino, where you can gamble away your chips at poker, blackjack, bingo, or the slots. (Both of these games require additional software to run.) If your entertainment tastes are more conventional, you'll also find plenty of record, movie, and book reviews in this section.*

15. CRITICS' CHOICE   ▲▲ $
KEYWORD: CRITICS

Critics' Choice is where to go for reviews of all major new releases in movies, books, videos, games, and music. The reviews are thoughtful, detailed, and well written. There's no searchable database of past reviews, and for that reason the Critics' Choice isn't a comprehensive guide. Still, it'll help you find out about what's current, and whether you really do want to put down $7.50 for that movie you were considering, or $14.95 for a new CD. If you want to discuss or dispute a review, click on the button labeled You're the Critic! to check out the Critics' Choice message board.

Learning & Reference
Here's where to come for your general reference needs, or to find educational resources useful to teachers, students, and parents. AOL has a good selection of general-purpose reference resources, but since it lacks large, industrial-strength databases, it's not suitable for more intensive (professional or academic) research.

16. SMITHSONIAN ONLINE   ▲▲ $
KEYWORD: SMITHSONIAN

Want to see photos from the space program or learn more about American art? Smithsonian Online provides information about the Smithsonian Institution's many museums, special exhibits, and publications. There is an abundance of information here for educators, students, or just interested people. You can find out what's currently on display and learn more about the museums' collections. Or examine the Smithsonian's catalog of books, pamphlets, and other educational resources. The National Museum of American Art in this case is a virtual museum, with "galleries" you can tour, GIF images to download, information about artists, and a database for research into U.S. art and artists. And if you're traveling to Washington, D.C., you can find out about current and upcoming special exhibits, and look up each museum's hours.

17. *COMPTON'S ENCYCLOPEDIA*   ▲ $
KEYWORD: ENCYCLOPEDIA

Whether you want to read up on RAM or Rainer Maria Rilke, *Compton's Encyclopedia* is the place to turn. It's got 5,200 full-length articles, supplemented by over 26,000 shorter "capsule" articles. Of course, the advantage of an electronic encyclopedia like this one is that you can search through it quickly, and with AOL's interface that's a simple matter. The major drawback to Compton's Encyclopedia is that—unlike Grolier's—it's not cross-referenced, so you can't easily jump from one article to related ones. You have to return to the search window and enter a new search term each time you want to see something else. This lack of cross-references is surprising, especially since Compton's recently was awarded a patent for hypertext technology. Other than that, it's a fine encyclopedia, useful for most every subject.

18. LIBRARY OF CONGRESS ONLINE   ▲▲▲▲ $
KEYWORD: LIBRARY

This virtual museum brings some of the Library of Congress's most exciting exhibits to on-line users. When we visited, the Vatican Library exhibition was on display, along with a wonderful presentation about the Dead Sea Scrolls. Other exhibits covered interactions between European explorers and American people from 1492 to 1600, and the recently opened secret archives of the former Soviet Union. Each exhibit has several "galleries" where you can read background material, learn about related history, and find out what various scholars think about the texts and artifacts on display. You can also download GIF images of objects from each exhibition. The resources here are well organized, and anyone who's ever been to a museum will find it easy to browse the Library's exhibits. A discussion area and conference room complete the Library's offerings. Don't miss this fascinating and well-designed informational resource!

CHAPTER 7

Delphi

Delphi has fewer subscribers than the other commercial information services covered in this book—but don't let its membership size fool you. Delphi boasts a lot of useful resources and, dollar for dollar, is one of the best on-line values available. Its news and reference services are quite comprehensive. There are many forums and special-interest groups with lively discussions, making Delphi a good place to meet people, get advice on a variety of subjects, and share information. Perhaps best of all, Delphi provides more complete access to the Internet than any other major information service. (See Chapter 9 for details on the Internet.) Delphi has plenty to interest the on-line traveler, and its rates are among the lowest.

Delphi uses a simple, plain-text menu system to provide access to its resources. Though easy to use, the menus can be unwieldy at times. There's no "command mode" for experienced users who want a quick way to navigate the service without wading through the menus, nor is there a graphical interface for novices who need a little help getting around—you're stuck with the plain-text interface. (There is an off-line message reader available that simplifies the use of Delphi's forums, e-mail service, and Internet newsgroups. It's called D-Lite; see item 5, "D-Lite Support SIG," under the "Inside Delphi" section, later in this chapter.) On the other hand, most resources are no more than one or two levels down from the main Delphi menu, so it doesn't take long to get anywhere in the service. Help is available at almost every prompt, in case you get confused or need more explanation.

There's a good selection of news, reference resources, computer information, and downloadable files on Delphi. The news menu includes stories from United Press International (UPI), the Business Wire, PR Newswire (for press releases), and Reuters, to name a few. You can get stock and market information here, too. Delphi's reference

resources include Grolier's Encyclopedia, the Dictionary of Cultural Literacy, and the CAIN AIDS Information Network, among others. The reference menu also gives you full access to Dialog, one of the largest and most comprehensive information resources anywhere on line (see the sidebar later in this chapter).

Delphi's plain-text menus are visually unappealing, but they're easy to use.

Delphi's special-interest groups (SIGs) cover a variety of topics: The Computing menu has discussion groups for almost every brand of personal computer, for example, and the Groups and Clubs menu includes SIGs devoted to various hobbies, professions, and interests. Each SIG has a forum (a bulletin board area where you can post and read messages), a conference area (for real-time discussions), and a database area (where you can download files). In addition, many SIGs provide additional features such as special announcements, news, and access to Usenet newsgroups.

The conferences on Delphi—one of its more popular features—are widely used. There are many regularly scheduled meetings in addition to impromptu get-togethers; it's a good way to meet peole on line. Delphi's conferencing software can be awkward to use, but once you get used to it, it's not too difficult to manage.

One of Delphi's most useful features is its Internet access. In addition to sending and receiving

Internet e-mail from your Delphi account, you can use gophers, telnet, ftp, and other utilities for accessing the Internet's many resources. Delphi also gives you access to Usenet newsgroups, either through the standard UNIX newsgroup reader, nn (see Chapter 9 on the Internet for an introduction to nn), or through Delphi's own easy-to-use newsgroup reader. So if you're looking for access to the Internet, Delphi is a good alternative to commercial providers. Its prices are comparable to the dedicated providers, but with Delphi you also get its own array of information resources for the same price—which is a pretty good deal!

In addition to all these features, Delphi also boasts an excellent selection of on-line games. You'll find logic games, text adventures, and card games here. Long-time computer users will recognize some old classics (for example, Lunar Lander and Wumpus), but there are new games, too. Some interactive games make use of Delphi's conferencing features to let several people play at once. And one unique feature that Delphi offers is modem-to-modem game support. Instead of dialing your competitor directly, you both connect to Delphi and then use it to connect your computers and play against each other. Delphi supports modem-to-modem versions of many popular games, including chess, Go, and space battle games. You need to have the proper software to play these games, but some of these games are shareware programs that you can download from Delphi.

One shortcoming of Delphi is its lack of high-speed access numbers. As of this writing, there was only one way to connect to Delphi at rates faster than 2400 baud, and that was by direct-dialing their 9600-baud access number in Cambridge, Massachusetts. More widespread 9600-baud access is planned for the near future.

Some on-line travelers may find Delphi's size limiting, and will be frustrated by the less than abundant selection of resources. But if you

don't need hundreds of forums or special features, you don't mind the text interface, and you want extensive Internet capabilities, then Delphi is just the ticket.

Subscribing to Delphi

To sign up for a free trial membership to Delphi, set your comm software to 8N1; then dial by modem (800) 365-4636. If you currently have Internet access, telnet to delphi.com instead (see Chapter 9 for an explanation of telnet). After you've connected, press return once or twice. At the Username: prompt, type JOINDELPHI, and when the system prompts you for your password, type R993. Then enter the information requested by Delphi, and follow the instructions to find out your local access number. You can also call Delphi's service representatives at (800) 695-4005 (voice). The trial membership gives you five free hours of connect time in the first month; additional hours are billed at $1.80/hour.

If you live in Boston or Kansas City, you can connect directly to Delphi with a local phone call. Just set your comm software to 8N1 and dial (617) 576-0862 for Boston or (816) 421-6938 for Kansas City. In other parts of the world, you'll probably want to use SprintNet or TYMNET to connect to Delphi. SprintNet and TYMNET are packet networks (see "The Traveler's Dictionary" at the end of this book) to which you can connect with a local phone call. You can then connect to Delphi through the packet network, thus saving the cost of a long-distance call. SprintNet and TYMNET carry surcharges during business hours (6:00 a.m. to 6:00 p.m. local time on weekdays) but are free of surcharges for callers from the continental U.S.

during nonbusiness hours. When you register for Delphi, you'll be able to look up the packet network access number nearest you, and you'll also receive instructions for connecting to Delphi using that network.

If you already have Internet access, you can use telnet to connect to Delphi: Just telnet to delphi.com and log in. This costs you nothing (though you still have to pay any applicable fees to your Internet access provider).

Fees

Delphi offers two pricing plans. The 10-4 Plan gives you four hours of use per month for a monthly fee of $10.00; additional connect-time in that month is billed at $4.00/hour. The 20-20 Plan offers 20 hours of use per month for $20.00, with additional connect-time billed at $1.80/hour. Delphi charges no enrollment fee; however, you will be charged a one-time fee of $19.00 to switch from the 10-4 Plan to the 20-20 Plan if you make the switch any time after your first month of membership. In addition, you'll pay packet network fees if you use SprintNet or TYMNET to connect to Delphi.

Packet Network Fees for Connecting to Delphi

	Home Time Per Hour	Business Hours Per Hour
Continental U.S.		
via SprintNet	No charge	$9.00
via TYMNET	No charge	$9.00
via PC Pursuit	No charge	No charge
Canada		
via TYMNET	$3.00	$9.00
via Datapac	$25.80	$25.80
Hawaii		
via TYMNET	$5.40	$12.00
via SprintNet	$12.00	$12.00
Guam	$30.00	$30.00
Alaska, Puerto Rico	$12.00	$12.00
Prepaid International	$1.80	$1.80

In the table of packet network fees "business hours" are 6:00 a.m. to 6:00 p.m. local time on weekdays, except holidays. "Home time" is all other times (6:00 p.m. to 6:00 a.m. local time on weekdays, plus all day on weekends and holidays).

Delphi charges an additional $3.00/month for Internet access, bringing your total monthly fee to $13.00 on the 10-4 Plan or $23.00 on the 20-20 Plan. In addition, some services within Delphi (such as Dialog) carry additional surcharges, indicated on the opening menus of each service.

Note Unlike many other commercial information services, Delphi has no "basic services" area where you can browse without accumulating hourly charges. Every minute you're connected to Delphi counts toward your monthly allotment. Once you've used the monthly allotment of connect-time, you'll have to pay for every additional hour you're connected. The only exception is the member assistance area (the Using Delphi menu), which is free of connect-time charges.

Getting Around Delphi

Delphi's menus are easy to use: Just type the full name or the first few letters of the item you want to select, and press Enter. You'll only need to type as many letters of the menu item as are necessary to distinguish it from other menu items (usually no more than three letters, often only one or two).

To move quickly through several levels of menus and submenus, type the main menu's name (or abbreviation), followed by a space, and then the name (or abbreviation) of the item on the submenu that you want. You'll go directly to the menu or item you've selected. For example, to select the PC Compatibles/IBM item on the Computing menu, type **COMPUTING PC**, or simply **COM PC**, and press Enter. If you're not at the main menu, enter **GO COM PC**. You can combine three or more menu selections at a time, if you like. On the Delphi map in this chapter you'll find the abbreviations you need to get to any part of Delphi.

Most menus in Delphi include a HELP selection and an EXIT selection. HELP provides context-sensitive help and brief explanations of the menu items and commands available to you. EXIT returns you to the previous menu, or logs you off of the service if you're at the Main menu. Ctrl-Z also exits you from whatever menu or application you're currently using, but it doesn't log you off of Delphi, even at the Main menu. If you want to return to the Main menu, just type **MAIN**.

For more information about using Delphi, go to the Using Delphi menu. You'll also find member assistance and billing information there.

Note You should be aware that the on-line world is a very dynamic place. It's a good practice to check the Using Delphi area if you ever have trouble accessing resources.

See this table for other commands you can use anywhere in Delphi.

Delphi Commands

Keystroke or Command	Result
Ctrl-C	Cancels current activity and returns to previous prompt
Ctrl-O	Stops text from scrolling and takes you to next prompt
Ctrl-Q	Resumes text flow from Delphi (after Ctrl-S)
Ctrl-R	Redisplays line you're currently typing (useful in conferences)
Ctrl-S	Pauses text flow from Delphi (resume with Ctrl-Q)
Ctrl-U	Cancels current input
Ctrl-Z	Exits current application or menu
BYE	Logs you off Delphi
MENU	Redisplays current menu
PAGE name	In conference area, notifies member name that you'd like to chat with them
/ACCEPT	Accepts another member's PAGE (request to talk)
/BUSY	Turns off PAGEs, conference messages, and new mail notifications
/BYE	Logs you off of Delphi (used in conference areas or forums)
/EXIT	Exits current application or menu (useful for leaving conference area)
/HELP	Displays a list of available commands
/LENGTH n	Sets your screen length to n lines
/NOBUSY	Allows PAGEs, conference messages, and mail notifications to reach you
/REJECT	Tells member who paged you that you are unavailable
/TIME	Displays current eastern (standard or daylight) time
/WHOIS name	Displays information about member name

Dialog: The Mother of All Databases

Dialog is one of the biggest information databases in the world, and you can access it right here on Delphi. It's a massive research tool that brings together over 450 separate databases on a wealth of topics, from medicine to philosophy to trademarks and more. Dialog not only offers access to a staggering quantity of information, it also provides highly sophisticated tools for searching that information.

For serious research needs, Dialog is the way to go.

However, this service is not for the faint of heart—its complicated command structure and high fees mean you won't be able to learn how to use Dialog by mere trial and error. Delphi, unfortunately, doesn't offer much assistance beyond a rudimentary sample Dialog session. Dialog's parent company does offer a wide range of manuals and training seminars—for a fee, of course. If you plan to use Dialog for your business or for personal research, you should invest in some of these training materials and ser-

vices *before* you get started. For more information (including a list of the databases Dialog offers), contact Dialog directly at (800) 334-2564 or (415) 858-3792.

Dialog is a surcharged service. You'll be charged $21.00/hour, or $0.35/minute. In addition, most databases within Dialog carry additional surcharges, from about $0.50 to more than $3.00/hour; some also charge for each query and for lists of search results. In short, it's not cheap—but when you need a heavyweight information source, Dialog can't be beat.

DELPHI Travel Guide

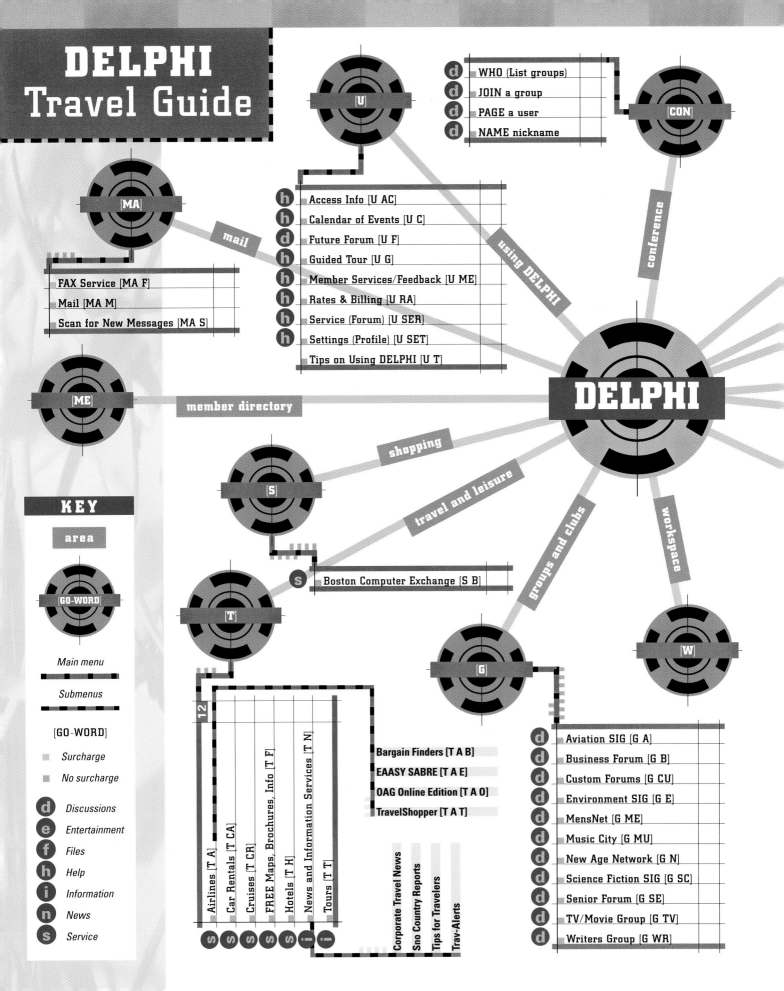

[U]

- **d** WHO (List groups)
- **d** JOIN a group
- **d** PAGE a user
- **d** NAME nickname

[CON]

conference

[MA]

mail

- **h** Access Info [U AC]
- **h** Calendar of Events [U C]
- **d** Future Forum [U F]
- **h** Guided Tour [U G]
- **h** Member Services/Feedback [U ME]
- **h** Rates & Billing [U RA]
- **h** Service (Forum) [U SER]
- **h** Settings (Profile) [U SET]
- Tips on Using DELPHI [U T]

using DELPHI

FAX Service [MA F]
Mail [MA M]
Scan for New Messages [MA S]

[ME]

member directory

DELPHI

[S]

shopping

travel and leisure

s Boston Computer Exchange [S B]

[T]

groups and clubs

workspace

[G]

[W]

KEY

area

[GO-WORD]

Main menu

Submenus

[GO-WORD]

- *Surcharge*
- *No surcharge*

- **d** *Discussions*
- **e** *Entertainment*
- **f** *Files*
- **h** *Help*
- **i** *Information*
- **n** *News*
- **s** *Service*

12

	Airlines [T A]	Car Rentals [T CA]	Cruises [T CR]	FREE Maps, Brochures, Info [T F]	Hotels [T H]	News and Information Services [T N]	Tours [T T]
	s	**s**	**s**	**s**	**s**	**i**	**i**

Bargain Finders [T A B]
EAASY SABRE [T A E]
OAG Online Edition [T A O]
TravelShopper [T A T]

Corporate Travel News
Sno Country Reports
Tips for Travelers
Trav-Alerts

- **d** Aviation SIG [G A]
- **d** Business Forum [G B]
- **d** Custom Forums [G CU]
- **d** Environment SIG [G E]
- **d** MensNet [G ME]
- **d** Music City [G MU]
- **d** New Age Network [G N]
- **d** Science Fiction SIG [G SC]
- **d** Senior Forum [G SE]
- **d** TV/Movie Group [G TV]
- **d** Writers Group [G WR]

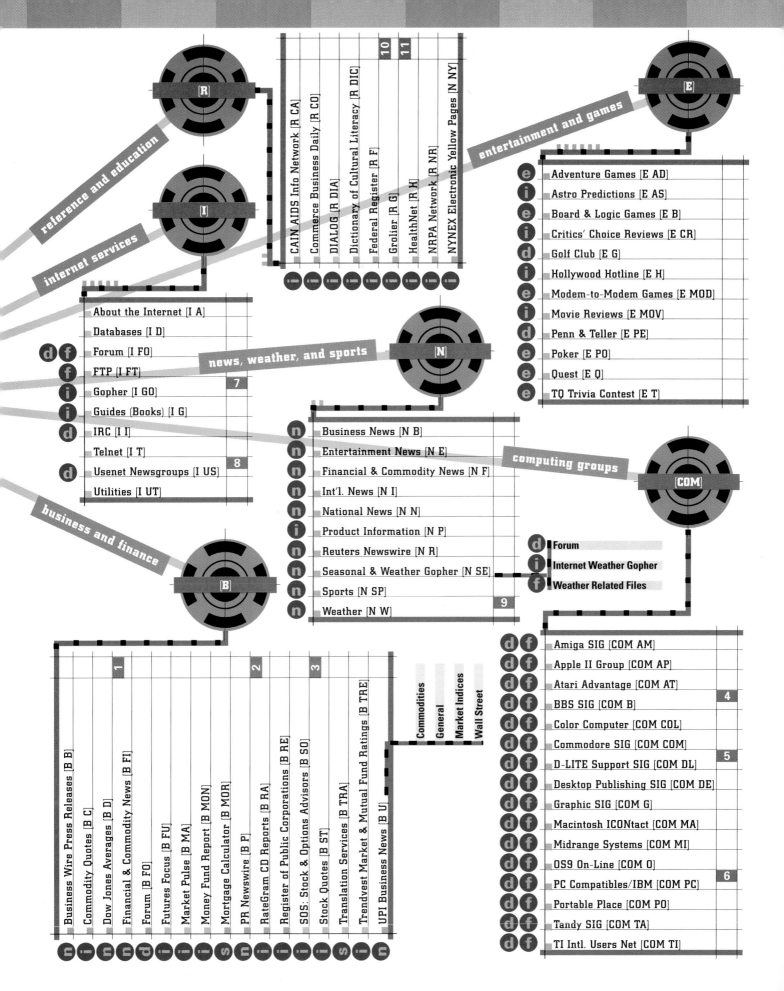

reference and education

R

I

10
11

CAIN AIDS Info Network [R CA]
Commerce Business Daily [R CO]
DIALOG [R DIA]
Dictionary of Cultural Literacy [R DIC]
Federal Register [R F]
Grolier [R G]
HealthNet [R H]
NRPA Network [R NR]
NYNEX Electronic Yellow Pages [N NY]

entertainment and games

E

Adventure Games [E AD]
Astro Predictions [E AS]
Board & Logic Games [E B]
Critics' Choice Reviews [E CR]
Golf Club [E G]
Hollywood Hotline [E H]
Modem-to-Modem Games [E MOD]
Movie Reviews [E MOV]
Penn & Teller [E PE]
Poker [E PO]
Quest [E Q]
TQ Trivia Contest [E T]

internet services

About the Internet [I A]
Databases [I D]
Forum [I FO]
FTP [I FT]
Gopher [I GO]
Guides (Books) [I G]
IRC [I I]
Telnet [I T]
Usenet Newsgroups [I US]
Utilities [I UT]

7
8

news, weather, and sports

N

Business News [N B]
Entertainment News [N E]
Financial & Commodity News [N F]
Int'l. News [N I]
National News [N N]
Product Information [N P]
Reuters Newswire [N R]
Seasonal & Weather Gopher [N SE]
Sports [N SP]
Weather [N W]

9

computing groups

COM

Forum
Internet Weather Gopher
Weather Related Files

business and finance

B

1
2
3

Business Wire Press Releases [B B]
Commodity Quotes [B C]
Dow Jones Averages [B D]
Financial & Commodity News [B FI]
Forum [B FO]
Futures Focus [B FU]
Market Pulse [B MA]
Money Fund Report [B MON]
Mortgage Calculator [B MOR]
PR Newswire [B P]
RateGram CD Reports [B RA]
Register of Public Corporations [B RE]
SOS: Stock & Options Advisors [B SO]
Stock Quotes [B ST]
Translation Services [B TRA]
Trendvest Market & Mutual Fund Ratings [B TRE]
UPI Business News [B U]

Commodities
General
Market Indices
Wall Street

Amiga SIG [COM AM]
Apple II Group [COM AP]
Atari Advantage [COM AT]
BBS SIG [COM B]
Color Computer [COM COL]
Commodore SIG [COM COM]
D-LITE Support SIG [COM DL]
Desktop Publishing SIG [COM DE]
Graphic SIG [COM G]
Macintosh ICONtact [COM MA]
Midrange Systems [COM MI]
OS9 On-Line [COM O]
PC Compatibles/IBM [COM PC]
Portable Place [COM PO]
Tandy SIG [COM TA]
TI Intl. Users Net [COM TI]

4
5
6

INSIDE DELPHI

Delphi contains a variety of resources, from news services to references to special interest groups (SIGs) on a variety of topics. The SIGs are perhaps one of Delphi's best features—each one includes a public message board, a live conferencing area, and databases of files you can download. Read on to learn more about Delphi's offerings.

The following pages describe and evaluate the best and most popular of Delphi's many resources. Each description is preceded by a number that you can use to find that resource on the map. Or, when you see a number on the map, you can look for that number among the resource descriptions. This listing not only gives you a sense of what's inside Delphi, but it will also help you quickly find the best resources as they appear on the map.

For an estimation of the quality and usefulness of each resource described, look for the following symbols:

▲▲▲▲   Outstanding—don't miss it!
▲▲▲   Excellent—worth going out of your way to see it.
▲▲   Very good—worth a look.
▲   Above average—stop by if it's on your way.
▼   Disappointing—don't bother.

You'll also find an indication of the cost of each described resource. The exact amount of surcharges, if any, are specified at the end of each description, and the dollar icons give you a general idea of how its price compares to other features inside Delphi.

$$$ Steep—hang on to your wallet!
$$ Moderate—not a bargain, but reasonable.
$ Cheap—a good value, easy on your pocketbook.
✛   Free—no surcharges or connect time charges!

If you need direct access, you'll find the GO-word for each resource in the listing as well as on the map. Finally, each resource is classified by type. The types for Delphi are News, Discussion, Files, Information, Entertainment, Help/member assistance, and Service and are represented by the same type symbols that appear on the map.

Business and Finance

Here's where to turn for business, investment, and financial information and news. From the UPI Business News stories to the investing advice offered by RateGram and Trend-Vest, you'll find plenty here to help manage your personal finances and keep you on top of the latest trends. And for keeping abreast of new mergers, ventures, and products, the Business Wire and PR Newswire give you access to the world of press releases. Bear in mind that many features on the Business and Finance menu are surcharged, although the rates are generally quite reasonable.

1. FINANCIAL AND COMMODITY NEWS   ▲▲▲ $$
GO B FI

There's a wealth of news about various financial markets here on News-A-Tron's menu. You can get commentary on the dollar's recent performance, reports on various money market funds, the latest foreign currency rates, world interest rates, and the market prices of many commodities. Plus, there's at-a-glance information about the New York Stock Exchange and other major stock markets. This is also the place to go for current commodity quotes and for information about agricultural markets. The surcharge applies each time you visit News-A-Tron's menu (unless you leave without selecting any options except for the HELP option), but you can stay as long as you like and view as many reports as you need for that one fee. A good deal!

Surcharges: $1.25 per session; a subscription plan is also available that provides three months of unlimited access for $45.00.

2. RATEGRAM CD REPORTS   ▲▲▲ $$
GO B RA

RateGram provides valuable information about the money market funds and CDs with the highest rates. It's a simple way to find the best investment—just choose the category you're interested in, and capture or print the list that RateGram gives you. Each fund listed includes a contact phone number, percentage rate, yield, minimum investment, and term. Choose from Liquid Money Market Accounts, CDs, Jumbo CDs, Money Market Mutual Funds, the week's top CDs, and RateGram's Rate Almanac.

Surcharges: $1.00 per report

3. STOCK QUOTES   ▲ $$
GO B ST

Simple and straightforward: You type a ticker symbol, and Delphi gives you the current price of that stock. If you can't remember the symbol, just type the company's name followed by a question mark to see a list of possible symbols, and enter the one you want. The stock quotes are 15 minutes behind the current prices while the market is open; when it's closed you get the closing prices. Unfortunately, there's no easy way to automate getting large numbers of quotes, and if you use this resource frequently, the fees can add up.

Surcharges: $0.07 per quote

Computing Groups

Here's where you'll find SIGs dedicated to the discussion of various computer platforms and applications. Turn here for informal advice, help solving a problem, or just to share your experiences with computer users like yourself.

4. BBS SIG   ▲▲▲ $
GO COM B

If you're interested in bulletin board systems (BBSs), this is the place to come for more information—whether you're a bulletin board operator (sysop), thinking about starting your own BBS, or just looking for BBSs in your area. The

forum's discussions are aimed mostly at BBS operators and sysops, and those who frequent this area seem to have plenty of technical knowledge. But this forum isn't the only place to find BBS discussions: One of the most convenient features of the BBS SIG is that it also gives you access to a dozen Usenet newsgroups dealing with BBSs, including alt.online-service, alt.bbs.lists, and others. You can find out about new BBSs, search for bulletin boards in your area, or talk to other BBS aficionados. Delphi's BBS SIG also has submenus for *Connect* magazine and NOMA, the National Online Media Association.

Surcharges: None

5. D-LITE SUPPORT SIG   ▲▲▲ $
GO COM DL

D-Lite is the unofficial off-line reader for Delphi. D-Lite facilitates your use of Delphi's e-mail, SIGs, and Usenet newsgroups by letting you specify off-line what you're interested in. D-Lite then logs on to Delphi, gets what you've requested, posts messages that you want to send, and logs off. Because it can do all this much more quickly than you can manually, it can save you a lot in connect-time fees. Although D-Lite isn't marketed or supported by Delphi, it does have a SIG here, where you can download the PC or Mac versions of the program, learn how to use it, and get technical support from its author. D-Lite is a shareware program, and registration is inexpensive. If you use Delphi a lot, you owe it to yourself to check out this SIG.

Surcharges: None

6. PC COMPATIBLES/IBM SIG   ▲▲▲ $
GO COM PC

This is the forum for everyone with an IBM-compatible PC, and there are a *lot* of participants here. Whether you're having trouble with DOS, Windows, or your hardware, there are experts here who will probably be able to answer your questions and help you get everything working right. The databases contain lots of PC software you can download—shareware, freeware, and demos, as well as informational files, comm program scripts, and more. The PC SIG's menu also gives you access to a special menu of Usenet newsgroups relating to PCs—more than 20—covering Windows, OS/2, DOS, programming, telecommunications, and other topics. There is a special section for *PCM*, a magazine for Tandy computer users, and the Tandy SIG can also be reached from the PC SIG's menu. And if you're looking for peripherals, a second computer, or even a programming job, be sure to check out the classified ads.

Surcharges: None

Internet Services
Delphi's Internet services are one of its best features. You'll find plenty of information about the Internet in the forum and in the databases, but perhaps the best way to find out about the Internet is just to jump in. Check out the gopher and the Usenet newsgroups. If you like live chat sessions, try IRC (Internet Relay Chat), an Internet-wide, real-time conference. And look on the Utilities menu

for some useful Internet utilities; finger, for instance, gives you information on many Internet users, if you know their e-mail address. Remember that before you can use Delphi's Internet capabilities, you need to sign up for them—it'll cost you an extra $3.00 a month, but it's well worth it.

See Chapter 9 of this book for details on the Internet.

7. GOPHER   ▲▲▲ $$
GO I GO

A *gopher* is a program that simplifies access to Internet resources by putting them on a menu. There are gophers all over the Internet, and they're all connected—making up, in effect, one enormous, complicated menu of Internet resources. (See Chapter 9 for a more detailed description of gophers and a map of the gopher universe.) Delphi's gopher provides a large menu of useful information and services, and you can use it to connect to any other gopher in the world. It's easy to use; just enter the number of the menu item you want to select. The right-hand column of the menu tells you the category of each item: a text file, another menu, a newsgroup, or a telnet connection to another computer. To go to the previous menu, just type BACK. Experiment with the gopher—it's probably the easiest and fastest way to roam the Internet. Delphi's gopher also boasts a Personal Favorites feature you can use to customize the gopher with your favorite gopher sites to visit.

Surcharges: None (after monthly Internet access fee)

8. USENET NEWSGROUPS   ▲▲▲▲ $$
GO I US

Usenet is the part of Internet that has to do with *newsgroups*, bulletin board-like discussion areas where you can read or post "articles" (messages) about a specified topic. There are literally hundreds of newsgroups, covering every imaginable topic, and with participants from all over the world. Delphi gives you two options for reading Usenet newsgroups: either the traditional newsreader called nn (found at many Internet sites), or Delphi's own newsreader. Delphi's reader is simpler and easier to use, but nn is more powerful and provides more options for customizing the way you follow discussions on the newsgroups. Choose either program; both give you access to all the newsgroups you could want. All you have to do is find the name of a newsgroup you're interested in, and start reading. If you want to download batches of newsgroup articles and read them off line, get D-Lite, the off-line reader for Delphi. GO COM DL to find out more about D-Lite, and read the description earlier in this chapter (item 5 on the map).

Surcharges: None (after monthly Internet access fee)

News, Weather, and Sports
This menu provides up-to-date news from a variety of news services. The business, entertainment, financial, international, and national news menus give you all the stories from UPI, with new articles added throughout the day. The

Reuters news service has its own menu of stories here, too. Of course, you can also get sports and weather.

9. WEATHER
GO N W

Delphi's weather service gives you the latest weather forecasts for your area or for the entire U.S., but it falls short of being a complete resource. There are no weather maps available here—you have to go to the Seasonal & Weather Gopher (GO N SE), and search through its menus for weather maps that interest you. That gopher is also where you need to turn if you want more detailed forecasts or descriptions of conditions. Still, if all you want is a quick forecast for a city in the U.S., the Weather menu is adequate.

Surcharges: None

Reference and Education *The Reference and Education menu includes a rich selection of reference resources, including Grolier's Encyclopedia, the health resources HealthNet, the CAIN AIDS Information network, and Dialog, a massive reference resource (see sidebar earlier in this chapter). There are also a few extras such as the Dictionary of Cultural Literacy and the NRPA (National Recreation and Park Association) Network, where you can get information on U.S. National Parks.*

10. GROLIER
GO R G

Grolier's Encyclopedia is an easy-to-use, searchable encyclopedia that contains over 31,000 entries. Most of these articles are cross-referenced, so it's easy to move from one article to a related one just by picking a menu option. Grolier's is available on many other commercial information services, but Delphi's is one of the simplest and friendliest implementations of this encyclopedia that we've seen. A good source for current information on general topics.

Surcharges: None

11. HEALTHNET
GO R H

HealthNet is an on-line medical reference for medical consumers. You'll find some useful articles on home care, first aid, and sports medicine, as well as detailed descriptions of various diseases in HealthNet's menu-driven database. Also, there's a bimonthly on-line newsletter that discusses one topic in depth. Unfortunately, contrary to what the introductory information claims, HealthNet's database isn't searchable—you just have to wade through the menus until you find what you're looking for. Also, the data here doesn't go beyond the basics. If you want more detailed information, or access to current medical journals, you will need to look elsewhere.

Note: For an excellent database of information about AIDS, see CAIN (the Computerized AIDS Information Network) here on Delphi: GO R CA.

Surcharges: None

Travel and Leisure *Delphi provides the traveler with many services, from EAASY SABRE, which lets you make your own air travel reservations, to travel news and information, to a list of free brochures and maps you can order on line (they'll be mailed to you free). There's also the VIP club, which offers discounts on many travel services.*

12. AIRLINES
GO T A

If you want to make your own plane reservations or are just interested in searching for the lowest fares to a given destination, go to the Airlines menu. You'll find several services here that will meet your needs. There's Bargain Finders International, which you can use to search for discounts and special offers on travel throughout the world. Or use EAASY SABRE, the Official Airline Guide (OAG), or WORLDSPAN Travelshopper to find flight information and order tickets for any airline. EAASY SABRE and Travelshopper are both free of surcharges, and their menu-driven interfaces are easy to use. OAG provides a similar ticketing service, but it carries a surcharge. For corporate users who need to make flight reservations for their company, there's also Commercial SABRE, a version of EAASY SABRE designed for business use.

Surcharges: None; OAG carries a surcharge of $0.59/minute during business hours, and $0.42/minute evenings, weekends, and holidays

eneral Electric started GEnie (the General Electric Network for Information Exchange) in 1985 as a low-cost alternative to CompuServe, and it remains a good value. GEnie offers dozens of news and information services, special interest groups, games, and databases, for an hourly rate that's the lowest among the major information services. Although GEnie doesn't boast fancy graphics or a graphical front-end, it has plenty of resources to satisfy the frugal on-line traveler.

GEnie has a text-based, menu-driven interface that is easy to use. (A new Windows-based front end program was released in June 1993—too late for us to review it.) Unlike most on-line services with text interfaces, GEnie's menus often are two columns wide. This means you can see more options at once—but it sometimes also makes for a cluttered screen, especially when you encounter very long menus. Exploring GEnie using its menus is a simple matter because most resources aren't more than one or two levels down. So look around, and see what you find!

GEnie's RoundTables (RTs) are among its central features. RTs are discussion areas devoted to specific topics; they include a bulletin board and file libraries, as well as real-time chat (RTC) rooms where you can talk "live" with other members of that RoundTable. Many of the menus you'll find in RTs include related resources from other areas of GEnie. The Computing Services area includes a large number of RTs for users of various computers and operating systems; you can also get technical support from some companies who maintain RTs in this area. In addition, there are dozens of special-interest groups (SIGs) on the Leisure Pursuits & Hobbies menu, where you'll find RTs devoted to cars, planes, writing, gardening, and many other interests.

If you use GEnie's RTs very much, you'll probably want to get the Aladdin shareware program, an automated off-line reader program. To use it, you specify the bulletin boards and topics you're interested in, and Aladdin logs on to GEnie, retrieves the pertinent messages, and then logs off. You can then read and respond to messages off line, without incurring connect-time charges. Aladdin is available in PC, Mac, and Amiga versions.

GEnie's selection of real-time games is another feature that attracts many new users. You need to download special software to play these games, but once you've got the software running, you can play graphical, interactive games with GEnie users from all over. There's Air Warrior, an air combat game; Cyberstrike, a three-dimensional action game; a complex simulation of the Hundred Years' War; plus about a dozen others, including several role-playing games.

GEnie's two-column menus fit a lot of information onto your screen, and they're easy to use. Keywords appear at the top of most pages; just type the keyword to move to that page.

GEnie's reference offerings grew substantially with the addition of Dialog in mid-1993. Dialog is one of the most powerful information resources in the country (see "Dialog: The Mother of All Databases" in Chapter 7). You can access the entire Dialog service directly through GEnie. Often, however, you'll want to access the more specialized database offerings, such as the Educator's Center, the Law Center, the Trademark Center, or Quotations Online, where you can look up familiar quotations. These resources

just one database. They're easier to use than the full Dialog service—and cheaper, too, since you're not paying for access to databases you don't need. Grolier's Academic American Encyclopedia, the CIA World Fact Book, and several additional databases are also available on GEnie as reference resources.

GEnie's basic news services are rudimentary: You get access to the Reuters newswire, Newsbytes, and The Sports Network, a sports news service. There's no weather service on GEnie, although you can download daily weather maps from the Weather KnowledgeBase in the Space and Science Information Center. If you want more news than this, you have to sign up for GEnie's QuikNews service, which costs $25.00 per month and lets you specify up to ten search terms. It then scans news stories from many major world newswires for the search criteria you specified, and collects the matching stories in your folder. It's a useful service, and the flat monthly rate is reasonable for frequent users. If you need additional resources beyond these, turn to the GEnie NewsStand, a Dialog database containing stories from 12 U.S. newspapers and hundreds of magazines.

One of GEnie's biggest flaws is its e-mail service, which is difficult to use despite the menu-driven interface. Even tasks as simple as reading and replying to messages are more complicated than they should be. The menus are not easy to figure out, messages scroll by too fast when you're reading them, and on-line message editing is difficult. However, GEnie does offer an e-mail gateway to the Internet. And, with the ability to include attached files and send messages to multiple recipients, it's a fully capable e-mail system—you just have to put up with the fact that it's hard to use.

Although lacking a few features, GEnie is a fairly complete on-line service. Its reference and game resources are excellent, and it boasts the lowest hourly rate of any on-line service. For economical on-line traveling, GEnie is a good bet.

Subscribing to GEnie

To sign up for GEnie by modem, set your communications settings to 8N1. Also, specify the "local echo" or "half-duplex" setting in your comm program. Then dial (800) 638-8369, or in Canada (800) 387-8330. As soon as the modem connects, type **HHH** and press Enter. When the U#= prompt appears, type **SIGNUP** and press Enter. Then follow the instructions to open your GEnie account.

For questions about GEnie, call their customer service number at (800) 638-9636 (voice).

Fees

GEnie's price structure is ideal for anyone who only spends a few hours per week or month on line. There is no initial fee to sign up. The monthly subscription rate is $8.95 (Can$10.95), which gets you four free hours of non-prime time connect time. There are no basic services that are free from connect-time charges, and GEnie doesn't offer any discount pricing plans. Connect-time charges accrue in all areas of GEnie except the main menu (keyword: TOP) and the member services area under the About GEnie menu (keyword: GENIE).

The hourly rates (after your allotment of four hours) are listed in the following table. GEnie is considerably more expensive during prime time (business) hours. However, its non-prime time rates are quite low. Some access numbers in the

U.S.—those in GEnie's Extended Network—carry an additional $2.00/hour surcharge. There is also an additional surcharge for using 9600-baud access, GEnie's toll-free 800-number access, and packet networks (SprintNet or Datapac). GEnie's 800-number access is available only in the U.S., and the surcharge is waived if you connect to it at 9600 baud.

GEnie Connect-Time Fees

Type of Access/ Surcharge	U.S. Hourly Rate	Canada Hourly Rate
Non-prime time	$3.00	Can$4.00
Prime time	$12.50	Can$16.00
Extended Network	$2.00	n/a
9600 baud	$6.00	Can$8.00
800-number	$6.00	n/a
SprintNet	$2.00	n/a
Datapac	n/a	Can$6.00

Prime time is 8:00 a.m. to 6:00 p.m. local time on weekdays. Non-prime time is everything else: evenings, weekends, and some holidays.

Be aware that many GEnie resources, including the QuikNews news-clipping service and all Dialog databases, carry additional surcharges. If you use these features much, you'll soon use up what you save in connect-time charges!

Finally, some resources within GEnie are designated Premium Services and carry additional surcharges. To avoid unpleasant surprises, be sure to find out the rates for a Premium Service before using it.

Getting Around GEnie

GEnie's menus are straightforward: just type the number of the item you want to select and press Enter. To move directly to an item, type its keyword, or type **M** followed by the page number of the item you want. Each item's keyword is displayed at the top-center of its menu, and the item's page number is displayed in the upper-right of the menu.

Many GEnie customer service features have their own keywords, as shown in the following table.

Customer Service Features

Keyword	Result
BILL	Displays your current bill
HELP	Provides more help on using GEnie
INDEX	Displays an index of resources, including keywords and page numbers
MAIL	Takes you to the GEnie e-mail area
PHONES	Finds local access numbers
RATES	Displays current GEnie rates
SET	Lets you change your password, terminal settings, and account information
TOP	Takes you to the top (main) GEnie menu

Many screen displays on GEnie are not "paged," or presented to you one screenful at a time. This means a lot of information can scroll off the top of your screen before you have a chance to read it. To temporarily pause the flow of information, press Ctrl-S or the Break key. To resume scrolling, press Ctrl-Q or Ctrl-Break.

Listed below are several commands you can use throughout the service. Most GEnie

CHAPTER 8 : GENIE 103

commands can be abbreviated to their first three
letters.

GEnie Commands

Command	Result
BYE	Logs you off the GEnie service
COM	Toggles command mode on and off (in command mode, menus aren't displayed)
HEL	Displays on-line help
PAS	Lets you change your password
PRE	Goes to the previous menu

Note that the PRE command can be abbreviated to simply P. Also, bear in mind that this command doesn't take you to the last menu you visited, but rather to the menu above the current *item* in the menu structure. Since many GEnie resources appear on several menus, the next menu you see after using PRE may not be the one you last saw.

GEnie
Travel Guide

[GENIE]

[COMMUNICATE]

[ENTERTAIN]

[BUSINESS]

Worldwide Patent Center [PATENTS]
Trademark Center [TRADEMARKS]
Trade Names Database [TRADENAMES]
Business Resource Directory [DIRECTORY]

about GEnie

business services

communications (GE mail & chat)

entertainment services

i Astro News & Events [ASTRO]
i Astrology RT [ASTROLOGY]
i CINEMAN Entertainment Info. [CINEMAN]   10
i Comics RoundTable [COMICS]
i Hollywood Hotline™ [HOTLINE]
d Science Fiction & Fantasy RTs [SFRT]
d Sports RT [SPORTS]

Enter GEnie Mall
GEnie Classified Ads   7

GEnie
[TOP]

KEY

area

[GO-WORD]

online shopping services

[SHOPPING]

GEnie games

leisure pursuits & hobbies

education services

news, sports & features

Main menu

━━━━━━━━━

Submenus

━ ━ ━ ━ ━

Cross-listed items

• • • • • • • • •

[GO-WORD]

The Sports Network [SPORTSNEWS]
Reuters Newswires [REUTERS]
Newsbytes News Network [NEWSBYTES]
GEnie QuikNews (Clipping Svc) [QUIKNEWS]
GEnie NewsStand [NEWSSTAND]
Dow Jones News/Retrieval® [DOWJONES]
Columnists & News Features [FEATURES]

Surcharge
No surcharge

d Discussions
e Entertainment
f Files
h Help
i Information
n News
s Service

[LEISURE]

[EDUCATION]

[NEWS]

d Automotive RT [AUTO]
d Aviation RoundTable [AVIATION]
d Collectibles RoundTable [COLLECTIBLES]
d Food & Wine RoundTable [FOOD]
d Gardening RoundTable [GARDEN]
d MIDI & Computer Musicians RT [MIDI]
d Modeling RoundTable [MODEL]
d Pet-Net RT [PET]
d Photo & Video RT [PHOTO]
d Radio & Electronics RoundTable [RADIO]
d Writers' RoundTable [WRITERS]
d Zymurgy RoundTable [BEER]

8

s College Aid Sources for Higher Education [CASHE]
s Computer Assisted Learning Center [CALC]
d Education RT [ERT]
d Educator's Center [EDUCATORS]
d i f Space & Science RT [SPACERT]   9

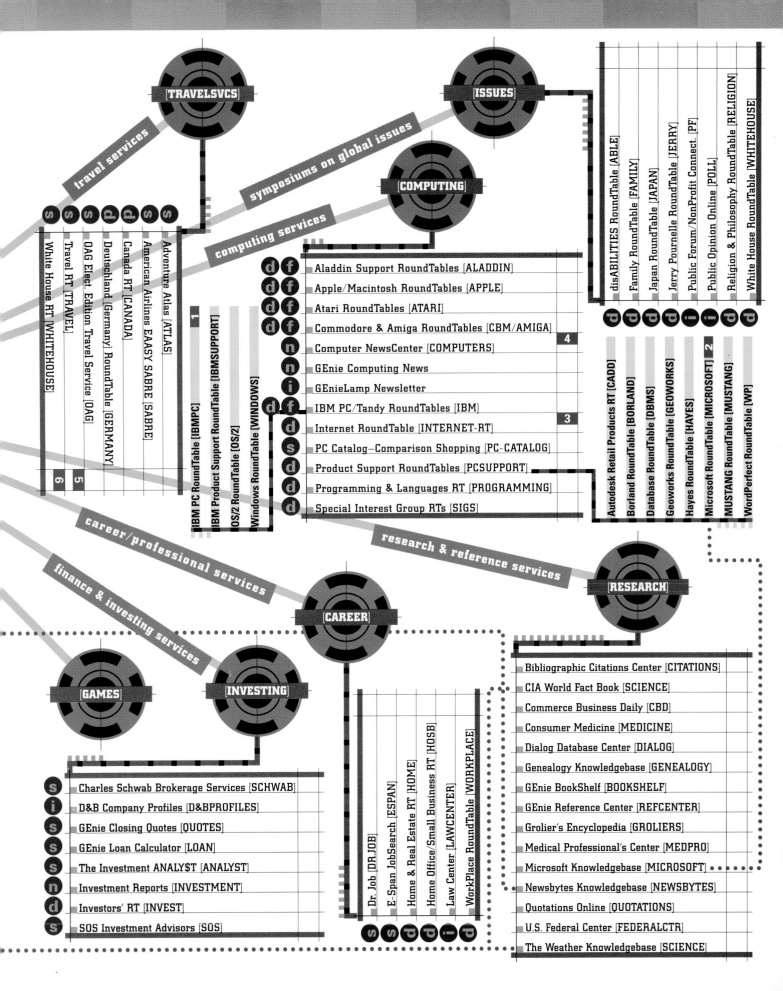

INSIDE GENIE

GEnie offers a wealth of resources that are arranged in the 15 categories shown on the GEnie main menu. You can choose from computing, finance and investing, news, careers, leisure, entertainment, research and reference, communications, travel, shopping, games, business, education, symposiums on global issues, and general information about GEnie. As you can see, you're likely to find something to interest you.

The following pages describe and evaluate the best and most popular of GEnie's many resources. Each description is preceded by a number that you can use to find that resource on the map. Or, when you see a number on the map, you can look for that number among the resource descriptions. This listing not only gives you a sense of what's inside GEnie, but it will also help you quickly find the best resources as they appear on the map.

For an estimation of the quality and usefulness of each resource, look for the following symbols:

▲▲▲▲▲ Outstanding—don't miss it!
▲▲▲▲ Excellent—worth going out of your way to see it.
▲▲ Very good—worth a look.
▲ Above average—stop by if it's on your way.
▼ Disappointing—don't bother.

You'll also find an indication of the cost of each described resource. The exact amount of surcharges, if any, are specified at the end of each description, and the dollar signs give you a general idea of how its price compares to other features inside GEnie.

$$$ Steep—hang on to your wallet!
$$ Moderate—not a bargain, but reasonable.
$ Cheap—a good value, easy on your pocketbook.
✛ Free—no surcharges or connect time charges.

If you need direct access, you'll find the keyword for each resource in the listing as well as on the map.

Finally, each resource is classified by type. The types are news, discussion areas, information, and service and are represented by the same type symbols that appear on the map.

Computing Services
GEnie's Computing Services menu includes many SIGs for users of various computers, operating systems, and application software. You'll also find several software and hardware vendors represented on the Product Support RoundTables menu—turn here for technical support directly from the companies themselves.

1. IBM PC ROUNDTABLE ▲▲▲ $
Keyword: IBMPC

Need to resolve an interrupt conflict? Looking for the scoop on the latest PC industry news? In this RT you can chat with fellow PC users, get or give advice, and learn more about IBM PCs and compatibles. The bulletin board is popular and includes categories for many aspects of PC hardware, software,

and peripherals. You can also get technical support from Gateway 2000, Boca Research, and Quarterdeck Office Systems. The file library contains a vast quantity of shareware, files describing technical problems and their solutions, and product reviews from a variety of sources. There are also plenty of shareware and freeware games and utilities here; you're sure to find a few "goodies" to add to your hard drive.

Surcharges: None

2. MICROSOFT ROUNDTABLE ▲▲ $
Keyword: MICROSOFT

The Microsoft RoundTable is the place to turn when you need technical support for any Microsoft product, on any platform. The bulletin board here has categories for all of Microsoft's major products, where you can post questions and get answers from Microsoft staff. In addition, this RT has a software library containing updated printer and video drivers, information files, and other useful material. Perhaps best of all is the Microsoft KnowledgeBase, a vast database of technical information that Microsoft has compiled over the past several years. Although it may take you a few tries to formulate just the right query to produce the articles you want, it's well worth the trouble. The technical notes available here are truly insider information—you won't find these details anywhere else.

Surcharges: None

3. INTERNET ROUNDTABLE ▲▲ $
Keyword: INTERNET-RT

If you're interested in the Internet, be sure to check out this RoundTable. GEnie doesn't offer Internet access other than an e-mail gateway, but you can get lots of information about the Internet here. Look on the bulletin board for discussions of the various ways you can access the "Net." Once you're on the Internet, this RT offers helpful discussions about using Internet utilities such as ftp, WAIS, and other programs. If you don't have access to Usenet newsgroups, but you want to find out what's going on in them, look into this RT's software libraries, where you'll find "digests" of many newsgroups. These digests are updated periodically and contain all the messages posted to a newsgroup since the last digest was compiled. The libraries also contain Internet utilities that run on many different kinds of computers, and more information about how to get connected to the Internet.

Surcharges: None

4. COMPUTER NEWSCENTER ▲ $$
Keyword: COMPUTERS

A Dialog service, the NewsCenter gives you access to databases of articles from hundreds of computer magazines, high-tech publications, press releases, and newsletters. You'll find product announcements, reviews, and other useful

information within these easily searched databases. The per-search cost can be quite steep, so make sure you read the instructions before starting. There's also a practice area where you can run searches on a smaller database for just $1.00 per search and $1.00 per record displayed.

Surcharges: $2.50 per search; $4.50 per list of ten matching articles in a "summary" database, $6.00 per list of ten matching articles in a "fulltext" database; $4.50 per summary record displayed, $6.00 per full-text record displayed. No-hit searches cost $1.25.

Travel Services
GEnie's Travel menu offers access to two airline ticketing systems: American Airlines's EAASY SABRE, and the OAG Electronic Edition Travel Service. With both, you can get flight information, make reservations, and make hotel and rental car arrangements—all without a travel agent. Before you start your trip, though, be sure to check out the various travel RoundTables for first-hand information about your destination.

5. TRAVEL ROUNDTABLE
Keyword: TRAVEL

Expert advice from seasoned travelers is yours on the Travel RoundTable. The bulletin board has categories for many aspects of traveling in general: how best to travel by rail, sea, or air; camping tips; and advice on getting the best accommodations. In addition, there is a category for each continent, where people who are interested in that part of the world stop to share their experiences. Look in the file library for the text of past discussions—you may find some invaluable tips!

Surcharges: None

6. WHITE HOUSE RT
Keyword: WHITEHOUSE

The software libraries in this RT contain all the latest White House press releases, speeches, and statements, so this is the place to be if you want to check up on the President and the rest of the Executive Branch. New files are posted here daily as soon as the White House releases them. After you've read the news, stop in at the bulletin board to debate the current administration's policies with other interested people. It's a lively board; political positions across the spectrum are represented, and the debates can get a bit heated!

Surcharges: None

Online Shopping Services
The centerpiece of GEnie's shopping resources is the GEnie Mall, where you can browse the wares of nearly 30 stores, buy products on line, or request catalogs you want mailed to you. The Shopping Services menu also lets you order GEnie-related products, such as manuals and T-shirts.

7. GENIE CLASSIFIED ADS
Keyword: ADS

GEnie's Classified Ads are easy to browse and to respond to. The categories include Aviation, Computers, Personals, and Business, and there's also a special section listing job openings at General Electric. It's inexpensive to place an ad, too. The volume of ads posted here is not great, but check it out if you're looking for used computer equipment, business opportunities, or if you want to find out about jobs with GE.

Surcharges: None to browse. To place an ad for 7 days costs $0.10/line; a 14-day ad costs $0.15/line, and a 30-day ad is $0.20/line. There is an additional $1.00 charge if you don't want your e-mail address shown on the ad.

News, Sports & Features
GEnie has a respectable selection of news and sports offerings. For general news, go to the Reuters news service (keyword: REUTERS). To look up stories from many U.S. newspapers and magazines, use the GEnie NewsStand—a surcharged service that gives you access to several Dialog databases. Unfortunately, there's no weather resource here, but you can download recent weather maps from the Space and Science Information Center (see item 9 below).

8. NEWSBYTES NEWS NETWORK
Keyword: NEWSBYTES

Newsbytes is one of the best sources of computer industry information. It's an independent news service devoted solely to computer and high-tech industries, and it covers that news better than any other resource. You'll find information about new technologies and the latest products; stories covering company actions and mergers; and other news of the business. Newsbyte's menu lets you read just the current day's news, or search the last two weeks' worth of stories. You can search by bureau, subject, or story type, or search for words in the text. Newsbytes is one of the best ways to stay on top of the computer industry!

Surcharges: None

Education Services
GEnie's education services include the Education RoundTable, Grolier's Encyclopedia, and several databases on educational topics: the Educator's Center, the College Aid Sources for Higher Education, and the GEnie Bookshelf. These databases come from Dialog and carry additional surcharges, but the RoundTables and the Encyclopedia are free of surcharges.

9. SPACE & SCIENCE ROUNDTABLE
Keyword: SPACERT

The Space & Science RT, known as "Spaceport," is primarily a place for people interested in astronomy, space exploration, and related issues. Come here to find out more about the universe or just to share your views with other space and astronomy buffs. Many of the Spaceport's sysops are writers and editors associated with major astronomy magazines,

so you'll find plenty of expertise here. One of the Spaceport's best features is the Space and Science Information Center (keyword: SCIENCE). It offers a variety of science information resources: a weather information database from which you can download the latest weather maps and data; the Planetary Report Knowledge-Base containing information on the solar system; and the CIA World Fact Book, a compendium of information about the world's nations.

Surcharges: None

Entertainment Services
GEnie's Entertainment menu includes resources for music, movies, television shows, and more. Get the latest dish on Hollywood, or use CINEMAN (item 10) to see movie reviews. You can even have your horoscope read. Note: If it's games you're after, go to GEnie's Games menu (keyword: GAMES).

10. CINEMAN ENTERTAINMENT INFO ▲▲ $
Keyword: CINEMAN

If you're a movie buff—and even if you only occasionally go to movies—take a look at this resource from CINEMAN Syndicate, a corporation providing movie reviews and information. CINEMAN offers two-line capsule reviews of all recent releases so you can quickly scan what's now showing, as well as in-depth reviews of most major recent movies. And you can also find out what the most successful movies are, with the Box Office Report. CINEMAN is a handy guide for today's movies; unfortunately, though, it doesn't have a database where you can look up reviews of older movies—you're limited to what's current.

Surcharges: None

CHAPTER 9

The Internet

The Internet is the largest computer network in the world. It provides access to a vast amount of information and computing power, and communication with more people than any single commercial on-line service. It's estimated that over 15 million people use the Internet, and that number is growing exponentially. You can use the Internet to send e-mail to just about anyone, get data and files from computers thousands of miles away, talk with people from around the globe, search library catalogs at many universities, see weather maps, find out about space shuttle missions, and much more.

The Internet is not a commercial on-line service; it is not run by a single company. The Internet lacks a standard interface; nor does it have a central menu or set of commands. The Internet consists of a vast number of connections among thousands of computers all over the world—each of which is owned and maintained by a different institution or person. There are many networks that together make up the Internet, including Usenet, Bitnet, ARPAnet, and NSFNet. Today these individual networks can be considered part of a single network because they are sufficiently integrated. If you connect to one computer on the Internet, you can probably get access to all the others—and that's the key to the Internet's power.

There are several very different types of resources available on the Internet. Some resources are simply programs running on computers connected to the Internet. To use these programs you first need to log on to the designated computer, using a program called *telnet*. Once you're connected through telnet, you can use the remote computer as if you were logged on to it directly—you type commands at your keyboard and the computer displays its responses on your screen. Programs you can access via telnet include useful Internet utilities, programs to search for data throughout the Internet, and interactive games.

The file library is another type of resource available on the Internet. File libraries are one of the Internet's most powerful features. Many Internet computers store large collections of publicly accessible file libraries that contain truly staggering quantities of data, software, and much more. You use the *ftp* (file transfer protocol) program to connect to the computer that has the file library you want to access. (See the section "Getting Files via ftp" later in this chapter for details.)

If you want to participate in discussions with other Internet users, there are several Internet resources available. *Newsgroups*, the Internet's equivalent of bulletin boards or forums, are a popular discussion medium. There are hundreds of newsgroups covering every imaginable topic. You can access newsgroups through a *newsgroup reader* program, which lets you read messages and post your own.

You can also take part in discussions through e-mail. Programs called *list servers* are used to simplify group discussions: You send your message to a special list address and the list server distributes it to everyone on the list. To join a discussion, you send a command to the list server and it adds you to the list of subscribers; from then on you receive a copy of any messages sent to the list's address. Discussion lists exist for almost as many topics as there are newsgroups. The main difference between discussion lists and newsgroups is the messages show up in your mailbox instead of through the newsgroup reader. (See the section "Taking Part in Internet-wide Discussions" later in this chapter for details.)

Finally, the *gopher* program is one of the most valuable Internet resources, especially for new users. A gopher provides menu-driven access to Internet computers. The most powerful feature of the gopher, however, is its ability to seamlessly connect to other gophers. If there's a gopher available on the computer you use to connect to

the Internet, you will be able to use it to access information and resources on that computer. And you can explore all of *Gopherspace* simply by using the gopher's menus. Gophers offer one of the easiest ways to access resources on the Internet because gopher programs are loaded on many computers. (See the section "Easy Access through Gophers" later in this chapter.)

The Internet is very disorganized because it's not run by a single, central company or agency. It can be hard to find the information you need, since there's no single "card catalog" where you can search resources throughout the network. However, there are search utilities that simplify finding programs and files, and there are also many helpful files that describe in detail where to locate various resources. Newsgroups are another good source of information and advice on this topic. In short, you stand a good chance of finding what you're after if you know how to use just a few Internet utilities.

So take the time to learn your way around the Internet, and you'll open up an almost limitless world of on-line information. Read on to learn how to get connected, travel around the Internet, and find what you're looking for. In no time, you'll be cruising the world's largest information highway.

Connecting to the Internet

In most cases, you don't need to put your PC directly on the Internet. All you really need to collect information and files, communicate with others, and generally explore the Internet is dial-up access to a computer that is on the network. Dial-up access allows you to connect to the Internet computer (which is often a minicomputer or mainframe) by modem. Once connected, you use the remote computer to access the Internet, get the information you need, and display it on your screen.

If you're a student or a member of the faculty or staff at a university, you may qualify for free dial-up access to an Internet computer. Many universities and other educational institutions have computers on the Internet. You can use these computers either through a terminal somewhere on campus, or by dialing in to them with your modem. If you can get an account on a campus computer that has Internet access, you will have all the Internet access you need.

If your school or company doesn't offer access to the Internet, you'll have to look for a commercial Internet access-provider. Some commercial on-line services and many bulletin boards offer access to certain Internet resources; among the services described in this book, Delphi and The WELL provide the best Internet access. In addition, there are services that specialize in providing Internet access and charge a monthly fee. The sidebar, "I Want My Internet Access," later in this chapter gives more information on these services.

Bear in mind that some computers connected to the Internet may not offer access to the full range of Internet resources. Owners of Internet computers often choose to restrict access to certain newsgroups, to the popular interactive games called MUDs or MOOs, and/or to the IRC (the Internet's worldwide chat utility). (See the later sections, "Taking Part in Internet-wide Discussions," and "Live Talk on the Internet," for details.) If your access-provider doesn't offer a particular resource you'd like to use, remember that some Internet resources can be very taxing on the computers on which they run, consuming lots of computing power and tying up communications lines. The owners of the Internet computer may decide that certain resources slow down their

system, and may therefore elect not to support them. Your only recourse is to try persuading those in charge of the computer to add the feature you want, or you can look for another Internet access-provider who does offer what you want.

Fees

The fees you'll pay for Internet access will depend on the type of access you have. If you connect through an educational institution or if your company provides Internet access, you may pay little or nothing. The rates for commercial access providers vary, so shop around. Happily, once you have Internet access, there will be no additional fees. The Internet is supported by the institutions and organizations that own and maintain the computers making up the network. Once you've connected to the Internet, you have unlimited access to everything your access provider allows.

Getting Around the Internet

Once you've got access to a computer on the Internet, start exploring! To make the most of the Internet, you'll need to know how to use the network's most powerful and essential tools.

I Want My Internet Access!

Unless you attend a school or work for a company that provides Internet access, you'll have to find a commercial provider of dial-up access. Fortunately, the list of these providers is growing all the time; with a little shopping around, you can probably find a good deal.

If you subscribe to an on-line service that provides Internet access, you may have all you need. Of the major commercial on-line services, Delphi (see Chapter 7) provides the most complete access, with a gopher, full newsgroup access, IRC (Internet Relay Chat, covered later in this chapter), and many useful Internet utilities. Another good choice may be The WELL (see Chapter 2), which also offers fairly complete access.

Commercial services that specialize in providing Internet access can be found all over the country. It pays to shop around because fees vary greatly. PDIAL (the Public Dialup Internet Access List) is the best place to start shopping; it is a list of U.S. and international Internet access providers. PDIAL can be found in many on-line locations, including the newsgroups alt.internet.access.wanted, alt.bbs.lists, alt.on-line-service, ba.internet, and news.answers. To receive a copy of PDIAL via e-mail, send a message to info-deli-server@netcom.com. In the body of the message, include only the command Send PDIAL.

InterNIC Information Services is another good source of data about public Internet access providers. InterNIC's Reference Desk offers information about the Internet, books on using it, and lists of access providers. Contact InterNIC at (800) 444-4345 (voice) or (619) 455-4600 (voice), or by e-mail at info@inter-nic.net. To receive the information via traditional mail, send a fax to InterNIC at (619) 455-5640 and include your U.S. Postal Service mailing address. InterNIC also has a gopher that provides lots of useful information; see Item 3 under "Inside the Internet" later in this chapter.

You may also be able to get Internet access through a *freenet*. Freenets are bulletin boards that cater to their local communities, providing an electronic forum where the residents of that city or area can meet, obtain information, and make announcements—and some freenets also provide Internet access. So if you live within the same area code as a freenet, find out if it has Internet connections. For a list of freenets and more information about them, contact the National Public Telecomputing Network (NPTN) at (216) 247-5800 (voice), or via e-mail at info@nptn.org. NPTN also maintains an anonymous ftp site at nptn.org, where you'll find information in the directory /pub/info.nptn.

With the following instructions and a little practice, you'll have no trouble finding what you're looking for.

Remote Log-on with telnet

The telnet program helps you connect to other Internet computers, log on, and run programs and commands on remote computers. It's one of the most useful Internet tools, because if the computer you're using doesn't offer a gopher, for example, you may be able to use telnet to connect to a computer that *does* have one.

The telnet program is very easy to use: Just type **telnet** followed by the name or address of the computer to which you want to connect. For example, to connect to the hypothetical computer andy.tech.edu, you would type **telnet andy.tech.edu**. Once you're connected, you need to log on and, in some cases, provide a password. Thereafter, what you type is sent to the remote computer, and what's displayed on your screen comes from that computer. When you're done, type **quit** or **bye** or **off** to disconnect from the remote system and return to your local computer.

Internet computers can be identified in one of two ways. Each computer connected to the Internet has an *IP* (*Internet Protocol*) *address*, which follows the format of the numbers in this example: 134.72.8.250. This set of numbers uniquely identifies a specific computer, and sometimes you'll need to use it to start a telnet session with that computer. *Domain name addresses* are the other means by which computers are identified on the Internet. Domain name addresses are easier to remember than IP addresses. Here are two examples: andy.tech.edu and conglomo.com. The computer's domain name address also tells you something about the computer: The edu suffix signifies an educational institution such as a university (in this case, the hypothetical Tech University); and com means a commercial system or company (in this case, the imaginary Conglomo

Corporation). Other suffixes you may see include org for nonprofit organizations, mil for military computers, and gov for government computers other than the military's. You may also encounter suffixes that specify the country in which the computer is located; for example, us is the United States, de is Germany (Deutschland), and so forth.

The leftmost term in a domain name address is the computer's name. In the above examples, andy.tech.edu signifies the computer named andy in the domain tech.edu, which is Tech University. There may be other computers at Tech University, such as physics.tech.edu or rocko.tech.edu.

Occasionally, you will have to specify a particular port on the destination computer. The telnet program typically connects you to a default port on the remote computer, but some applications require that you connect to a specific one. To connect to a specific port, just type its number after the remote computer's domain name or IP address. For example, if you're instructed to connect to sunshine.ucsb.edu, port 550, simply type **telnet sunshine.ucsb.edu 550**. Don't worry about specifying a port number unless the instructions for connecting to a service specify a particular one.

Easy Access through Gophers

The telnet program may be the most basic way to get around the Internet, but it's not very convenient because you have to specify each computer you want to access and you must know its domain name or IP address. Then, once you do get connected, your options are often limited. Gophers, on the other hand, make navigating the Internet as easy as picking items from a menu. (The map of Internet Gopherspace at the back of this book will help you explore the world available through gophers.)

If there's a gopher on the computer you use for Internet access, you can probably activate it by typing **gopher** (or a similar command). If you

don't have a gopher on your own system, however, you can connect to one through telnet. Public-access gophers are available at the following locations:

- ▶ *consultant.micro.umn.edu (log-in: gopher)*

- ▶ *ux1.cso.uiuc.edu (log-in: gopher)*

- ▶ *gopher.msu.edu (log-in: gopher)*

- ▶ *panda.uiowa.edu (log-in: panda)*

Be aware that these sites are often very busy, and you may experience delays when you use them.

Using Gopher Menus

The first thing you see when you start a gopher (either locally or via telnet) is the main menu for the computer on which the gopher is running. If you're running a gopher locally, you may be able to specify a different gopher server's menu as your opening menu. To start a gopher with a different menu, type **gopher** followed by the domain name address of the gopher server whose menu you want to start with. For example, the University of Minnesota gopher server's address is gopher.micro.umn.edu. To start your gopher with the University of Minnesota gopher's main menu, type **gopher gopher.micro.umn.edu**.

Here's how you would select an item from the menus of the public-access gophers mentioned above:

1. Use the Up Arrow and Down Arrow keys to move to the item.

2. Press Enter or Right Arrow key to select the item.

Alternately, type the number of the item you want to see, and then press Enter.

To retreat one menu level, press u or Left Arrow.

If a menu or document is too long to fit on one page, press the spacebar, the + key, or Page

Down to see the next page. To go back to the previous page, press b, the – key, or Page Up. To return to the gopher's main menu, press m.

You can determine a menu item's type by looking at the last few characters of its description. These characters are explained in the following table.

Types of Gopher Menu Items

Characters	Type and Description
/	Directory. When you select a directory item, you get another menu of choices.
.	Documents—a text file that the gopher will display on screen a page at a time. After displaying a document, the gopher returns you to the most recent menu.
<?>	Searchable resource—for example, a dictionary or other reference work—that prompts you for a search term and returns with a menu of items matching your query.
<TEL>	telnet connection to another computer. When you select a <TEL> item, you are automatically connected to another computer via telnet, and you cannot use the gopher while you're connected. You'll be returned to the gopher as soon as you end the telnet session.
<CSO>	CSO phone book server—use this to search for Internet users at a variety of locations.

To simplify access to gopher features you use frequently, add them to a personal list of bookmarks. By doing so, you'll be able to get to them more quickly, since you'll avoid many menu levels. Press a to add the currently selected menu item to your bookmark list. Press A to add the currently displayed *menu* to the list of bookmarks. To view your bookmark list, press v. You'll get a

gopher menu listing all your bookmarked items, which you can select in the normal way. This will take you directly to items that otherwise would be buried many menu levels deep. To delete an item from this bookmark menu, select it and press d.

See the following table for other commands you can use with gophers.

Gopher Commands

Command	Result
=	Show technical information about current item
/	Search for an item in the current menu
D	Download a file
n	Find next item matching the last search
O	change gopher options
q	Quit, with prompt for confirmation
Q	Quit immediately (no prompt)
s	Save current item to a file

The foregoing commands are case-sensitive.

Look for a menu on your gopher called Other Gopher and Information Servers, or something similar. This is the menu that lets you connect to the rest of the gopher universe. One of the gophers that is usually at the top of this menu, the University of Minnesota gopher, is especially useful. It was the first gopher ever, and it remains a central gopher from which you can easily connect to sites all over the world, even if they're not available directly from your own gopher.

Searching Gopherspace with Veronica

Because Gopherspace is huge, finding the items you're looking for can be difficult—and it's also hard to know if what you're looking for even exists! Fortunately, there is a utility called Veronica that helps you search through all of the world's gophers for items matching your interests.

Veronica is available on most gophers, from the same menu that gives you access to other gophers around the world. (Veronica is listed under "Other Gopher and Information Servers" on the University of Minnesota gopher, which appears on the map of the Internet Gopherspace at the end of this book.) Just select Veronica and type your query. Veronica will display a menu of items throughout Gopherspace that match your search terms, and you can then select the items you want in the normal way. If you'd like to find out more about the gophers on which these items are located, use the gopher = command.

Veronica queries aren't case-sensitive. You can include parentheses, and the logical operators AND, NOT, and OR. You can also use the asterisk as a wildcard. For instance, the query cyber* will match any item containing a word that begins with cyber, such as cyberspace, cypberpunk, or cybernetics. In addition, you can use several switches to adjust your queries. For example, the -mX switch limits the number of entries returned by your search to a maximum of X. If you don't specify the -mX switch, you'll get a maximum of 200 entries. Use the -m switch by itself, without an X number, to specify an unlimited number of entries.

If you'd like to restrict your search to a certain type of gopher item, include the switch -t followed by one or more codes for the item type or types you want. See the following table of gopher item types.

Gopher Item Type Codes

Item	Type
0	Text document
1	Directory
2	CSO phone book server <CSO>

Item	Type
4	BinHexed Mac file
5	DOS binary archive
6	UNIX uuencoded file
7	Searchable resource <?>
8	telnet session <TEL>
9	Binary file

Note Item types 4, 5, 6, and 9 in the foregoing table specify binary files of one kind or another. Putting these types of files on gophers is discouraged, so you probably won't find many of these items through a Veronica query. Unix uuencoded files are binary files that have been encoded for transmission using only ASCII characters; to convert them back into binary files, you need a program called uudecode.

You can put the switches either before or after the search string. For example, the query "-t01 -m100 nafta" returns a menu of text documents or directories whose names contain the word *nafta*; the menu will be no more than 100 items long. When we tried this query, there were nearly 2,000 matching items. So you can see that the –m switch can be very useful! The query "nafta AND gatt -t0" returns only text documents whose names include the words *nafta* and *gatt*. This search produced a list of 37 items when we tried it.

Getting Files via ftp

One of the Internet's most powerful programs is ftp, the file transfer protocol that lets you move files between remote computers and your local Internet computer. With ftp, you can get access to enormous libraries of data files, software, electronic books, and valuable information.

Keep in mind that ftp only transfers files between two Internet-connected computers; ftp won't help you get files onto the personal computer on your desk. You can use ftp to transfer files into your account on the Internet computer you dial into, but then you'll have to use a modem-based protocol, such as Kermit, in order to transfer the file to your PC. Also, be aware that ftp can transfer megabytes of files in mere minutes. But the transfer rate to your PC is limited by the speed of your modem connection—so downloading, say, the complete works of Shakespeare might take hours. This would be true even if you were able to download them via ftp in only a few minutes.

The ftp program works much like telnet: You type **ftp** followed by the name of an ftp archive, and then press Enter. For example, to connect to the NPTN information archive at nptn.org, you type **ftp nptn.org**. Once you're connected, type in a user name and password to get access to the archive.

Tip Many ftp archives allow "anonymous ftp," which allows anyone free access to selected files. If it's allowed, you simply log in with the user name *anonymous* and give your own e-mail address as the password. Note that most anonymous ftp sites don't allow you to *put* files into their archives. Throughout this chapter you'll learn more about making use of anonymous ftp sites.

The following table lists the most useful ftp commands.

ftp Commands

Command	Result
ascii	Enters ASCII mode in order to transfer text files
binary	Enters binary mode in order to transfer binary files
cd	Changes the current directory; cd .. moves to the parent directory of the current one

dir *[files]*	Lists files in the current directory (file specification is optional)
get *file*	Gets the specified file (transfers it to the local computer)
help	Prints help
lcd	Changes the current directory on the local computer
mget *files*	Gets the specified multiple files (transfers them to the local computer)
mput *files*	Puts the specified multiple files from the local computer onto the remote computer
put *file*	Puts the specified file from the local computer onto the remote computer
pwd	Displays the name of the current directory
quit	Ends the ftp session

When using the dir, mget, and mput commands, you can use wildcards within the file specifications: * stands for any number of characters, and ? stands for any single character. With the mget and mput commands, you can specify a list of files, separated by spaces.

Using ftp via E-Mail

Even if you can't use ftp on your Internet access system, it still may be possible to get files from anonymous ftp sites, by using e-mail. Simply send a properly formatted message to the ftp mail server at the e-mail address ftpmail@decwrl.dec.com; the server will connect to the anonymous ftp site you specify and return the files you request. You can include as many commands as you like, but place only one command on each line, and don't include any extra text. Be sure to end your command list with the quit command to ensure that the ftp mail server doesn't interpret any other text, such as your signature file, as commands.

The following table lists the ftp mail commands.

ftp Mail Commands

Command	Result
ascii	Switches to ASCII mode in order to transfer text files
binary	Switches to binary mode in order to transfer binary files
chdir *directory*	Changes to the specified directory
chunksize *N*	Specifies the maximum length of return messages as *N* characters; use to break large files into several smaller messages if your e-mail system has a maximum message length
connect *hostname*	Connects to the specified ftp host
dir *[directory]*	Lists the files and directories in the current directory (if you don't specify one), or in the specified directory
get *file*	Requests that the specified file be sent to you via return e-mail
quit	Marks the end of your list of commands
reply *address*	Specifies your return e-mail address (useful because return address headers don't always work correctly)
uuencode	Specifies that binary files should be encoded with the uuencode program instead of the default program (btoa)

A typical message to the ftp mail server might look like this:

```
reply dtweney@conglomo.com
connect ftp.netcom.com
ascii
chdir pub/dharma
dir
get README
quit
```

This message specifies the return address, connects to the ftp server ftp.netcom.com, and specifies that ASCII files are going to be transmitted. It then switches to the directory /pub/dharma, gets a directory listing, and retrieves the text file

README. If all goes as planned, the directory listing and the README file will be returned to the specified e-mail address in a day or so.

Note The ftp mail server will not let you request more than ten files per message. Also, you are only allowed one chdir command per session. If you want files from several different directories, send multiple messages.

Searching ftp Sites with archie

The utility called archie helps you search through the world's anonymous ftp sites in order to locate a specific program. The archie program maintains a database of file information collected from anonymous ftp sites all over the world, and provides tools for effectively searching this database. Once you've found what you're looking for, you make a note of the ftp site and the directory in which the file is located, and then use ftp to connect to that site.

There are three ways to use archie: You can connect to an archie server via telnet, or use an archie client program on your local Internet computer, or you can send e-mail to an archie e-mail server.

The following table lists many of the archie servers you can access via telnet or e-mail.

archie Servers

Address	Location
archie.ans.net	ANS server, New York
archie.au	Australia
archie.doc.ic.ac.uk	United Kingdom
archie.edvz.uni-linz.ac.at	Austria
archie.funet.fi	Finland
archie.internic.net	AT&T server, New York
archie.kr	Korea
archie.kuis.kyoto-u.ac.jp	Japan
archie.luth.se	Sweden
archie.ncu.edu.tw	Taiwan
archie.nz	New Zealand
archie.rediris.es	Spain
archie.rutgers.edu	Rutgers University, New Jersey
archie.sura.net	SURAnet, Maryland
archie.unl.edu	University of Nebraska
archie.mcgill.ca	McGill University, Montreal, Canada

Once you've connected to one of these servers using telnet, log on as **archie**. Before starting your search, you should specify the type of search you want.

- ▶ *If you want the prog search to return only file names that match your search expression exactly, type* **set search exact**—*this is the fastest search method.*

- ▶ *To search for any file name that contains a substring matching your search expression (case-insensitive), type* **set search sub**—*although it's slow, this is the most useful search type.*

- ▶ *To perform a case-sensitive substring search, type* **set search subcase**.

- ▶ *Finally, for a search that utilizes UNIX regular expressions, type* **set search regex**. *For information on regular expressions, type* **help regex**.

To search for files and programs in the archie database, type the **prog** command followed by the expression you want to search for. The prog command looks for file names matching your query. For example, if you set the search type to exact, the command prog com will return from

the database a list of files named com. However, if you set the search type to sub, the same prog com command will return files such as computer, communicate, and color.com. If you need help, type **help**.

The prog command only searches through archie's list of file *names*. To search the database of file *descriptions*, use the whatis command. It works just like prog—you type **whatis** followed by a string you want to search for. If there are any matching entries, archie lists them by file name, along with their description. The whatis command doesn't provide information about where the files are located, however, so you'll need to do a prog search on any file names that look interesting.

Note The whatis and prog databases are not always properly synchronized, so your prog command may not always locate all the files that you've found using whatis.

If the computer you dial into for Internet access has an archie client program, you can perform archie searches right from the client computer's command line. Type **archie** followed by the command-line switches you want, a space, and then the string you want to search for. (When running archie on a local client, you can only perform prog file-name searches.) To get help, just type **archie** with no switches or search string.

The switches you use on the archie command line tell the archie client what kind of search you want to perform, which archie server to access, and what size a list of files you want. The following table lists switches you'll use most often.

Common archie Switches

Switch	Description
-c	Do case-sensitive substring search
-e	Get exact string match (default search type)

-m *N*	Return a maximum of *N* matches (default is 95)
-N *X*	Set query "niceness" level of *X* (0 to 35765)
-r	Do regular expression search
-s	Do case-insensitive substring search
-t	Sort in reverse date order
-h *hostname*	Use archie server specified
-L	List known archie servers and current default

The "niceness" level set with the –N switch determines the priority for your search when processed by the archie server. The higher a "niceness" level you set, the less strain you'll put on the remote system, and the longer your search will take. It's polite to set a high number, like 30000, especially if you're not doing essential research.

Finally, one of the most convenient ways to perform archie searches is via e-mail. Because archie searches can take a long time (several minutes to half an hour), it's often easier to send your search request by e-mail and then pick up the response later. The results will be sent via return e-mail directly to you, usually within a few hours to about one day.

To run an archie search via e-mail, send a message to archie@*archie-server*. For example, to use the archie server at the University of Nebraska, you'd send mail to archie@archie.unl.edu. Put the commands you want to use in the body of the message, without any other text. Following is a list of a few of the commands you can use.

Commands for Using E-mail in an archie Search

Command	Result
prog *search-term*	Perform a file-name search for *search-term*

Command	Result
help	Get help on using archie by e-mail
servers	Get a list of all known archie servers
whatis *search-term*	Search the whatis database for keywords matching *search-term*

Note archie e-mail searches always interpret your search terms as UNIX regular expressions. To get help on constructing UNIX regular expressions, e-mail the command ***help regex*** to any archie server.

Searching Text Databases with WAIS

WAIS is short for Wide Area Information Server, a program for maintaining and searching text-based databases. There are currently more than 500 WAIS databases worldwide. You can use the WAIS program to locate the WAIS databases that are most likely to contain the information you're interested in, and then to search one or more of these databases for specific articles matching your interests.

Probably the easiest way to use WAIS is through the gopher system. When you use the gopher interface, you can search only one WAIS database at a time. Most gophers contain an item named WAIS-Based Information on the Other gopher and Information Servers menu. If your local gopher doesn't have this or a similar menu, connect to the University of Minnesota gopher (see the map of Internet Gopherspace at the back of this book for directions to the WAIS menu). With the gopher, you first locate the WAIS database you want, on a subject menu or on the alphabetical list of databases. Then enter your query, and the gopher will display a menu of matching items in that database.

If you want to search several WAIS databases at once, you'll need to connect to a WAIS server using telnet rather than through a gopher. There are WAIS servers at quake.think.com and nnsc.nsf.net; when you connect to either of these systems, log on as wais. Both of these systems use a version of WAIS called SWAIS, which is designed for text-only terminals. Other interfaces are available, but SWAIS is one of the simplest and most common.

The first thing you'll see when you connect to SWAIS is the database called directory-of-servers.src. This is the database you search to locate the WAIS databases that contain the information you're after; once you've got a list of relevant databases, you can search them.

1. Make sure the directory-of-servers database is selected. Press the spacebar; an asterisk will appear next to the database, indicating that it's selected.

2. Press w for a keyword search, enter your search term, and press Enter. WAIS doesn't understand logical operators such as AND and OR, so you're limited to a simple keyword search. You can enter multiple keywords, however, separated by spaces.

Tip When searching the directory-of-servers database, it's a good idea to use the broadest possible search terms. Once you've successfully identified the databases you want to search, you can switch to more specific queries.

3. The results of your keyword search are displayed on screen. Each listed database is accompanied by a number indicating how closely it matches your query—a score of 1000 means a perfect match; lower numbers indicate a partial match. To see the description of a particular database, use the arrow keys to move to it and then press the spacebar. To add the selected database

to the list of databases you want to search, press u to "use" it.

4. After you've specified all the databases you'd like to use, press s (lowercase) to return to the list of sources. This list now shows the directory-of-servers database, plus all the databases you selected with the u command.

5. Move to the directory-of-servers database and deselect it by pressing the spacebar.

6. Select the databases that you added to this list with the u command. Then press w to modify your original keyword query, and press Enter to perform the query on the selected databases.

This time, the search results list will show articles in the selected databases that match your query. As in the first search, they're scored from 1 to 1000 based on how closely they match your search terms. To view a particular article, move to it with the arrow keys and press the spacebar. To save an article to a file, move to it and press S (uppercase). Or, to mail it to yourself, press m and specify an address.

To see additional commands, press ? at any time. When you're done searching the WAIS databases, press q to leave the program and log off.

Taking Part in Internet-wide Discussions

If you want to meet Internet users from around the world, take part in discussions on just about any topic under the sun, get advice, and read news you might not hear about anywhere else, there are two Internet resources you'll find indispensable: newsgroups and discussion lists. Newsgroups are

the Internet's bulletin boards, and you need a special program to read the messages posted on them. You can also join a discussion list and participate in discussions through Internet e-mail.

Using Newsgroups and the nn Reader

The Internet's newsgroups are part of a subnetwork called Usenet. Originally used for posting news articles of interest to various groups, newsgroups quickly evolved into a popular discussion medium. Currently, there are hundreds of newsgroups where anyone can read or post messages on a variety of subjects.

In newsgroup names, such as alt.bbs.lists and comp.sys.ibm.pc.software, the elements of the name are grouped hierarchically, with the leftmost element representing the highest-level category. The following table lists the newsgroup categories.

Newsgroup Categories

Category	Subject
alt	Alternative
bionet	Biology-related
bitnet	Popular Bitnet discussion lists, in newsgroup format
biz	Business
comp	Computers
de	Discussions in German (Deutsch)
fj	Discussions in Japanese
k12	Subjects for students from kindergarten through 12th grade, and their teachers and parents
misc	Miscellaneous (including For Sale and Help Wanted)
soc	Discussions of social issues
talk	Discussions of current issues

Note The alt newsgroups are unmoderated. There are no restrictions on what can be posted on them, and an "anything goes" atmosphere exists on many. If you're easily offended, you may not want to subscribe to some of these alt newsgroups; some Internet access providers don't offer the more racy or offensive ones. Bitnet, the third category listed in the previous table, is discussed in detail later in this chapter.

To access the newsgroups, your Internet access-provider must have a program to read the newsgroups. One of the most common newsgroup readers is nn. Before you start nn, you must specify the newsgroups you're interested in. A menu-driven program called nnprep simplifies this process. If nnprep is available on your system, run it first to set up nn. Otherwise, you have to manually edit nn's initialization file, .newsrc, to specify the newsgroups you want.

Start nn, and then press Q to quit immediately. Then open the file called .newsrc using a text editor. This file lists all of the newsgroups available to you, one per line. The newsgroups followed by a colon will be read by nn when you run it, and newsgroups followed by an exclamation mark will be excluded. The .newsrc list initially has colons on each line, so for every newsgroup to which you *don't* want to subscribe, change the colon to an exclamation mark. Then save this file, and restart nn.

Once you start nn, it displays a list of articles from the first newsgroup. Each line in the list is labeled with a letter and displays either the subject of the article, or a right-angle bracket if the article is a response to the one just above it. To mark an article you want to read, type the lowercase letter that labels the article. After you've marked the articles you want to see from the first page of the list, press the spacebar to see the next page of articles. When you reach the end of the article list, nn displays the articles you selected, one at a time,

and then displays the article list for the next newsgroup you have designated.

To see a list of possible nn commands, press ? or type **:help** at any time. The following table lists some of the commands you can use when selecting articles with nn.

Commands for Selecting and Reading Articles

Command	Result
@	Reverse (toggle) all article selections
~	Deselect all articles
<	Show the previous page of articles
>	Show the next page of articles
^	Show the first page of articles
$	Show the last page of articles
C or U	Cancel (unsubscribe) the current newsgroup
N	Go to the next newsgroup without reading articles in the current one
P	Go to the previous newsgroup without reading articles in the current one
Q	Quit nn
X	Show selected articles immediately, then continue with the next newsgroup
Z	Show selected articles immediately, then return to this article selection menu

Note Commands in nn are case sensitive. As you read articles, press the spacebar to page forward, or to get the next selected article if you're at the end of one. To move back a page, press Del. To jump to the next selected article, press n; to move to the previous article, press p.

When you want to reply to an article, you have several options: To reply with an e-mail message to the article's author, press r. To post a

follow-up article on the newsgroup, press f. To post a new message, starting a topic of your own, type :post. Here are some other commands you can use while reading articles in nn:

=	Go back to article selection menu
m	Forward current article via e-mail
s	Save current article to a file

Of course, you can type ? or :help here, too, if you want more information on these commands.

Note Occasionally, you may find newsgroup articles that have been encrypted with rot13 encryption. This is a preventive measure to protect newsgroup readers who might be offended by the message. If you come across a message that has rot13 in its subject line, or that appears unintelligible when you read it, you can decrypt it with the D command. Likewise, if you're posting a possibly offensive message, you should encrypt it with the D command before posting it.

Joining Discussion Lists

If you'd prefer to avoid the hassle of using nn, there's another way to participate in discussions on the Internet: Subscribe to a discussion list on a Bitnet list server. Bitnet—another one of the networks that make up the Internet—specializes in list servers, or *listserv* programs. A list server maintains a mailing list of people interested in a particular topic. When one of the list members sends a message to the list server, it automatically routes the message to everyone on the list.

To subscribe to a discussion list, you send a message to the e-mail address of the list server. For example, suppose you want to join a discussion list called pynchon on the list server at listserv-request@ucsb.bitnet. You send an e-mail message to that mailing address, with nothing in the subject line and only one line in the body of

the message: subscribe pynchon *your name*. Use your full name in the message; the list server will get your e-mail address from the return address on your message. The listserv program adds you to its list, and you'll start receiving messages from other list members.

Be aware that list servers usually use an address for subscribing that is different from the regular list address. In other words, you might subscribe by sending a message to listserv-request@ucsb.bitnet, but your subsequent messages would be sent to pynchon@ucsb.bitnet. When you subscribe to a list, you'll receive complete instructions on how to use it.

Some list servers maintain databases of past discussions and related information. You can get this information by sending special commands to the list server's address. To find out about the format of these commands, send to the list server a message that contains only the command help in the body of the message. You'll receive a list of instructions and commands by return e-mail.

For a searchable list of all discussion lists and Usenet newsgroups, check out the WAIS database called lists.src. WAIS is discussed earlier in this chapter.

Live Talk on the Internet

Although space limitations prohibit more detailed descriptions of these features, let's take a brief look at talk, IRC, and MUDs—three ways you can talk interactively, in real-time, with other Internet users.

The talk program and its newer version, ntalk, let you speak one-on-one with any other Internet user who also has access to one of these

programs. To use talk or ntalk, just type **talk** *person@domain* or **ntalk** *person@domain*, where *person@domain* is the Internet e-mail address of the person with whom you want to talk. If the person is currently logged on to their Internet account, they'll receive a message saying you want to talk. Once they start the talk or ntalk program, the two of you can exchange messages in real-time.

IRC is the Internet Relay Chat, a multichannel "CB simulator," where at any time you're likely to find hundreds of people talking to each other. Because it's so resource-intensive, many Internet access providers don't allow access to IRC. But if you have access to it, try it out. The interface can be daunting at first, but with some practice you'll be able to chat with people thousands of miles away.

Finally, MUDs (Multi-User Domains or Multi-User Dungeons) are interactive, real-time games where you can explore a virtual "world," interact with other players, collect treasures, create objects, and more. Also called MUCKs, MUSHes, and MOOs, these games are quite popular among Internet users. To join one, you must use telnet to connect to the MUD. Each MUD has its own set of commands and rules, so you need to find out as much as you can about the MUD before you log on. For more information about MUDs and a list of some of the most popular ones, see the Games menu on the University of Minnesota gopher (look for it on the map of Internet Gopherspace at the back of this book).

INSIDE THE INTERNET GOPHERSPACE

The following pages describe and evaluate a few of the best and most popular of the Internet's many resources. The resources that you can access through the Internet gopher are numbered. Each number refers to a location on the map of the Internet Gopherspace at the back of this book, so you can use the map to find that resource. Or, when you see a number on the map, turn to the corresponding number among the resource descriptions. Resources that can't be accessed through the gopher are described later in this chapter. They are not numbered, but their descriptions include detailed instructions on how to get to them.

For an estimation of the quality and usefulness of each resource, look for the following symbols:

▲▲▲▲   Outstanding—don't miss it!
▲▲▲   Excellent—worth going out of your way to see it.
▲▲   Very good—worth a look.
▲   Above average—stop by if it's on your way.
▼   Disappointing—don't bother.

Each resource is classified by type. The types are news, discussion, information, entertainment, files, and service, using the same symbols that appear on the map.

Gopher Resources *Gophers provide one of the easiest ways to navigate the Internet's many resources. In addition to providing you with menu-driven access to substantial quantities of textual information, many gophers also include access to ftp sites, WAIS databases, telnet sessions, and more. You may be able to find many of the following resources on several different gophers, and your own gopher may offer direct access to a great many of them. Since the University of Minnesota gopher is fairly central, however, our map of the Internet Gopherspace shows how to find these resources from there. Just use your own gopher to connect to the University of Minnesota gopher, and then follow the menus depicted on the map to find the resource you're looking for. If you can't find the University of Minnesota on your gopher menu, try connecting directly to it: Start your gopher program with the command gopher gopher.micro.umn.edu.*

The University of Minnesota gopher is often overloaded with users, and is sometimes slow as a result. So once you discover a path to a resource that doesn't take you through the Minnesota gopher, you should take that route instead.

1. IBM ACIS HIGHER EDUCATION INFORMATION SERVER   ▲▲

Also known as IKE, this gopher provides a wealth of information about using IBM computers in education. Along with collections of IBM press releases and product information, there's a very useful software library with dozens of shareware and freeware educational programs for IBM PCs and compatibles. Each program can be downloaded to your local Internet computer right from the gopher. Check out GEOCLOCK, a nifty program that displays a map of the world showing what areas are currently in sunlight. There are also several planetarium programs,

software to teach mathematical functions and principles, and programs to help you learn French, German, Greek, Italian, and Spanish. You'll also find a telnet connection to the IKE BBS, where you can exchange ideas with other IBM users involved in higher education.

2. INFO-MAC ARCHIVES   ▲▲▲

This very popular collection of Macintosh software contains hundreds of programs, from antivirus utilities to Newton software to word processors. It's an easy way to get freeware and shareware, because using the gopher program eliminates the need to connect via ftp. You just select the program you want, and the gopher transfers it to your local Internet computer. Unfortunately, the archives are very heavily used, and while it's busy you may not be able to access some or all of Info-Mac's menus.

3. INTERNIC   ▲▲▲▲

InterNIC is the Internet Network Information Center, a public service offering lots of Internet information to the general public. The InterNIC Information Services menu here is a gold mine for new Internet users. It contains a comprehensive explanation of the Internet and how to use it. If you're just starting to use the Internet, this gopher should be one of your first stops because it will give you up-to-date information that you'll find indispensable. If you don't have access to a gopher, you can contact InterNIC by phone or by e-mail—see the section "Connecting to the Internet," at the beginning of this chapter.

4. POPULAR FTP SITES VIA GOPHER   ▲▲▲▲

This convenient menu on the University of Minnesota gopher gives you access to more than 20 popular ftp file libraries, including an archive of U.S. Supreme Court rulings, a library of popular music lyrics, information about the Internet's many resources, and a lot more. This is only a small sample of the many ftp sites throughout the Internet, but it's an easy way to get many interesting files without having to deal with the ftp program. Browse around and see what you find—it's well worth it!

5. ELECTRONIC JOURNAL COLLECTION FROM CICNET   ▲▲▲

This is a one-stop newsstand for electronic journals from all over the Internet. It's maintained by the Committee for Institutional Cooperation, a conference of midwestern universities. This collection compiles dozens of electronic journals on every imaginable topic. It's organized alphabetically, by subject, and by Library of Congress call letters. Unfortunately, you can't perform searches for titles or keywords. If you want to get an idea of the incredible wealth of information to be found for free on electronic journals, be sure to check out this resource.

6. ELECTRONIC NEWSSTAND ▲

The Electronic Newsstand is a commercial service providing stories and information from over 50 national and international magazines, from *American Demographics* to *Yoga Journal*. Each magazine's entry on this gopher features a few articles from the current issue, an archive of articles from past issues, plus information on how to subscribe—often at a discount. The Newsstand also features book and movie reviews, as well as an electronic bookstore where you can order books. Though not a complete database of magazine articles, the Electronic Newsstand is an interesting place to visit and provides a convenient way to get information about many magazines.

7. U.S. GEOGRAPHIC NAMES DATABASE ▲

This is a convenient way to look up ZIP codes anywhere in the United States. Enter a place name or a ZIP code, and you'll get a gopher menu listing all of the matching items in the database. Select any item to find out more about that place. Information you can get includes the state it's located in, its latitude and longitude, population, and elevation. Next to the Geographic Names database on the gopher menu is a U.S. Telephone Areas Codes database that you can use to look up area codes in a similar fashion.

8. MTV GOPHER ▲

This gopher is part of MTV.COM, an Internet computer run by MTV VJ Adam Curry. It's got plenty of information about MTV schedules, music stars, the current music and video charts, concert dates, and more. You can download pictures of your favorite stars, or music and video clips that you can play on a multimedia-capable computer. For those who just can't stand being away from MTV while they're using the computer, this gopher is a perfect compromise.

9. CORNUCOPIA OF DISABILITY INFORMATION ▲▲▲

This gopher brings together a large collection of information for, about, and from people with disabilities. It includes government publications, databases of resources, newsletters, health information, legal information, advice, and bibliographies—it's truly a rich source of facts relating to many disabilities. There's also a useful search menu that lets you scan this large gopher for the information that interests you.

10. NATIONAL AERONAUTICS AND SPACE ADMINISTRATION ▲▲

Want to find out what those billions of taxpayer dollars are going for? Check out the NASA gopher, which offers plenty of information from the space program and other NASA projects. Although some parts of this gopher are incomplete or poorly organized, there's a wealth of data here. Much of it is of interest primarily to scientists, but there are features for students and teachers, too—the Ames Research Center K-12 Gopher is especially useful. Select the NASA News menu item for an up-to-date status report on current space missions. You can even download photographs taken during recent space shuttle missions, through the Space Shuttle Earth Observations Project menu item.

11. THE WELLGOPHER ▲▲▲

Think of this as the gopher equivalent of an independent weekly newspaper. The WELL's gopher tells you about events in the worlds of art and music (especially Grateful Dead concerts), environmental issues, politics, and more. It also gives you access to some choice documents on cyberpunk, including stories by Bruce Sterling, articles from *Mondo 2000*, and similar sources. There's even a newsstand of sorts, on the Publications menu, that features such eclectic items as the Buddhist *Diamond Sutra*, a review of the French press, stories from the *Whole Earth Review*, and even an electronic version of *Factsheet Five*, a guide to independent 'zines. Although it may not appeal to everyone, the WELLgopher features a wealth of unusual data you won't find anywhere else on the Internet.

12. GOPHER TO NETFIND GATEWAY ▲▲

The Netfind server is the closest thing to an Internet phone book. You can use it to look up e-mail addresses for people just about anywhere on the Internet. The catch? It doesn't always work. Netfind is a pretty smart program that uses several Internet utilities to perform searches for you, but those utilities don't always turn up the information you need. Still, it's a good way to start and it's easy to use. This gopher menu item connects you by telnet to a Netfind server. Log in as netfind and use the menus to start your search. Hint: read the Help menu item first for some very useful tips on constructing queries.

Anonymous ftp Resources

A s useful as it is, a gopher doesn't give you access to one of the Internet's most powerful features: ftp. This chapter has described how to use archie to find information and programs in anonymous ftp sites throughout the Internet. But to give you some idea of what's available, the following table lists ftp sites you may want to investigate. Although only six sites are listed, you can find enough files in the these libraries to keep you occupied for weeks!

ftp Sites

Site   **Directory**
Description

coombs.anu.edu.au   **/coombspapers**
This ftp server comes from Australian National University and contains a wealth of research papers, reports, and technical information of interest to scholars in the social sciences and humanities. The collection is particularly strong in Asian religions, especially Buddhism and Taoism.

ftp.cdrom.com   **/pub**
Maintained by Walnut Creek CDROM, a company that produces CD-ROMS, this archive contains a lot of interesting material. There's a very large selection of games for all kinds of computer platforms, plus electronic books, and more.

ftp.eff.org   **/pub**
This is the ftp server of the Electronic Frontier Foundation (EFF). It carries lots of information about using the Internet, about legal aspects of electronic communications, and more. You can get information about the EFF from the directory /pub/EFF. Look in /pub/Publications for magazine articles, stories, and interviews.

ftp.uwp.edu   **/pub/music**
This archive contains lots of music information. You'll find reviews, scores, lyrics, MIDI files, and more. The emphasis seems to be on classical and folk music, probably because of copyright restrictions. However, the /pub/music/lyrics directory contains the lyrics to thousands of pop songs, sorted by group or artist.

mrcnext.cso.uiuc.eud   **/pub/etext**
Come here to get electronic texts from Project Gutenberg, a group that is putting many works of literature into electronic form and making them publicly available, for free. They've been converting books to ASCII files for decades now, and the collection is quite large.

obi.std.com   **/obi**
This ftp archive is owned by The World, an Internet access provider based in Massachusetts. The /obi directory contains even more electronic versions of public-domain texts than you can find in the Project Gutenberg files. There's a lot of material here!

Further Down the Information Highway

T his book lists a fraction of the resources available on the Internet, just enough to give you an idea of the vast quantity of material that you can find on the net. Of course, the best way to learn about the Internet's vast and rapidly changing geography is to get connected and start exploring. The Internet, like the commercial information services described in previous chapters, is a fascinating, entertaining, and even habit-forming place. And the better you know your way around the Internet, the more useful it will be for you.

Whether you use the Internet or a commercial on-line service, you'll find that the on-line world is almost as big and as varied as the real world. With this book, you've got plenty of information to simplify navigation of these complicated information highways. So what are you waiting for? Hit the road and start exploring!

The On-line Traveler's Dictionary

ANSI (American National Standards Institute) *A text transmission format that includes special codes to change the color or position of text on the terminal window. If you set your comm software to ANSI emulation, bulletin boards that use ANSI graphics will have more colorful and sophisticated menus. (See also* emulation; terminal window.*)*

archive file *A single file containing many files in compressed form, making it faster and easier to transfer these files by modem. You usually need special software (such as PKZip, Unstuffit, or LHA) to extract the files from the archive file when you receive it.*

ASCII (American Standard Code for Information Interchange) *A text-only file format. An ASCII file contains plain text without any formatting codes.*

AT command *Commands used with Hayes and Hayes-compatible modems to control the modem's behavior, change its settings, and so forth. AT commands all begin with the letters AT, to get the modem's ATtention.*

attachment *A file (often binary) included with an e-mail message. Not all e-mail systems support attachments.*

baud rate *Commonly used as a synonym for* bits per second, *a measure of how fast a modem can transmit information over a telephone line.*

binary file *A file containing digital information (not just text). You can't view a binary file in your terminal window unless you first download the file to your own computer. Binary files can be graphics images, word processor documents, executable programs, or compressed data files. (See also* download; terminal window.*)*

bulletin board *A computer system you can dial into, to read publicly posted messages, post messages of your own, or download files. Also known as a BBS (bulletin board system). Some larger commercial on-line services have bulletin boards where members can exchange messages. (See also* forum.*)*

chat mode *Real-time conversation with another person or people through an on-line service or bulletin board. As you type at your computer, the words appear immediately on the other participants' screens. Also called CB mode.*

compression *A technique used to reduce the size of data files, so that they require less hard disk space and can be transmitted more quickly via modem. You need a compression program to compress files into archive files and then to uncompress them (remove them from the archive file). (See also* archive file.*)*

download *To transmit a file from a remote computer to your own.*

emulation *The type of terminal your communications software is pretending to be in order to communicate with a remote host. Common emulations are TTY (Teletype, or text only), DEC VT52, DEC VT100, and ANSI (text with ANSI codes).*

FAQ *Stands for Frequently Asked Questions (pronounced "fack"). Common term for a file containing many frequently asked questions on a particular subject, along with their answers.*

flame *A nasty on-line argument. Also known as* flame war.

forum *A message area for discussions within an information service. Most forums operate like bulletin boards, allowing members to post and read public messages.*

freeware *Free software.*

gateway *A connection between two on-line services or networks. A gateway may only allow the two services to exchange e-mail, or it may allow members of one service to access features of the other.*

host *The computer that receives your modem's call. Once you're connected to a host computer, you're like a "guest" there. The host computer provides you with menus or command prompts (displayed on your screen), so you can get access to the host's services, programs, and files.*

interface *The text, menus, or graphics a computer or on-line service uses to communicate with you.*

Kermit *A protocol for uploading or downloading files. It's relatively slow, but especially useful for communicating with mainframes and minicomputers, such as those on the Internet.*

local *On the same end of the line as you; refers to the computer you are currently using.*

log on *Once you've connected to an information service or bulletin board, you need to log on, to communicate who you are by entering your name or ID number and password. After the remote computer has accepted your password, you're logged on and ready to use the service.*

log off *Telling the system to which you're connected that you're ready to leave and want to hang up. Logging off usually means typing BYE, QUIT, or LOGOFF. The system usually responds by telling you your total time on line or your total charges, and then hangs up or waits for you to hang up.*

off line *Not connected to any information service, network, or computer.*

on line *Connected to an information service, network, or computer via modem.*

packet network *A data network to which you connect with a local call; the packet network then connects you to an on-line service that may be quite far away. Usually it's less expensive to use a packet network than to make a long-distance call.*

protocol *The system of codes used by two computers to transfer binary files, and to verify that the data is being transferred correctly. Both computers must use the same protocol. Popular protocols include Kermit, XModem, and ZModem, among others.*

remote *On the other end of the line from you; refers to the computer to which you're connected by modem.*

self-extracting archive file *An archive file that can be opened without using special software. The self-extracting archive file is an executable program, and when you run it, it decompresses and extracts the files archived within it.*

shareware *"Try before you buy" software. There's no charge to download the software, but if you keep using it, you have to pay for it.*

sysop *Abbreviation for* system operator, *the person in charge of a bulletin board or forum. Sysops maintain the bulletin board or forum's files, watch over its message areas, and provide help if you're having trouble working with the system.*

terminal window *The part of your communication program's screen that shows the text sent by the host computer and the text you type. Here is where you're "talking" with the remote computer.*

thread *A topic of discussion on a bulletin board. Usually all messages in a thread will have the same Subject: or Topic: line.*

upload *To transmit a file from your computer to the remote computer.*

virtual *Simulated by a computer.*

XModem *A common file-transfer protocol.*

ZModem *A file-transfer protocol that allows "batch" transfers—uploading or downloading several files at one time.*

Index

Note: Page numbers in italic denote figures or illustrations.

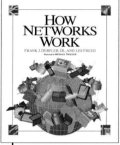

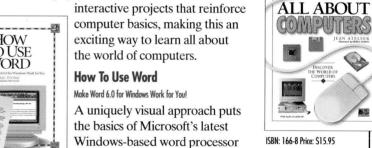

Ziff-Davis Press Survey of Readers

Please help us in our effort to produce the best books on personal computing.
For your assistance, we would be pleased to send you a FREE catalog
featuring the complete line of Ziff-Davis Press books.

1. How did you first learn about this book?

Recommended by a friend . . . . ☐ -1 (5)

Recommended by store personnel . . . . ☐ -2

Saw in Ziff-Davis Press catalog . . . . ☐ -3

Received advertisement in the mail . . . . ☐ -4

Saw the book on bookshelf at store . . . . ☐ -5

Read book review in: _____ ☐ -6

Saw an advertisement in: _____ ☐ -7

Other (Please specify): _____ ☐ -8

2. Which THREE of the following factors most influenced your decision to purchase this book? (Please check up to THREE.)

Front or back cover information on book . . . ☐ -1 (6)

Logo of magazine affiliated with book . . . . . . ☐ -2

Special approach to the content . . . . ☐ -3

Completeness of content . . . . ☐ -4

Author's reputation. ☐ -5

Publisher's reputation . . . . ☐ -6

Book cover design or layout . . . . ☐ -7

Index or table of contents of book . . . . ☐ -8

Price of book . . . . ☐ -9

Special effects, graphics, illustrations . . . . . . ☐ -0

Other (Please specify): _____ ☐ -x

3. How many computer books have you purchased in the last six months? _____ (7-10)

4. On a scale of 1 to 5, where 5 is excellent, 4 is above average, 3 is average, 2 is below average, and 1 is poor, please rate each of the following aspects of this book below. (Please circle your answer.)

Depth/completeness of coverage	5	4	3	2	1	(11)
Organization of material	5	4	3	2	1	(12)
Ease of finding topic	5	4	3	2	1	(13)
Special features/time saving tips	5	4	3	2	1	(14)
Appropriate level of writing	5	4	3	2	1	(15)
Usefulness of table of contents	5	4	3	2	1	(16)
Usefulness of index	5	4	3	2	1	(17)
Usefulness of accompanying disk	5	4	3	2	1	(18)
Usefulness of illustrations/graphics	5	4	3	2	1	(19)
Cover design and attractiveness	5	4	3	2	1	(20)
Overall design and layout of book	5	4	3	2	1	(21)
Overall satisfaction with book	5	4	3	2	1	(22)

5. Which of the following computer publications do you read regularly; that is, 3 out of 4 issues?

Byte . . . . ☐ -1 (23)

Computer Shopper . . . . ☐ -2

Corporate Computing . . . . ☐ -3

Dr. Dobb's Journal . . . . ☐ -4

LAN Magazine . . . . ☐ -5

MacWEEK . . . . ☐ -6

MacUser . . . . ☐ -7

PC Computing . . . . ☐ -8

PC Magazine . . . . ☐ -9

PC WEEK . . . . ☐ -0

Windows Sources . . . . ☐ -x

Other (Please specify): _____ ☐ -y

Please turn page.

PLEASE TAPE HERE ONLY—DO NOT STAPLE

6. What is your level of experience with personal computers? With the subject of this book?

	With PCs	With subject of book
Beginner...............	☐ -1 (24)	☐ -1 (25)
Intermediate..........	☐ -2	☐ -2
Advanced.............	☐ -3	☐ -3

7. Which of the following best describes your job title?

Officer (CEO/President/VP/owner)........ ☐ -1 (26)
Director/head.......................... ☐ -2
Manager/supervisor.................... ☐ -3
Administration/staff................... ☐ -4
Teacher/educator/trainer............... ☐ -5
Lawyer/doctor/medical professional....... ☐ -6
Engineer/technician................... ☐ -7
Consultant........................... ☐ -8
Not employed/student/retired........... ☐ -9
Other (Please specify): _____ ☐ -0

8. What is your age?

Under 20............................. ☐ -1 (27)
21-29................................ ☐ -2
30-39................................ ☐ -3
40-49................................ ☐ -4
50-59................................ ☐ -5
60 or over........................... ☐ -6

9. Are you:

Male................................ ☐ -1 (28)
Female.............................. ☐ -2

Thank you for your assistance with this important information! Please write your address below to receive our free catalog.

Name: _____

Address: _____

City/State/Zip: _____

Fold here to mail.

2060-07-08

NO POSTAGE
NECESSARY
IF MAILED IN
THE UNITED
STATES

BUSINESS REPLY MAIL
FIRST CLASS MAIL   PERMIT NO. 1612   OAKLAND, CA

POSTAGE WILL BE PAID BY ADDRESSEE

Ziff-Davis Press
ZIFF-DAVIS
ZD
PRESS
5903 Christie Avenue
Emeryville, CA 94608-1925
Attn: Marketing

CompuServe Travel Guide

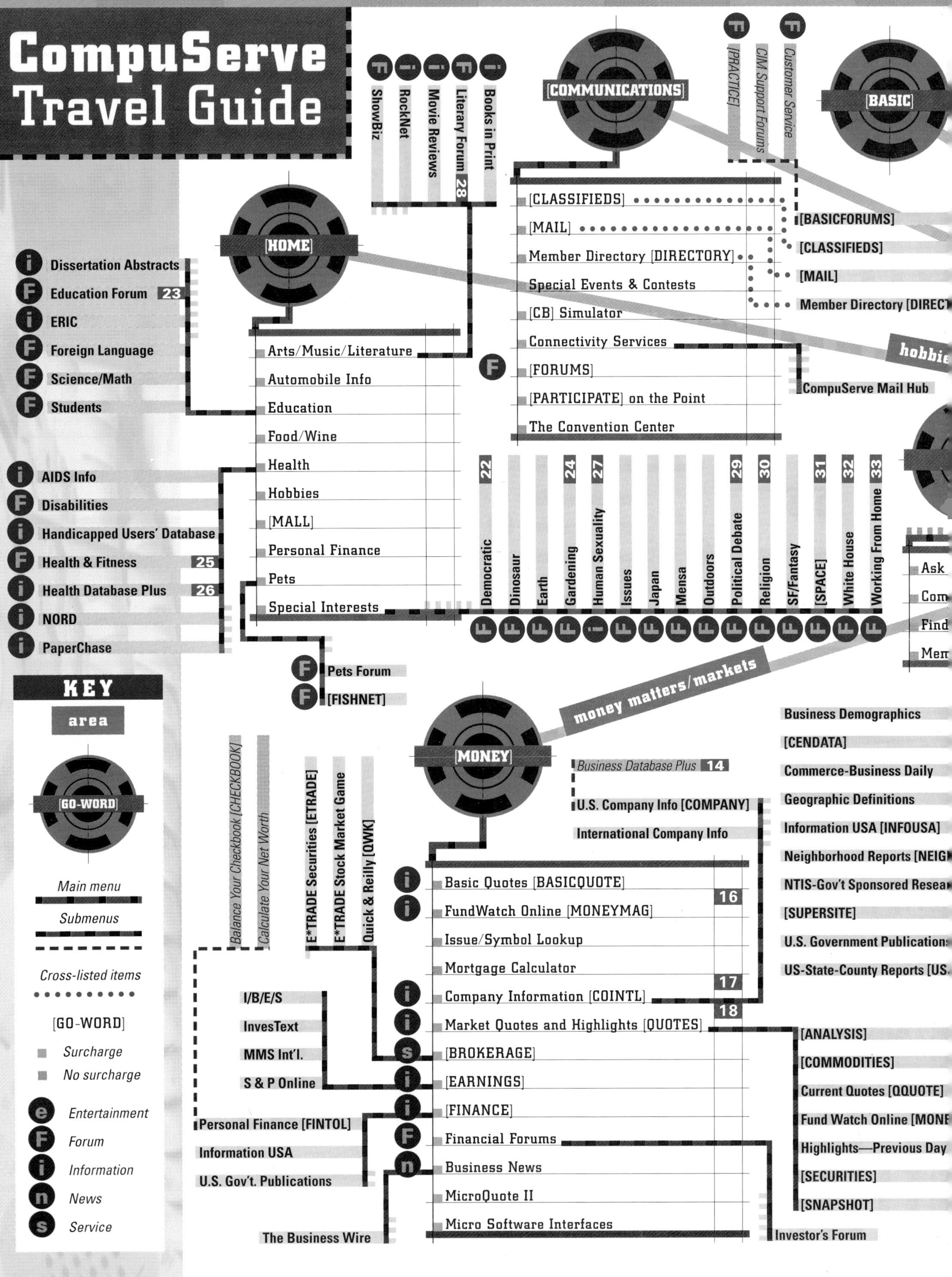

[F] [i] [i] [F] [i]
ShowBiz
RockNet
Movie Reviews
Literary Forum 28
Books in Print
[COMMUNICATIONS]
[F] [F]
[PRACTICE]
CIM Support Forums
Customer Service
[BASIC]
[CLASSIFIEDS]
[MAIL]
Member Directory [DIRECTORY]
Special Events & Contests
[CB] Simulator
Connectivity Services
[F] [FORUMS]
[PARTICIPATE] on the Point
The Convention Center
[BASICFORUMS]
[CLASSIFIEDS]
[MAIL]
Member Directory [DIRECT
hobbie
CompuServe Mail Hub
[HOME]
[i] Dissertation Abstracts
[F] Education Forum 23
[i] ERIC
[F] Foreign Language
[F] Science/Math
[F] Students
Arts/Music/Literature
Automobile Info
Education
Food/Wine
Health
Hobbies
[MALL]
Personal Finance
Pets
Special Interests
[i] AIDS Info
[F] Disabilities
[i] Handicapped Users' Database
[F] Health & Fitness 25
[i] Health Database Plus 26
[i] NORD
[i] PaperChase
22 Democratic [F]
Dinosaur [F]
Earth [F]
24 Gardening [F]
27 Human Sexuality [i]
Issues [F]
Japan [F]
Mensa [F]
Outdoors [F]
29 Political Debate [F]
30 Religion [F]
SF/Fantasy [F]
31 [SPACE] [F]
32 White House [F]
33 Working From Home [F]
Ask
Com
Find
Mem
[F] Pets Forum
[F] [FISHNET]
money matters/markets
KEY
area
[GO-WORD]
Main menu
Submenus
Cross-listed items
[GO-WORD]
■ Surcharge
■ No surcharge
[e] Entertainment
[F] Forum
[i] Information
[n] News
[s] Service
[MONEY]
Business Database Plus 14
U.S. Company Info [COMPANY]
International Company Info
Business Demographics
[CENDATA]
Commerce-Business Daily
Geographic Definitions
Information USA [INFOUSA]
Neighborhood Reports [NEIG
NTIS-Gov't Sponsored Resea
[SUPERSITE]
U.S. Government Publication
US-State-County Reports [US
Balance Your Checkbook [CHECKBOOK]
Calculate Your Net Worth
E*TRADE Securities [ETRADE]
E*TRADE Stock Market Game
Quick & Reilly [QWK]
[i] Basic Quotes [BASICQUOTE]
[i] FundWatch Online [MONEYMAG] 16
Issue/Symbol Lookup
Mortgage Calculator
[i] Company Information [COINTL] 17
[i] Market Quotes and Highlights [QUOTES] 18
[s] [BROKERAGE]
[i] [EARNINGS]
[i] [FINANCE]
[F] Financial Forums
[n] Business News
MicroQuote II
Micro Software Interfaces
I/B/E/S
InvesText
MMS Int'l.
S & P Online
Personal Finance [FINTOL]
Information USA
U.S. Gov't. Publications
The Business Wire
[ANALYSIS]
[COMMODITIES]
Current Quotes [QQUOTE]
Fund Watch Online [MONE
Highlights—Previous Day
[SECURITIES]
[SNAPSHOT]
Investor's Forum

CompuServe

basic services

- n [BASICCOM]
- e [BASICNEWS]
- i [BASICGAMES]
- i [BASICQUOTES]
- s [BASICREF]
- s [BASICTRAVEL]
- s [SHOPPING]
- [HELP]

Peterson's College Database
Handicapped Users' Database
[HEALTHNET]
[CONSUMER] Reports
[ENCYCLOPEDIA]
[DICTIONARY]

2

1

communications/bulletin boards

/lifestyles/education

[ORY]

[TRAVEL]

EAASY SABRE
WORLDSPAN Travelshopper
ABC Worldwide Hotel Guide
OAG Electronic Edition

EAASY SABRE
WORLDSPAN Travelshopper
OAG Electronic Edition

Information USA

West Coast Travel

F California

F Florida

Information USA
Dept. of State Advisories [STATE]
Travel Britain Online [TBONLINE]
Visa Advisors [VISA]

travel

- s Air/Hotel/Car Informa
- i Dept. of State Advisor
- i Travel Britain Online
- i Visa Advisors [VISA]
- s Zagat Restaurant Gui
- s Air Info/Reservations
- s Hotel Info [HOTELS]
- i U.S. Domestic Info
- i International Info
- F Travel Forums

California
Florida
Florida Today
Japan
Travel
UK

the electronic mall/shopping

member assistance

[HELP]

Customer Service
nand Summary
a Topic [TOUR]
bership Changes

reference

[REFERENCE]

Computer Database Plus [COMPDB]
Computer Directory [COMPDIR]
Support On Site [ONSITE]

computers/technology

news/weather/sports

entertainment/games

- i HHL Movie Reviews
- i Hollywood Hotline
- i Magazine Database Plus
- i Magill's
- i Roger Ebert's Movie Revie
- i RockNet
- F ShowBiz
- i Soap Opera Summaries

35
- i Academic American [ENCYCLOPEDIA]
- i America Heritage [DICTIONARY]
- i Consumer Reports [CONSUMER]
- i Consumer Reports Complete Drug Ref. [DRUGS]
- i Peterson's College Database [PETERSON]
36
- i Computer Library [COMPLIB]
BORHOOD]
- i [DEMOGRAPHICS]
ch
39
- i Directories
- i [HEALTHNET]
TCN] 34
- i [IQUEST]
37
38
- i Knowledge Index [KI]
- i Business Database Plus [BUSDB]
- i Health Database Plus [HLTDB]
- i Magazine Database Plus
YMAG]
- i Newspaper Library
MARKET]
- i Books in Print
- i Marquis Who's Who
- i New Car Showroom
- i Magill's Survey of Cinema

[GAM]

- e Biorhythms
- e Hangman
- e Roger Ebert's Movie Reviews
20
- e The Entertainment Center
- F Entertainment Forums
21
- F Fantasy/Role-playing/Adv. Games
- F Game Forums
- e Modem Games
- e Parlor/Trivia Games
19
- e War/Simulation Games

Biz*File
Dun's Electronic Business Directory
Phone*File

- n Associa
- n [WEAT
- n Online
- n UK New
- n Citiban
- n Enterta
- n Executi
- n NewsGr
- i Newspa
- n Reuter
- n Soviet
- n [SPORT

All-Music Guide Forum